One Day in Bethlehem

Jonny Steinberg

One Day in Bethlehem

13 Sept 2019

To Beth
with love
love
Jony

Johnathan Ball Publishers

JOHANNESBURG & CAPE TOWN

Originally published in South Africa in 2019 by
JONATHAN BALL PUBLISHERS
A division of Media24 (Pty) Ltd
PO Box 33977
Jeppestown
2043

ISBN 978 1 86842 934 9
ebook ISBN 978 1 86842 935 6

Every effort has been made to trace the copyright holders and to obtain their permission for the use of copyright material. The publishers apologise for any errors or omissions and would be grateful to be notified of any corrections that should be incorporated in future editions of this book.

The material quoted from the Amnesty Hearing in Chapter 19 is taken from the Truth and Reconciliation Commission Amnesty Hearing of Stephen Donald Makhura, 16 November 1998, Application No. AM 0014/96, Welkom, Day 1. It is available at http://www.justice.gov.za/trc/amntrans/1998/98111618%20_wlk_981116wel.htm.
The material quoted from Fusi Mofokeng's 1992 trial is taken from the court transcript of
S v TG Mokoena and Five Others 68/92, High Court of South Africa,
Free State Division, Bloemfontein.
The article quoted in Chapter 23, 'Where is the justice?' by Jacques Pauw, appeared in
City Press on 9 October 2009 and is reproduced with the permission of *City Press*.

Twitter: www.twitter.com/JonathanBallPub
Facebook: www.facebook.com/JonathanBallPublishers
Blog: http://jonathanball.bookslive.co.za/

Cover by publicide
Design and typesetting by Triple M Design
Printed and bound by CTP Printers, Cape Town
Set in 11/17pt Apollo MT Std

A thing is not necessarily either true or false;
it can be both true and false.

HAROLD PINTER

Part I

One

I could have sworn that I was in my office when I read the newspaper report that triggered this book. My memory has me reading the words on the monitor on my desk, then gazing out of the window at the brickwork on the building across the road. Indeed, I cannot picture that article except on my monitor, and I cannot separate my first thoughts about it from the view of the brickwork. They are forever fused.

When I return to the article I am astonished to learn that it was published on 31 December 2011, for I was on holiday then, in southwestern France, and must have read it on my laptop, sitting on a couch in front of a log fire. Of this I have no memory at all.

Salutary, that, for those who took part in the events that follow have told and retold the story so often that none has cause to believe what he remembers.

The article I read that day recounts an immense injustice. In April 2011, two South African men walked free after nineteen years in jail. They were black and poor and on the day they went to prison they were little educated. And they were innocent. A murder had been committed, of that there is no doubt, but neither man had had anything to do with it.

3

The crime had taken place in broad daylight on the outskirts of a rural town called Bethlehem in the province of the Free State. Two white patrol officers had approached a bakkie full of black men and were greeted with volleys of fire from an AK-47. One of the officers, Lourens Oosthuizen, aged twenty-one, died on the scene. The other, Johannes Joubert, aged twenty-nine, was left permanently disabled.

It was 1992, and white South Africans were crazy with fear, for they were about to lose power and in their thoughts they died a thousand deaths. But they still controlled the police and the courts, and could thus inflict their wild fears on two young men without the wherewithal to defend themselves. Fusi Mofokeng and Tshokolo Mokoena were convicted of murder, despite the fact that they had not been on the scene of the crime, on the grounds of common purpose. It was said that they had beckoned the murderers from Johannesburg to the rural town of Bethlehem to rob a wealthy white man. The luckless Constables Oosthuizen and Joubert had approached the would-be robbers just minutes before they were to descend on their prey. And so Mofokeng and Mokoena were convicted of murder on the grounds that they had orchestrated a crime that had ended in a killing.

Six years later, apartheid was dead, Nelson Mandela was president, and the four surviving men who had in fact committed the crime appeared, together with Mofokeng and Mokoena, at South Africa's Truth and Reconciliation Commission (TRC). The four had applied for amnesty on the grounds that they had shot their weapons as freedom fighters. They had been trained in combat by the armed wing of the African National Congress (ANC), they said, and were acting under military discipline. They had been moving across the country in a vehicle full of military weapons when the two police officers had approached them. Their standing orders were to resist surrendering either themselves or their weapons. And so they had opened fire.

4

If an applicant before the Amnesty Committee of the TRC could show that his motives were political and if he confessed the full extent of his crime, the law bound the TRC to grant him amnesty. The four were so granted.

Fusi Mofokeng took the stand. He and Tshokolo Mokoena had no crime to confess, he said. They were not trained in military combat. They were just ordinary young men. They had not beckoned the combatants to Bethlehem. They had played no role in the events that unfolded that day. Their four co-applicants confirmed that this was indeed the case.

The Amnesty Committee expressed its heartfelt sympathy for Mofokeng and Mokoena. But it could not grant them amnesty for they had committed no crime. And so the four who were guilty of murder walked free, while the two who were guilty of nothing remained in prison for another twelve years.

It could be that I and my fellow South Africans have become hardened to travesty. For I must confess that the story stayed with me, not for the injustice it recounted but for a casual remark Fusi Mofokeng reportedly made.

'The thing that most amazed him in his first seven months of freedom,' the reporter Rowan Philp, wrote, 'was not smartphones and Google, but that "a white lady actually served me at a restaurant and was very nice to me too".'

The moment I read those lines, I wanted urgently to meet Fusi Mofokeng. I wanted to borrow the eyes of a person who had walked into 2011 from the past. For I had it in mind that we'd forgotten what had changed and what had not since the end of apartheid; that it would take an insurmountable effort to distinguish the old from the new. What an opportunity, I thought: to consult a person who has been as if asleep all these years.

I wrote Fusi Mofokeng a letter. I wished to get in touch while the world around him was still surprising.

Two

Between the sending of that letter and our first meeting, five months passed. Fusi Mofokeng was not one to proceed on impulse, it appeared; he had felt it necessary to take advice before acting upon correspondence from out of the blue. And, besides, I was living in the United Kingdom and some time passed before I could make it to South Africa.

Having set aside a day and a time many weeks in advance, I finally phoned him on the afternoon of 18 June 2012, on the road from Johannesburg to Bethlehem, to ask for directions to his house.

'You will get lost in the black township,' he said, the voice in my ear deliberate and courteous. 'Even myself, I am still getting lost.'

And so, at rush hour, at an intersection in the very centre of Bethlehem, a middle-aged man in a golf shirt waved to me from the other side of the street. I crossed and went to him and shook his hand and he invited me into the passenger seat of his car, an old red Toyota Camry.

He drove out into the traffic with great caution, his body bent towards the windscreen, his shoulders a little hunched. We exchanged pleasantries – about my drive from Johannesburg, for instance, and about his day at work. He had spent much of it under the bonnets of various Bethlehem municipal vehicles.

'I like to be alone with a broken machine,' he said. 'You concentrate hard. You look at your watch and are surprised because the day is done. If, by then, you have fixed the machine, it has been a good day.'

From out of the blue, on the open road leading out of town, he gasped suddenly and ducked his head, his hands still firm on the steering wheel. I swivelled instinctively to see if a missile had been thrown into the car.

He recovered his composure and smiled at me, somewhat embarrassed.

'There is a speed camera in this spot,' he said conspiratorially, pointing a finger at the side of the road, 'right as you descend the hill and pick up speed. They have caught me here three times. I have learnt to slow down. But now I was chatting to you and not paying attention. I think I was doing sixty-five kilometres per hour.'

A forgotten feeling came over me. I took in his shaven head and cheeks, his even-tempered face, his maroon golf shirt and his polyester slacks, the gentle bulge of his soft stomach and the smell of soap. I felt I had met him many times before. He was a middle-aged workingman who doffs his cap at strangers and on Sunday mornings sings in a steady baritone in the church pews.

I was transported back nearly a quarter of a century to the days when I met such men every Tuesday evening, at the Congress of South African Trade Unions Johannesburg Shop Stewards Local, during the dying days of apartheid. These modest men more than twice my age, men who seemed to shuffle rather than to walk, and who greeted me with a decorum so deep and so strange that they seemed to come from another world.

Bohlokong, Bethlehem's black township, was as labyrinthine and hard to navigate as Fusi Mofokeng had suggested. We zigzagged through a warren of dust roads crowded with pedestrians: men and women returning from work, boys and young men huddled in circles, their backs to the world. At his house, Fusi Mofokeng told me, Tshokolo Mokoena, his fellow innocent, the man who had walked out of prison with him the previous year, was waiting.

Fusi Mofokeng, Tshokolo Mokoena and I met that evening and the next. We sat at a table in the house the government had built for Fusi's mother while he was in prison. In the same room, his sister, Victoria, watched a Sesotho-language drama on television. The house was tiny, thirty-one square metres in all, identical to three million other houses the government had built for the poor since coming to power in 1994. As we sat there talking, some twelve million human souls sat in precisely the same house, most of them, I imagined, watching television.

I confess that I struggled to connect with Tshokolo Mokoena during that first evening. He spoke in short bursts of what seemed to me self-pity and accusation, his words collecting in a heap on the table before us. Looking at the notes I made, they are filled almost entirely with Fusi Mofokeng's words. During his years in prison, he said, the world outside slowly emptied of the people he loved: first, his beloved brother Amos, then his father, then his mother. He was not permitted to attend any of their burials, he said, and could thus not truly comprehend that they were no longer out there in the world.

For nineteen years, he said, you fight to get out of prison. Finally, a fax comes from on high authorising your release. The day draws near. You dress up in a borrowed suit and walk out to cameras and politicians – for the two of you are now famous for your innocence.

'My main feeling was sadness,' Fusi Mofokeng said. 'I thought to myself: I am walking on the streets of Bethlehem, but my father and my brother and my mother are no longer here and so are they still my streets? I wanted my brother to see my release. Everyone was shaking my hand and slapping my back. But what was I thinking was I must go as soon as I can to my brother's grave. I wanted to see it. He had been gone eighteen years and six months but I had not yet accepted that he was dead.'

Later in the evening, he suggested again that the world had become unfamiliar in the profoundest of ways.

'People we had known were dead,' he told me. 'Others who greeted us had not yet been born when we were last here. People from the past came to see us but I did not recognise them. Others were nearly familiar, but not quite.

'On my first night home, I could not sleep. I lay listening to the wind. I imagined the empty street outside. It was my home street now, but it seemed foreign and dangerous.'

As Fusi Mofokeng spoke, I turned away and looked at Victoria. In retrospect, I see that something must have drawn my attention: a glint, or a flash, as the overhead light caught the moisture on her face. She was gazing at the television screen, exposing her profile to me. A tear was running down her cheek and her eyes were blinking.

Fusi clocked that something in the living room had captured my attention for he turned in his chair. On seeing his sister crying he stood up and drew the interview abruptly to a close.

'I am sorry we didn't speak longer,' he said, as he drove me back to my car. 'You have come a long way and were maybe expecting to speak for a long time. I noticed while we were talking that our discussion had upset Victoria. I did not want her to keep listening to things that made her sad. And in any case, I have had flu for the last week. I think I should get an early night.'

I was very happy with the evening, I said, and did not think that the discussion had ended too soon. And I asked him how he had dealt with having flu when he was in prison.

'I was never sick in prison,' he replied. 'I was always healthy. Except for stomach ulcers. I was told that I got them because I was depressed.'

We drove in silence for some time.

'I was depressed,' he continued, 'because I was struggling alone. Tshokolo could not help me; he only has a Standard 3. I was struggling on our case and I was alone and it made me depressed. In prison, I finished high school, I did it by correspondence. The subjects I did for matric were mainly law subjects. I had to understand why we were in jail. Tshokolo could not write. I didn't want someone else to write for me because they would have got what I was saying wrong. I wanted to express my own feelings.'

'It is amazing to me that you are not angrier,' I said.

He stared straight ahead, about his mouth the vaguest hint of a smile.

'I was very angry,' he replied. 'I realised that if I did not stop being angry, I was going to die. It was a slow thing, to come to understand that my anger was making ulcers inside me, that the ulcers would turn into something worse, that I was busy dying.'

'Do you remember how it came to you?' I asked. 'The connection between your anger and your health.'

'I was shown the connection,' he said, 'by a warder, a very good man, a white man. His name was Steyn. One morning he came to me and said, "Fusi, I am watching your face. It is grey. You need to accept what has happened to you. If you do not, you will get very sick and you will not recover. I can see it in your face."

'I started to learn to step away, to watch myself from the other end of the room. I am still learning. It is an ongoing process. Even tonight, when I saw that Victoria was upset, I grew very angry. You maybe could not see it because I speak softly, but underneath I was wondering whether I will ever properly learn to control my anger.'

We did not speak again on that journey. I stared out of the window at the yellow and white lights of Bethlehem, the pulse in my temple pumping swollen feelings into my head. I was rehearsing how I might ask his permission to write this book.

Three

The way Fusi Mofokeng remembers it now, he was woken that day, 2 April 1992, when his brother-in-law, Sikhalo Ncala, knocked on his front door. It was late to be in bed, about 7:45 a.m.; but Fusi had booked himself off work sick and had no reason to tear himself from his blankets at dawn.

Bethlehem was unseasonably hot that day – by early afternoon the temperature would have climbed to thirty degrees – and when he opened the front door, a warm breeze must have washed over his face.

The two men greeted. Sikhalo lived outside Johannesburg, a good two-and-a-half-hour drive from Bethlehem. He said that he had left home before dawn, that he was on his way to Inanda in what was then still called Natal (today's KwaZulu-Natal) and had stopped in Bethlehem to see Amos, Fusi's elder brother. But Amos was gone. He had left for work at least an hour earlier, and would not be back until late afternoon.

Sikhalo stepped aside and nodded at the driveway to reveal a bakkie, its cargo area covered by a white canopy. It was full of men, he informed Fusi: one in the front seat, two behind, and another four in the back.

'I must see Amos,' Fusi remembers Sikhalo saying, 'even if we must wait all day.' And so Fusi invited them in.

From the moment the men climbed out of the bakkie, it was clear that something was not right. Each greeted Fusi furtively, absently, brushing past him with barely a word. Once they were in the house – eight grown men crowded into a small home – Fusi smelled their unease.

I am telling the story as Fusi first told it to me – we were sitting opposite each other at a chain fish restaurant in the centre of Bethlehem, a plate of hake and chips in front of each of us, at the surrounding tables white people who had come to eat from the surrounding suburbs. I think of that evening now as one of innocence, both mine and his. For in the coming years I would take him back to that morning often and his account would shift and buckle. [years -]

But a truth certain beyond doubt is that the men who walked into Fusi's home that morning had come from a civil war.

Many years earlier, Sikhalo had left Bethlehem with his newly wedded wife, Fusi's sister Victoria, and settled on the East Rand of Johannesburg; he had found work in the building industry and, after some time, established a modest construction business of his own. Having lived for several years in the backyards of other people's homes, he and Victoria erected a shack in a newly formed shantytown called Phola Park and were living there when the apartheid government unbanned its foe, the ANC, in 1990. In the uncertainty, fear and sheer malice the interregnum unleashed, the East Rand descended into warfare, armed civilian against armed civilian, one side supporting the ANC, the other the Zulu nationalist Inkatha Freedom Party (IFP), the apartheid police and army playing a murky and by no means impartial role in between.

Sikhalo was among the residents of Phola Park who chose to fight. By day he ran a construction business; by night he was a member of a self-defence unit (SDU) aligned to the ANC. He had become a soldier-workingman whose military training consisted of learning to assemble and fire an AK-47 in secret in the dead of night.

When his brother-in-law arrived in Bethlehem that morning, Fusi assumed that it was the civilian Sikhalo who had come.

'He had done construction work in Natal before,' Fusi told me. 'I thought that the ones with him were the labourers he had employed.'

Only once the men had filled the house with their aggression and their fear did Fusi begin to suspect that it was the soldier Sikhalo who had come to his house.

Normally, Fusi would have been out of the house by 7:45 a.m. He would have been at work behind a cash register at Checkers, one of the large supermarkets in the centre of the white town. Sikhalo would have knocked on the door of an empty house, prowled around for a while, and then left to make other plans. But Fusi was ill and he had taken time off.

There was no food in the house; some of the Phola Park men took the bakkie into town to buy breakfast. Where exactly they went and why, precisely what was in the sausages they brought back to cook on Fusi's stove: these questions would linger for years.

Fusi left, too, to visit his father, who was also sick, and to shop. He returned in the early afternoon.

Several people came to see him during the course of the day and each of these visits would come to matter; each would be contorted to tell a story. First, a young man called Thabo Motaung arrived. Fusi's father had sent him to see if his ailing son required attention. He was warmed by his father's thoughtfulness; he had remembered that his son was ill.

Two women visited in the early afternoon: Amos's girlfriend and another. They idled away an hour or two, drinking tea, talking about nothing in particular. In the mid-afternoon, shortly after they had gone, the Phola Park men, who had been hanging about the yard, prepared to depart. Fusi was not sorry to see them go. He washed the dishes they had dirtied and swept the house.

The dying sun brought Tshokolo Mokoena, as it had done every day since Fusi had been ill. Mokoena sat down and rolled a joint out of newspaper.

'He was a great dagga smoker,' Fusi recalled. 'He was a welder. He had a job at a workshop in town. He knocked off at 4:45. He would walk across the fields straight to my house. By 5:15 he would be sitting next to me, smoking his dagga.'

They had met about a year earlier. Opposite Checkers was an establishment where people bet on horses. During his lunch hour one day, Fusi had eyed a young man heading into the betting store, his jaw clenched, the tips of two bank notes protruding from his fist. The tension in the young man's face and in his gait had amused Fusi. He had waited for him to come out, stepped into his path and introduced himself, his eyes full of mirth.

Now, Mokoena sat in Fusi's yard on an upturned crate, smoking his joint. The sound of police sirens filled the two men's ears, first from far away, then very close, then far again. As they sat there talking, Mokoena smoking, their conversation was stopped short by a deafening noise, mechanical and unfamiliar, and before they had time to register what it might be an aircraft flew over Fusi's yard, so low that he glimpsed the crown of the pilot's head. It was a crop-sprayer, Fusi noted, but the nearest wheatfields were several kilometres away.

Fusi left Tshokolo Mokoena on his upturned crate and went out into the street. People had shot the police somewhere – that is what Fusi heard: he does not remember now who said it. In the twilight, army trucks began rolling into the township and disgorging one soldier after another. By nightfall, Bohlokong, Bethlehem's black township, was swarming with uniformed men and their guns and their machines.

The sight was not unfamiliar. For the last seven years, ever since young people had taken to the streets, marching, throwing stones, enforcing boycotts of white businesses, armed personnel had periodically swept the township. Sometimes they came at 5:00 on a Friday morning, hundreds of them, knocking on every door. Any young man sixteen years or older they dragged from his home, threw into a van and drove to the police station in town. There, the young men of Bohlokong would be crammed into holding cells, only to be led out one by one, their fingerprints taken, some of them pushed and slapped, before being sent home.

When news came that a raid had begun, young men would bolt from their parents' homes. Some went to hide in the township graveyard, others in churches and schools where they would lock the doors. On one of these raids, the police had marched into the house, ordered Fusi from his bed and threatened to take him away. His aunt, who was living with Fusi at that time, had stood between him and the police, her hands on her ample hips.

'This boy works at Checkers,' she had shouted. 'He must be at work at 8:00 a.m. If he is late he will be fired. You can take him, but then you must pay his wage.'

Now, with a plane flying overhead and the soldiers in the township, Tshokolo decided to chance the streets and go home, leaving Fusi to prepare food for Amos, who arrived several minutes after Tshokolo had left. Before Fusi could serve dinner, there was a quiet rapping on the door. It was Sikhalo's younger brother, a shy, stuttering man whom Fusi had known for as long as he could remember.

His message was so strange that at first Fusi did not understand what he was saying.

'My brother is here,' he kept repeating. 'He wants to talk to you.'

'Where exactly is your brother?'

'Here. Outside. On the street. He will not come in. You must go and talk to him.'

They went outside and the young man pointed down the street. Sikhalo was standing there on the corner. Fusi looked at him and Sikhalo looked back; they stood that way for some time before Sikhalo finally came.

In the safety of the house, in a murmur they could hardly make out, Sikhalo told the brothers his news. On the outskirts of Bethlehem, he said, a police van had stopped him and his comrades; two patrol officers had approached the bakkie, which was full of AK-47s, for the men were on their way to fight a battle against the IFP in Inanda. Under instruction from their commander, they had assembled one of their weapons and opened fire and hit both officers. Later, as they were fleeing, they had shot a farmer.

The way Fusi remembers it now, Sikhalo recounted his news in a voice so quiet that one had to strain to hear him. He was sitting at the kitchen table, his body very still, his hands fiddling with a fork.

The men had split up, Sikhalo explained. Five had stayed with the bakkie and were now on the road to Natal. But Sikhalo and the remaining two had made their way, on foot, to Bohlokong, and the others were somewhere out there now. Unlike Sikhalo, they knew nobody in the township; they would never find their way to Fusi and Amos's place and there was no safe house in which they might hide.

'They will be caught,' Fusi remembers telling Sikhalo. 'And they will be tortured. It will not be long before they give you up.'

Sikhalo shook his head slowly. 'They are highly trained,' he replied. 'It will not be so easy for them to get arrested.'

Amos and Fusi consented to hide Sikhalo. They were hardly going to turf him out into the night. In the morning they would assess what to do.

They made Sikhalo a bed and he promptly went to sleep. Fusi, who knew by now that he was not going to sleep at all, listened to the Sesotho news. It was first item: two members of Umkhonto we Sizwe, the armed wing of the ANC, had been arrested in Bohlokong, the township of Bethlehem.

Fusi woke Sikhalo. He told him that his comrades were with the police now; he was in great danger.

17

'They are highly professional,' Sikhalo said. 'They have been trained how to handle interrogation. They will say nothing.'

He climbed back into his bed and laid his head on the pillow: in less than a minute his breathing had slowed and deepened. That his brother-in-law could simply lie down and sleep in these circumstances astonished Fusi. He himself sat on a chair and waited.

It was about 11:00 p.m. when they came and although he had not yet given up expecting them, their manner of announcing themselves shook him to the core: a heavy knocking on the front door and all of the windows simultaneously, as if a creature with many arms had wrapped itself around the house and was banging with its many fists.

He got up and looked out of the window. A long barrel of a rifle was pointed at him. Habitually, he went to the kitchen to fetch a knife from the drawer. The handle on the front door had come loose weeks earlier and nobody had bothered to fix it. To open the door, one had to slide a knife into the mechanism and push the lock aside.

As he made his way to the door, knife in hand, it burst open, slammed against the kitchen wall and fell to the floor.

They were a great many of them, and they filed into the house, one after the other after the other. They pushed Fusi aside and stopped before Sikhalo, who had now got up and was standing in the middle of the house.

'*Hier's hy*,' one of them said, and they descended upon him.

Sikhalo is no more than five foot six, a slight, narrow-chested man. He now has a modest paunch, but I imagine that back then he was quite scrawny.

The way Fusi remembers it, one of them stood behind Sikhalo, hooked his forearms under Sikhalo's armpits and lifted him up into the air, his bare feet scrambling to find solid ground. Taking turns, the others laid into him with the barrels of their guns: in the stomach, in the crotch, in the ribs, in the chest. He was screaming for them to stop. The one who was holding him dropped him hard onto the floor and he rolled up in a ball.

Fusi does not remember how many policemen were in his house that night. He recalls only the three whom he would come to know well. Captain Colin Robertshaw, a striking man, tall and strong. His Afrikaans was stilted, his accent English. Warrant Officer Johannes Steyn, a more nondescript white man who belted out abuse in rapid Afrikaans. And Sergeant Mapalala, a towering oaf of a black man, the bottom of his trench coat dancing around his heels. They were all members of the Security Branch, he guessed, the political intelligence arm of the South African Police.

They searched the house. Everything they laid their hands on, they damaged. They tore open the backs of speakers and ripped up the bottoms of drawers. Fusi was made to stand up against the wall with his hands in the air. Mapalala guarded him. He put the barrel of his gun inside Fusi's mouth, right inside, so that he gripped it between his teeth.

The search took no more than an hour. At about midnight, Fusi, Amos and Sikhalo were loaded into a van and taken to the police station in town. Through the wire mesh at the back of the van Fusi saw that the soldiers were piling back into their trucks; the search was over; they were going back to barracks.

They have left the house in terrible mess, he remembers thinking. And they have destroyed many of our possessions. It will take time and money to put things right.

At 9:00 the following morning, a white man arrived at the police station clutching a briefcase. He was Amos's employer, the owner of the Mobil petrol station in town. Amos had worked a ten-hour shift the previous day, he said. And he ought to be at work now. If he was kept any longer, his employer would take legal action against the police. Amos was released at about 10:00 a.m. By lunchtime he was back at work.

The date was 3 April 1992. Fusi had now been in jail for about twelve hours. He would be released from this very building eighteen years and three hundred and sixty-four days later.

Four

It would have been a little after midnight when Fusi, Amos and Sikhalo Ncala were led into the police station. Fusi was separated from the others and locked in a room. For how long he sat there alone he does not recall, but some time later Robertshaw and Steyn came in and shut the door behind them. They did not lay a finger on him. They did not even raise their voices. What he recalls above all is their forensic interest in the last twenty-four hours of his freedom. Minute by minute, they wanted to know what he had done and whom he had seen.

He told them of being woken by Sikhalo's knock, of the men his brother-in-law had brought into the house, of his conviction that they were construction workers on their way to begin a project somewhere in Natal. He told of the two women who had come to visit him, of Thabo Motaung, sent by Fusi's father, of the visit Tshokolo Mokoena had paid him after work. He had done nothing wrong. He saw no risk in sharing the anodyne information his mere existence churned out each day.

In the women the police officers took only a brief interest. But the young men who came by, Thabo Motaung and Tshokolo Mokoena, concerned them a great deal. They wanted to know their places of work, their home addresses, with whom they lived. They wanted to know for how long Fusi had been acquainted with them, how often he saw them, and why.

He answered each question as narrowly as he could and no more. They would release him within a few hours, he thought. Whether they would pay the courtesy of taking him home was another thing; probably, they would disgorge him onto the streets of Bethlehem and he would make his way home on foot. By early afternoon he would be installed in his house, doing what he could to repair the enormous damage the police officers had wreaked.

Instead he was shackled, his left wrist to his left ankle, his right wrist to his right ankle. Thus chained, he was led to a cell and locked up alone.

It was truly a grim affair. There was no bed – he was to sleep on a thin mat on a concrete floor. Nor was there a tap. To drink, he soon discovered, he would have to scoop water from the toilet, using the bowl they gave him from which to eat his porridge.

For the following month this was to be his home. He would be kept here for twenty-three hours a day, unwashed, ungroomed, not so much as a bar of soap with which to clean his body, nor a mirror with which to see his face. As for his chains, they were kept locked, always, even when he was alone in his cell. They were long enough, to be sure, to permit him to walk, but whenever he took a step, or turned in his sleep, or raised his hand to scratch his face, they would spit metallic noise.

After breakfast each morning he was led into the yard for an hour of sunlight where he would join a handful of other prisoners. He would pace the yard's perimeter, his chains scraping about him.

Once, during exercise, whether on his second day in jail or the next he no longer recalls, a prisoner tapped him on the shoulder.

'They have brought in another of your people,' the man said.

'Where?' Fusi asked. 'Where is this other person?'

He heard his name being called – a disembodied voice, somewhere in the courtyard. He looked around but could not find its owner.

And then he saw Tshokolo. He was standing on a raised step at the other end of the yard.

'Why did you say what you said?' Tshokolo shouted.

'What?' Fusi replied.

'That we were planning to rob the Orsmonds. You and me. That we brought the men from Phola Park to rob the Orsmonds. You led the police to my door. You are a bastard.'

He wanted to reply, to say that he did not understand, that Tshokolo must explain further, but he had disappeared as suddenly as he had come.

Back in his cell, drinking the water into which he shat, growing increasingly aware of his own stench, he found, in a corner, a sharp-edged stone. With it, he carved a calendar onto his cell wall. Each morning as the sun rose, he would cross off a day. What exactly was he counting? The days left until he would regain his freedom, he remembers thinking. But to count the days he would have to know how many there were. And about this, Steyn and Robertshaw, who came to see him often, only confused him.

Sometimes they did little to mask their hatred for him. They did not believe that he was just an innocent boy from Bethlehem, they said. His story did not add up. By now they knew that he had spent a month with Sikhalo in Thokoza at the beginning of the year. What was he doing there for all that time? And in the company of a man who had now admitted to being a terrorist? Thokoza was awash with automatic weapons, with ANC guerrillas who had crept over the border and come to fight. He was one of them, they said. He was an outlaw.

At some point – he thinks it was a week after their detention – Fusi and Sikhalo were driven in separate cars to Johannesburg. Of the journey's purpose Fusi was told nothing. They drove in convoy along the N3, Fusi in the back of one car, Sikhalo in the back of another.

On the outskirts of Johannesburg, the car carrying his brother-in-law veered onto an offramp and disappeared, taking Sikhalo to who knows where. Fusi himself was led to one police station after another: first Germiston, not far from Thokoza; then Brixton, in the heart of Johannesburg; then Newlands. At each station, he was made to stand still for some time in front of a mirror. He did not understand the purpose of the procedure; he did not know of panes of glass that were see-through on one side, a mirror on the other. Only much later did the others inform him that behind the glass were people from Phola Park, picked up from their homes that morning.

The police clearly did not believe Fusi when he said that he was simply minding his business when Sikhalo knocked on his door. They were convinced that during his visits to his brother-in-law in Phola Park he had picked up a gun and fought. Behind the one-way glass were people the police hoped would tell them so.

Towards the end of that day, Robertshaw locked Fusi in a bare room and sat down at a table opposite him. From the questions he asked, it was clear that he had retrieved all the official documentation the quarter century of Fusi's existence had left. School records showed that he had lived in Thokoza until the end of 1982. In January 1984, he had begun school in Bethlehem. What had happened during that missing year? Where had he been? He was fifteen years old at the time, just the age at which a boy living amidst a growing insurgency might take to politics.

In a quiet voice, Fusi explained. He had in fact moved from Thokoza to Bethlehem in 1983, he said. But his passbook still recorded him as living in Thokoza and so he was not permitted to register at a Bethlehem school. It had caused the family immense anxiety. In the end, a social worker had had to intervene to secure his registration at a local school. But in the meantime he had missed a year.

Robertshaw lifted his hand as if to scratch his chin, but instead his arm flashed across the table, and Fusi found, to his astonishment, that he had been struck in the face.

'You are lying,' Robertshaw shouted. 'You were with the ANC in exile. You were receiving military training.'

'I was in Bethlehem,' Fusi said quietly.

It was an open-handed slap, more a half-hearted exploration than an earnest attempt to cause pain. The big man folded his hands in front him and was quiet for some time. When he spoke again, it was in a soft voice.

If Steyn and Robertshaw at times condemned him as a terrorist and a liar, at others they told him that he would soon be free. He needed only turn state witness, they said. He need only tell the court what his brother-in-law and his comrades had been up to in Bethlehem that day. If he was indeed not one of them, there was no reason that he should share in their fate.

At first, he agreed to testify. But to what, exactly, it is hard to say. At this moment in our conversations, he tells a story I cannot follow. For each round of ammunition we collect, from each AK-47 we find, the police told him, your reward money will increase. They wanted him to accompany them to the scene of the crime. To count shells? I am not sure. I tell him that I do not understand. And so he recounts the same story from the beginning, about the rounds of ammunition and the reward money, about them insisting that to be state witness he must take them to the scene of the crime. I leave the subject and return to it weeks later. The story he tells is the same.

Sometimes he tells me that he agreed to testify, but not to lie. He would say that he knew his brother-in-law to be a member of the Phola Park self-defence unit (SDU). But he would not say that he saw these men's weapons because in truth he did not; he noticed only that their shirts were untucked.

But at other times he intimates that he agreed to say much more. What exactly is buried in a wilderness to which he will not take me, and to which, I increasingly suspect, he himself will not go?

He can forgive anyone who turns state witness, he tells me, for he himself came close to betraying the Thokoza men. And how can he stand in judgment of those who did what he himself almost did?

It was sheer luck, he says, that he did not testify against the others. In our conversations, he repeats these words so often. Sheer luck.

At the heart of his explanation for his silence is a fellow prisoner. All these years later, he no longer has a face or a name.

'He was older than me,' Fusi recalls. 'He was knowledgeable about the police and their ways. He warned me. "Do not agree to testify. They will want to take you to the scene of the crime and they will take a picture of you there and use that picture against you in court. There the judge will see you at the scene holding a spent cartridge, or perhaps even a gun, and you will be convicted along with the rest."

'I had never visited the scene of the crime,' Fusi tells. 'Never in my life. I was not going to visit it now. That man taught me. He taught me not to trust Robertshaw and Steyn. They would betray me. They were not talking the truth.'

Who was this cipher-prisoner? Fusi recalls only that he was an older man, a man of some experience, a man who knew what's what.

Where did they speak? Was this man in the cell next door to Fusi's? Did they shout to one another through the wall? Or did the conversation take place during exercise time? Winter was coming and one can imagine the two men huddled in a patch of sunlight, the elder guiding the younger from great danger.

He does not recall. He remembers only the words, disembodied, their owner and their context long gone.

One morning in early May, he was driven across the Free State to the town of Kroonstad. There, in the town's large prison, he was placed in a cell and in the cells alongside him were Sikhalo Ncala, Tshokolo Mokoena and three of the strange men who had come to his house on the morning of 2 April. They were able to talk to one another through the bars and, at exercise time, to speak face to face.

He no longer recalls whether he knew by then the fate of the other four Thokoza men: that two had escaped and disappeared despite a nation-wide manhunt to find them, and that two more were dead, gunned down by the police on 2 April, somewhere under the Free State sky. He is almost certain that he knew this much earlier, that the presence of five men rather than nine came as no surprise, but he is not sure.

Within hours of his arrival, he discovered that he was the odd one out. Each of the others had been through hell. On the day that Fusi had been pushed in front of the one-way glass in Johannesburg, Sikhalo had been stripped naked, the tube of a tyre squeezed over his head. They had wanted to know about self-defence unit members: who had ferried guns, who had trained new soldiers, to whom in the ANC they reported. During the course of that long day, Sikhalo had resolved to die; in the cells at Brixton Police Station, he had attempted to end his life.

As for Tshokolo, one needed only look at him to see that he had been badly hurt. During his first interrogation they had taken to his face with the butt of a gun and he had not been right since. He suffered from recurrent headaches and blurred vision. Even now, he said, when he turned his head he felt a sharp pain flash through his face.

The first few days in Kroonstad were tough, Fusi says, for the others were aware that he might testify for the state. The homes of their friends and comrades in Thokoza had been raided. With whom had Fusi been talking? What sort of information had he been sharing? Why was he the only one among them who had not been badly beaten?

Sikhalo intervened on his behalf, Fusi says. Sikhalo assuaged them. It was not long before his co-accused trusted him. He was soon to consider each one of them a friend.

But of what did Sikhalo convince them? He says that his brother, Amos, paid for the services of a lawyer, a white man named Swanepoel. But his co-accused persuaded him to save his brother's money for the ANC had hired a lawyer for them all, a man named Denis Legodi who came all the way from Johannesburg to see his clients. What they discussed with him, what Fusi discussed with Swanepoel before Fusi dismissed him, he no longer recalls.

He remembers instead that, on their second and third mornings in Kroonstad, they were woken long before dawn and driven in the darkness to Bethlehem. They were being taken to attend their pre-trial hearing, they were told.

The hearing was convened each morning at daybreak. Fusi and his co-accused were considered very dangerous men, not just for what they had allegedly done, but for the agitation their presence in Bethlehem might cause. They were known guerrillas now and news of their crime was swarming across the black township. The presence of these men would surely draw unwelcome crowds. And so they were slipped into town on the quiet, the sun hardly risen. The proceedings were compressed and hurried; the court sat for no more than two hours each day so that the accused might be spirited away.

Of the proceedings Fusi recalls nothing at all. He remembers instead that on their arrival each morning the court building was surrounded by men in camouflage uniforms, the nostrils of their rifles facing the ground. Inside the court, glancing around, he realised with a jolt that an armed soldier was peering through each and every window, the barrel of his gun angling into the courtroom.

Sitting in the dock, he found himself thinking of a man called Gabriel

Mahakoe. He had never met Mahakoe, but he had read of him and had spoken so often about him that this stranger had come to live inside his being.

Mahakoe was the son of Free State farm labourers. So was Fusi. Had they ever met, they would have fallen easily into conversation – they were of the same world.

Throughout 1991, Mahakoe had worked as a farmhand outside the oddly named village of Verkeerdevlei, 'the wrong marsh', in the central Free State. His employers were an elderly couple, Willie and Bettie Engelbrecht.

On a morning in December 1991, Mahakoe broke into the Engelbrechts' farmhouse. They had left for Bloemfontein an hour or so earlier and he knew that they would not come back until the afternoon. He ransacked the empty house, found a rifle, loaded it with ammunition, lay down on their king-sized bed, and waited.

They returned a few hours later with their daughter and two grandchildren, aged eleven and twelve. Mahakoe killed them all, save for the elder child, Emily, whom he left for dead. He was arrested that same night in Bloemfontein. When asked why he had slaughtered a family, he was said to have replied: 'I was killing apartheid.'

By the following evening, his name had passed the lips of many thousands of Free Staters. In the townships of the poor, like Bohlokong, he became a legend, this lone black man announcing with such brutal clarity a changing of the guard. In the homes of whites, he became a virus, his name spreading stories grander and more terrible with each telling. It was said that he had been trained by the armed wing of the Pan Africanist Congress (PAC), or by Umkhonto we Sizwe, the ANC's army. While Nelson Mandela negotiated with the white government, it was said, his demeanour ever so genteel, his suit so very smart, his army had begun to slaughter his enemy.

Mahakoe's trial was to start in Bloemfontein in late May, just weeks after Fusi's pre-trial hearing. He would take the witness stand. For the first time he was to speak, in public, uncensored, to the world.

Sitting in the dock in the hush of dawn, the soldiers staring grimly through the windows, it occurred to Fusi that he had been swept into a story too strong, too deep. Despite himself, despite having done no more than wake up and answer a knock on the door, a tale was taking shape, and in that tale he was Gabriel Mahakoe.

Five

Late one night in the autumn of 1964, three years before Fusi's birth, his maternal uncle, Jan Mbele, fell into a hole.

He was in Johannesburg at the time working in a metal foundry. One evening he went out visiting and on his return crossed an empty field on the property of a gold mine. Somewhere in the middle of that field, in the pitch dark, he tumbled into a pit or a cavity or a hollow – nobody is certain any more. It was surely very deep, though, for he spent several weeks in hospital before leaving Johannesburg and returning to the farm that his family called home, his left arm mangled and useless.

When Mbele's employer, a white farmer named Snyman, caught sight of the shrivelled arm, he said, according to family legend: 'Jan, you are useless to me now. You and your family must pack your belongings and go.'

The farm was called Lucia. It lay in a long, narrow valley some fifteen kilometres southwest of Bethlehem. Aside from Jan and his wife, Tebello, the Mbeles of Lucia included Fusi's grandparents, Nono and Rose. Fusi's mother was still with his father then, and her three-year-old daughter, Victoria, in a rented room in Bohlokong.

It snowed heavily that winter, not just on the farms southwest of Bethlehem, but across South Africa's plateau. Mile upon mile of farmland and veld was lit up a brilliant white.

In Mbele family lore, the snow was falling and they had nowhere to go. Word spread among the black farm tenants of the valley, and into the kitchens of the white farmhouses, and, at the eleventh hour, the Greylings of Oorsprong said that they had use for the Mbeles, despite Jan's crippled arm. Old man Nono could still herd cattle, the Greylings said, and there were domestic chores aplenty for Tebello and Rose.

On a Saturday morning some time in July, a tractor came from Oorsprong trailing a wagon onto which the Mbeles piled their worldly possessions. It was not a long trip: Oorsprong lay at the other end of the valley.

What was in Jan Mbele's thoughts as the tractor dragged his family and his possessions to yet another farm? Perhaps he wondered whether those who wished him ill had sent a demon to steer his course that night. For why did he cross a wide field on the precise trajectory that would lead him into a hole? Maybe he cursed the mining company for leaving exposed a deep pit in a field that black workers used to get home. That is the significance his wife, Tebello, attached to the story of her husband's fall when she told it to me half a century later.

Men like Jan Mbele spent their lives sparring and ducking and feinting, as had their parents and their parents before them. The flesh of the story changed shape from one generation to the next, but the bare bones were the same: black people west of the Caledon River were dispossessed of their land in the late nineteenth century. From then on, the title deeds belonged to white people. If you were black and lived in the farmlands of the eastern Free State, you negotiated the terms of your existence with a landlord. He allowed you to live on his land, to grow maize and vegetables around your yard, to keep a small number of cattle. He allowed you to raise your family on his farm. In exchange, your landlord wanted your family's labour: yours, your wife's, your children's.

It was a deal against which you strained with all your being; and it was understood that you would break the rules when you could. Perhaps Jan Mbele had been breaking the rules when he fell into a hole – he had been working in a metal foundry in Johannesburg instead of on his landlord's farm. It is hard to know now the situation between him and Snyman. Perhaps the rules were malleable and rested upon a delicate balance of power. Perhaps the spectacle of Mbele's damaged arm shifted the balance in Snyman's favour and gave him licence to be cruel.

Jan's fall is a marker in the tales of injustice that have shaped the Mbeles' fate. It is a marker in this story, too. Among the tenants on Oorsprong was a family named Ncala. In 1973, their fourteen-year-old son, Sikhalo, would come to live there. By then, the Mbeles had been on Oorsprong nine years.

It was because of Jan's fall that Victoria and Sikhalo became neighbours. Had Jan not fallen, they might never have met, let alone married. And it would not have been on Fusi's door that Sikhalo knocked on 2 April 1992.

Six

When black people of a certain age reflect on their child-hoods on the eastern Free State's farms, their stories, invariably, turn to the *baas*, the white person on whose land they lived.

In Sikhalo's case, the boss was unusual indeed – not a middle-aged man with red neck and hairy arms, but an elderly widow. As the black tenants understood it, the Greyling son had had no appetite for farming and had gone to live in the nearby town of Harrismith. And the Greyling daughter had for many years lived on her husband's farm. In charge of Oorsprong's daily running was their mother, an old lady so frail, Sikhalo remembers, that she never once ventured into town alone. Instead, she would summon a team of black teenage boys, Sikhalo among them.

They would climb onto the back of her bakkie and feel the wind on their faces as she drove towards Bethlehem. In town, they would follow her into the farm supply stores and supermarkets and bakeries. She would bark instructions at the shop attendants and more instructions at her teenage underlings and by the time her business was done a veritable hoard of young black men followed in her wake through the streets, each burdened with fertiliser or tractor parts or fresh bread.

Her way was to shout and scream, Sikhalo says. He does not recall her ever talking in a soft voice. But he speaks kindly of her. She was hard because she was scared. To be an old lady running a farm alone – she dared not for a moment betray doubt.

Her name was Lettie, Lettie Greyling. Of this the black boys on Oorsprong were only dimly aware. They called her Madipela, 'Mother of the Rock Rabbits'.

Early on weekend mornings, the black boys of Oorsprong would scatter across the veld with their catapults and their stones. If they were still empty-handed by the time the sun hit their foreheads, they would turn reluctantly for home. But on those mornings of success, the one who had slain a rock rabbit would hold it up triumphantly in his fist. Right there, at the site of his conquest, he would skin it while the others made a fire. Rock rabbit meat was for the boys' mouths only, scoffed in the veld, out of sight, the product of the boys' own skills.

On seeing the smoke rising from the veld, Madipela would leave her farmhouse, march across her fields and storm the fireside gathering. '*Daai dassies is God se diertjies,*' she would shout. '*Julle is 'n klomp barbare.*' ('Those rock rabbits are God's little animals. You are a bunch of barbarians.') Then she would repeat what she had said in fluent Sesotho, in case the Afrikaans was not clear enough. The boys would bury their chins in their necks and stare sullenly at the ground.

After she was gone, her image remained, an old white lady, her hair unbrushed and streaked by the wind, her nostrils flared in anger. One of the boys would stand up and, in a screeching falsetto, shout out – *Daai dassies is God se diertjies!* – wagging a crooked finger in the air.

When Sikhalo came to Oorsprong he enrolled at the local school, a single-storey building at the other end of the valley, one side all windows, the other side all brick wall. At a trot, it was two and a half hours from Oorsprong. The kids would leave the farm at 6:00 a.m. and move briskly across the valley. When they passed the farm next door another half a dozen kids would join them, and then some more at the next farm and a few more at the next. By the time they were halfway there they were more than two dozen in all, some as young as seven, others as old as nineteen. Towards the end of the journey, each day, without fail, a white bakkie would slow as it passed. The window would be wound down and Snyman would poke out his head – the same Snyman who had once evicted the Mbeles from his farm.

'*Draai om! Draai om!*' he would shout. '*Skool maak swart kinders siek.*' ('Turn around! Turn around! School makes black children ill.')

The school itself stood in the middle of a vast field, flat and empty but for a towering blue gum. From more than a kilometre away, one took in the scene, the school building dwarfed by the field and the tree.

For two years, Sikhalo did this daily trip to school. There was just one teacher, a Mr Mokoena, and he often lost track of which student was in which grade, the student body melding into a seamless whole. Whatever Sikhalo learnt there, it was not enough – years later, when he would start a business, a wealth of experience in construction under his belt, his innumeracy was to keep him down.

Sikhalo was sixteen, he thinks, when Madipela ordered his father to take the boy from school. If he was to remain on Oorsprong, she said, he must earn his keep.

The work was gentle by the valley's standards. He milked the cows in the mornings and in the evenings, and did odd jobs around the farmyard during the days. And when Madipela went to town, he would be there, of course, in the back of her bakkie, ready to usher her through the streets of Bethlehem.

After three years of working for Madipela, Sikhalo ran away. Without his father's blessing he got a lift to Bethlehem one night, and the following morning took a minibus taxi to Johannesburg. A week later, he sent word to his father, apologising for his flight and assuring him that all was okay. As for when he would come back to visit, Sikhalo could not say. It was 1978. He was nineteen years old.

The eastern periphery of Johannesburg was full of neighbours and kin; young Basotho men from the farms of the eastern Free State had been settling there for generations. Within days Sikhalo had found a job in a white suburb called Brackendowns.

It was bullshit work, he recalls. He pushed a wheelbarrow around all day. He was, after all, a farm boy, barely literate, barely conversant in any language but his native Sesotho and the Afrikaans in which white people ordered him about. But even the very worst work in all of Johannesburg was a hundred times better than what he did for Madipela. She paid him a token R5 per month. Pushing a wheelbarrow around the suburban gardens of Brackendowns, he earned R4 a day.

None of the young men who grew up on those farms wanted their parents' lives. They regarded their fathers as little more than slaves.

Madipela is long dead now. And the Greylings have sold the land they once farmed.

But the farmhouse remains. It has been leased to a retired police officer who lives there with his wife and half a dozen dogs. He was an athlete in his time and on the kitchen walls hang a dozen photographs of his younger self, a skimpy athlete's vest showing off his fine young frame. Wiry and bent, with several large dogs at his heels, he points us to the grasslands where the tenants' *stat* once stood. It is empty and dead quiet and in the long grass we search in vain for the ruins of the Mbele house. It has left no trace.

We wander further up the hill and stumble over an outcrop. Only once on our knees do we discover that it is an untended grave. Searching through the long grass we find another and then another. We tear the growth from the crosses and the tombstones and we see the names: Ncala. Mbele.

Their descendants are gone now, scattered across the settlements of many cities and towns. Over the generations, the Mbeles and Ncalas must have lived on half a dozen farms. Fate brought them together right at the end, the last of the labour tenants buried side by side, their children flung out into the world.

Seven

That the souls on her land were God-fearing drew from Madipela a measure of respect. Each Sunday morning, a tractor would make its way up the hill towards the black tenants' homes, an open cart banging along behind it. An assortment of tenants, young and old, would climb on board, mindful of getting dust on their starched Sunday clothes. It was her duty, Madipela believed, to assist her fellow Christians to pray to the God they shared.

The Dutch Reformed Church was a twelve-kilometre journey along the valley basin and the tractor would make heavy progress along a dirt road. Their feet firmly planted, their fists gripping the cart's rim, the tenants would make their way to church. Madipela herself attended a service in the centre of Bethlehem and from the pews sang at full throttle. That, at least, is what her tenants had come to imagine.

At a church service in the early summer of 1978, Victoria Mbele, Fusi's elder sister, caught Sikhalo Ncala eyeing her. He had vanished nine months earlier, telling neither his employer nor his parents. Only now had he begun furtively to reappear.

When the service was over, Sikhalo suggested to Victoria that they let the tractor leave without them. Getting home on foot was no Sunday stroll – a three-hour journey if they were brisk – but in the tenants' crowded lives the walk from church was a rare opportunity to be alone. Many a farm tenant's child lost her virginity on the quietest reaches of a neighbour's farm, her discarded church dress at her side.

Victoria has nothing to say of the time between Sikhalo's Sunday court-ship and their marriage, only that it was brief, a couple of months at most. She has nothing to say of Sikhalo, except that she had known him since she was a small girl. By the time she spoke to me, she was angry with him beyond words.

Victoria was seventeen years old when they married, Sikhalo nineteen. He went back to his life in Johannesburg and she moved in with his par-ents on Oorsprong. Within twenty months, she was the mother of two children.

Victoria had grown up on Oorsprong under the care of her beloved grandparents, Nono and Rose. Her memories of them are so soft, so still, so filled with longing for another time, that one wonders how real they can be.

The last four years of Victoria's unmarried life had been hard by any-one's measure. She was thirteen when her granny Rose collapsed and died. If the Mbeles were to keep their home at Oorsprong, Victoria would have to take over her grandmother's duties. She was to wash Madipela's clothes and scrub her floors; she was to fetch firewood for the burner that lit the stove; each evening she would cook Madipela a meal.

She had been working this way for two years when she began attend-ing school. Why she started only then, at the age of fifteen, she cannot say, but her childhood was almost over and still she could neither read nor write; the opportunity to learn was slipping away. And so she spent the weekday dawns of her sixteenth, seventeenth and eighteenth years trotting the length of the valley. In the late afternoons, five hours of jogging to and from school behind her, she would begin her work for Madipela, cleaning her clothes, scrubbing her floors. When she returned home, her domestic duties would begin. She prepared her grandfather Nono's dinner and then made her way back to the main farmhouse in the dark. From the tap in Madipela's garden she would fill a great bucket to the brim and carry it home on her head. The following day's fresh water secured, she could rest.

By the time she married Sikhalo, she was exhausted and, who knows, she may have wed him for the change of routine.

It was not what she had expected. True, Sikhalo's mother was an unsmiling woman who thought little of the Mbeles. Victoria's family was famously poor. But the Ncalas were hardly rich and Victoria thought her mother-in-law's haughtiness unearned. MaNcala would settle, she thought. Once Victoria was a part of her household, the two would make their peace.

But the stubbornness with which the old lady clung to her sourness still surprises Victoria now. During the time she spent in the Ncala household, her mother-in-law did not for a moment forget to show her displeasure. Victoria recalls not a laugh, not an unexpected smile. With her daughter-in-law she refused to exchange anything but grim distaste.

The first child came, followed in haste by the second. Now that the two women were sharing in the care of infants, Victoria hoped, MaNcala might soften. It was not to be. Until now, Victoria had thought herself resilient. Her grandmother's death had struck her hard, but she had learnt to usher her sadness to the hinterland of her being. Her days were consumed by hard work, after all.

But the relentless presence of this malign spirit, day in, day out, sapped the life from her very marrow. When she woke each morning her bones were too heavy, her heart too grey. Her first contact with a human being, she well knew, would be scowling, distasteful, unpleasant. Two years into their marriage she handed Sikhalo an ultimatum. He was to bring her to Johannesburg or she would pack her bags and take her chances alone.

When Victoria handed Sikhalo her ultimatum he immediately conceded. But preparing for the arrival of his family, he warned, would not be easy. There was no space in Johannesburg. People lived on top of one another, inside one another's lives. And with such hunger for space came stiff rents. If his family were to live in Thokoza, they would need a room of their own. Finding one would take time.

Months went by and they did not discuss Johannesburg. Victoria at times wondered whether, in her state of unhappiness, she had conjured her ultimatum, the flesh-and-blood Sikhalo oblivious to her demands. She was about to raise the matter once more when, on a weekend visit to Oorsprong, he announced, unbidden, that he was to build a tin shack for his family in his uncle's Thokoza yard. To have kin as landlords was good, he said; at least this way there would be a degree of trust.

He vowed, too, that within a year he would start his own construction business. He would walk the white neighbourhoods of Alberton and Brackendowns and Benoni knocking on door after door, offering to pave patios, to install swimming pools, to see to the building of extra rooms. He was good at his work, he said. And his prices were more than fair. He did not see how he could fail.

In the winter of 1982 he came to fetch Victoria from his mother's home. More than a year had passed since her ultimatum. She left with two bags and two children, a third in her womb. She was twenty-two years old.

In Thokoza she was free of her mother-in-law. These many years later, she still recalls her escape from the old lady with relief. That she was together with her husband and children under one roof she enjoyed too.

But there was cause for alarm. Sikhalo had not built them a shack in his uncle's yard. Instead, they were installed in the main house. In each of its three rooms lived a family. Together with his wife and four of their children, Sikhalo's uncle occupied the largest room. The second was home to Sikhalo's cousin and his brood. Victoria and Sikhalo and their children were given the third.

They were simply too many human beings for so small a space, she recalls. No fewer than five toddlers waddled around the house, shitting and crying and jabbering – one cannot control a young child all of the time. In the yard was a single pit latrine and one of the older children would inevitably soil it, triggering shouts and threats. The house was ungovernable, its residents brittle; somebody was always about to explode.

Although she did not miss life on Oorsprong, she found herself dwelling upon the open spaces through which she once moved. For the streets of Thokoza were no respite from her crowded home. She spoke Sesotho and a smattering of Afrikaans. And yet, she soon discovered, a minority of Thokoza residents knew her mother tongue; the lingua franca on the streets was isiZulu, of which she did not speak a word.

And Thokoza was violent, too, she says – many of the people who lived there liked to fight. I press her to say more, but she repeats only that people took easily to fighting. Whether she chooses not to talk about politics, I do not know. But in the middle of her time in Thokoza the townships around her would host a fifty-month-long insurgency against apartheid. Children would boycott school and put up barricades. At times, soldiers would move into the streets en masse. Around the townships' taxi business, warfare would periodically erupt and the streets would fill with gunfire.

Of this she says little. Instead, it is the eternal question of accommodation of which she speaks. After a year in Sikhalo's uncle's house they could take no more. They moved, first to a shack in a shantytown on the edges of Thokoza. After several months there, Sikhalo hit hard times. They missed a month's rent and were evicted. Next, they moved to a shack in a stranger's backyard. The rent was manageable this time, but living on the property of people they did not know took its toll. By 1987 there was a fourth Ncala child and it seemed to Victoria that each day her landlords lodged a new complaint about the kids. They had damaged the communal tap and it would cost money to mend. There was a sick old lady in the house and the noise of the Ncala children kept her awake. Victoria fought back as best she could. Do you expect my children not to play, she asked. Must we not use the tap for fear that you will accuse us of breaking it? But she knew that the problem was not the malice of her hosts. Thokoza was simply too crowded.

There are aspects of her life in Thokoza about which Victoria will not speak. A sense of decorum holds her tongue. In her recollections, she complains about cramped spaces, about violence and strange tongues. What she holds back is her deep anger; Sikhalo was driving her to despair.

Sometime in the mid-1980s, he found construction work in Natal and would begin going there for long periods, first weeks at a time, then months. It was understandable: there was work in Natal and he would send his hard-earned money home – in the beginning, at least.

By the late 1980s, his trips to Natal had grown longer, and for months at a time he would send nothing home, not a penny. Victoria had no steady income. She was raising four children. They needed to eat. There were times when she feared that she and her children would grow hungry. It was not long before somebody whispered a terrible truth in her ear: Sikhalo had a woman in Natal, and with that woman he had had a child.

These were the grimmest of times. Her mother was very poor, and Victoria was loath to do it, but once in a while she sent two of her children to stay with their granny, for she feared that in her own care they might starve. And yet she remained with Sikhalo. Once, when I felt that the mood permitted it, I asked her, obliquely, very carefully, for she had an aura that held such questions at bay, why she did not leave him.

'I was not sure what else I might do,' she said.

Not far from the Ncalas' various temporary homes in Thokoza was a disused coalyard. Sometime in the mid-1980s, several families put up shacks there. The owner of the property might have called the town council and had the intruders removed. Instead, he demanded a modest rent from them and thus opened a tap he could not close. Word soon spread that this was a stable place, that one could pay something affordable and stay there; within a year, 150 families had settled on the property. The landlord took fright; he sold his coalyard to a company that would return it to the purpose for which it was built. The new owners, in turn, demanded of the municipal government that it remove the trespassers.

In June 1987, in the heart of winter, the Thokoza Town Council sent a team of men to demolish the shacks. The coalyard people watched the men destroy their homes, waited for them to leave, and then resurrected their shantytown several hundred metres away. It was municipal land, and the council did not want them there, but it also foresaw an endless game of cat and mouse. Reluctantly, it put up tents on vacant land behind two massive hostels that housed migrant workers. The people under the towers were told that they had until November to move to the new site. About a hundred families made the move.

At first, they called their new home Dunusa, which means 'to bare one's arse'; it had no services at all: no lights, no running water, no toilets. They extracted from the council an undertaking that the area would be provided with running water, sewerage and refuse removal. And they renamed their new home Phola Park. 'Phola' means 'to relax or cool down'. They were signalling their suspicion that the council's promises could not be trusted and that they would not move again.

Over the following year, people poured into Phola Park, thousands of them. They came primarily from the backyard shacks in the surrounding townships, people tired of fighting with their landlords over cramped space, people battling to pay rent. Among them were the Ncalas.

The decision was Sikhalo's. To live rent-free, he said, in the middle of Thokoza – it was not an opportunity a family in their circumstances had the luxury of turning down. Victoria was hardly in a position to protest. Without an income of her own, her views did not count for much. For the food in her children's stomachs and the roof over their heads she was beholden to her husband, a man funnelling part of his income to a family far away.

She recalls Phola Park as the worst place she ever lived. There were no lights, no toilets. And in this crowded settlement there was not a familiar face. When the sun set the world was thrown into a darkness into which she forbade her children to go. The youngest, Maria, was two years old. Mpho was four and Jonas six. The eldest, Boetie, was ten. At twilight she would gather them and bolt her door. If the children needed to wee or poo during the night they would do so in a bucket, sheltered by a make-shift curtain. She recalls waking each morning to a shack that smelled. Only once the sun had chased the darkness away would she open the door and take her two elder children to school.

Their physical safety aside, it was her children's hygiene for which she feared most. Phola Park had no refuse disposal service, and she recalls the rubbish piling up between the shacks. The children of others would play freely among the garbage and Victoria would shake her head in despair. Her own children were forbidden to touch anything another had thrown away. And so even in the glare of the highveld afternoons her children were confined, their mother, in her vigilance, scolding them for touching this and handling that. The daylight hours were no less dangerous, in her view, than the night.

Among her few pleasant memories of those early months was the daily journey to get water. With all four children at her side, the two elder ones carrying a bucket each, she would make her way to Khalanyoni, one of the two worker hostels alongside Phola Park. Taking her place in the long queue in front of the hostel's taps, she would listen to the sounds of the many tongues around her — isiXhosa, isiZulu, the Xitsonga of the Mozambicans, her own Sesotho.

Mostly, the strangeness of this place and its many people scared her. But around the tap at Khalanyoni there was, for reasons she at first could not fathom, a sense of peace. What passed between these waiting people was gentle, almost convivial. For all that we are strange to one another, she would think to herself, every one of us needs water. Our common thirst leads us to queue together at this one place where it might be quenched. Around this tap we are human beings together.

That Sikhalo supported a clandestine family tormented Victoria. But even when he was at home, living his life in full sight, he was a stranger. She struggled to understand his attitude to Phola Park. Everything she hated about their awful home he seemed to love. The foreign tongues, the hard men, the permanent strife: on all of these things her husband thrived.

For him, coming to Phola Park had been an act of will. On his daily commute to work he had watched the first tents go up and had decided immediately that he was going to live there. He was among the first to walk in and build his own shack. Among his new neighbours he did not know a soul. He simply erected a home, moved his family and resolved never again to live in someone else's backyard.

From the start, staying entailed fighting. The residents in the surrounding formal homes wanted the squatters out. When the town council offered to move them tens of kilometres away, to a site in the town of Heidelberg, Sikhalo was among those who refused to go. And in the cauldron of this battle he made friends.

Outside his shack was a fruit and vegetable stall run by a Mozambican man named Joe. At night, Joe would tell stories of his former life as a soldier fighting for Frelimo in his country's civil war. And when he and Sikhalo were alone, Joe would take out his automatic weapon, an AK-47 with its famous curved magazine, which he had bought from a group of Mozambicans who lived in a hostel a few kilometres away.

There was also an Mpondo-speaking man called Sebenzile who knocked one day on the Ncalas' door. He was a travelling salesman, he explained, and from his bag he produced household cleaners and body lotions and much else besides.

Within a week, Sikhalo and Sebenzile were great friends. Sebenzile would announce himself at the Ncalas' shack in the early evenings and he and Sikhalo would settle into deckchairs outside the shack's front door. Long after the night had become too thick to show one another's faces they would remain. Between them flowed stories: about growing up in Mpondoland and going off to work in the sugar cane fields of Natal; about coming of age on the farmlands of the eastern Free State under the reign of a fierce old protector of rock rabbits.

As a matter of course, Sikhalo addressed his non-Sesotho-speaking friends as Morena, the Sesotho word for Sir. And that is how he became known in Phola Park: the short, slight, jovial, Sesotho-speaking Morena.

As these friendships evolved, so did the battle to remain in Phola Park. In July 1989, when the Ncalas had been there almost two years, the Thokoza Town Council demanded that residents begin to pay a rental of R50 per shack. There was still not a single service in the settlement and a Residents' Committee formed to call for a boycott of the new rent. The council announced in turn that the land had been rezoned for industrial use and in December began demolishing shacks under police protection. Hundreds of residents surrounded the demolishers singing freedom songs and, on several occasions, threatened to storm the police line. Towards evening, a rumour circulated that a white man driving a tractor had destroyed a shack in which an infant was sleeping. Electric with anger, the crowd broke through the police line and mobbed the first tractor in their path. The driver was pulled from his seat and executed with a shot to the temple.

Sikhalo was among those defending their homes from demolition. And when, in the wake of the shooting, the Residents' Committee decided to hire lawyers to defend their right to remain in Phola Park, he was among those who went door to door raising money for the legal fees.

In the end, the funds were not necessary as a pro bono litigation service came to the residents' aid. On 18 January 1990, the Southern Transvaal Division of the Supreme Court ruled that the authorities had no grounds to demolish a shack unless it had been built without the consent of the owner of the land. The Thokoza Town Council owned the land and it had invited people to live there. The ruling ended the demolitions. Everyone could stay.

Victoria dimly remembers the evening of 18 January 1990. She thinks that Sikhalo went out celebrating, that he returned in the early hours happy and drunk. But that night is no great marker in the chronology she recalls. She was, after all, lukewarm about the prospect of remaining in Phola Park and the residents' victory was, for her, little cause for celebration. Besides, on the heels of the court victory other events were to follow, and their drama dwarfed all that had come before.

On 2 February 1990, the apartheid government unbanned the exiled

49

ANC. Nine days later Nelson Mandela walked out of prison. Legendary men who had devoted their lives to defeating apartheid, men once exiled and imprisoned, their images banned from view, were soon every night on television. Charming and well spoken, oozing prosperity, they were, above all, black men who carried about them the promise of power.

When I press her on what these momentous events might have meant, she says little. Perhaps she holds her counsel in front of the white man her brother has brought to her home. But I suspect, instead, that she weighs the course of history not by the deeds of famous men but by the will of God. And whether God applauded Mandela's release was not something she presumed to know.

She hoped, above all, that God would protect her children. For change was in the air, and with change, she recalls thinking, comes the prospect of trouble. She knew all too well by then that Phola Park was the most volatile of places, and she worried for what was in store.

If this retrospective memory is right, Victoria could not have been more prescient. For within months of Mandela's release, Phola Park would descend into a state of war.

The trouble began, she remembers, when residents of the two nearby hostels began fighting one another. Throughout the three years that Phola Park had been her home, isiZulu and isiXhosa speakers had lived in the hostel together. Now, the Zulus chased the Xhosas away, as she recalls, and they took refuge in Phola Park.

She did not like these new residents at all. From their new homes they would launch sorties into the hostels. They would bring back with them the property of the Zulu people they had raided: pots and pans, blankets, a portable gas stove. Once, she recalls, she saw among the crowd returning from the hostel the carcass of a cow.

At other times, they would return with pieces of the hostel itself. Window frames ripped from the hostel walls would adorn Phola Park shacks.

Bricks from a smashed hostel wall would be piled together to build a stove. These people are out to destroy the place where they once lived, Victoria recalls thinking. And if they do indeed raze the place to the ground, what will the Zulus do in turn?

The Xhosa people were claiming to be fighting for the ANC and for the freedom of black South Africans. And the people in the hostels supported the Zulu nationalist IFP. But she was sceptical of these grand political claims. The new residents of Phola Park, she observed, no longer had work. They lived for fighting now. In her memory, many among them were car thieves. They would bring stolen cars into Phola Park, strip them of their parts and then burn the carcasses in haste. She recalls the black smoke that spiralled each day above the shack roofs and the smell of melting metal.

The police and the military would now enter Phola Park in their hundreds. Shack by shack they would search the settlement from one side to the next. The shacks must be littered with stolen goods, she remembers thinking. Indeed, the very structures of many shacks were stolen. But perhaps all that interested the soldiers was weapons. She recalls their rifles and their tense faces and, indeed, their fear. For they were squarely on enemy territory now, and they worried when they turned their backs.

She recalls too that a time came when the Xhosa men began fighting back; on entering the settlement the police would be met by crowds of men and from the crowds would come the rattle of automatic gunfire. And she remembers that, after this happened twice, the police came no more. The shack settlement in which she lived was now a zone in which uniformed men dared not set foot.

By now Victoria was working. From the warzone that was her home she would depart every morning to take her place in the kitchen of a quiet suburban home. Sikhalo had found her the job; on the side of the house in which she worked was a patio her husband had recently laid.

She recalls work as a reprieve. The white suburbs, so quiet one could listen to the pulse in one's veins, were just half an hour's journey from the gunshots and the burning cars. She marvelled that she could step with such speed from one world into another.

On several occasions, in the taxi coming home from work, she would hear that the Zulus had attacked Phola Park. She would get off in the middle of Thokoza and make her way to a friend's place on Nhlapo Street. Her children would be there already, diverted from Phola Park on their journey home from school.

She does not recall ever fearing that the Zulus would attack her family. It was Xhosa people they were after, and as Sesotho-speakers she and her brood would surely be left alone. But for her children to lie down to sleep in a place where human beings were slaughtered was intolerable.

In her friend's house on Nhlapo Street she and the kids would sleep together under a single blanket. The following morning, she would wake and return to work. On the tip of her tongue was a request to her employer. Might her children move into the domestic worker's quarters in the backyard?

She kept the question inside. The lady seemed very kind. Around her neck she wore a thin gold cross. And in her face was a gentleness that made Victoria feel calm. But how would she respond to stories of mayhem and smoke and the sound of gunfire? Would she recognise as a Christian that no child should live in such a place? Or would the thought of four strange black children in her yard turn her heart cold? Besides, to make so heavy a request, even to a mother and a Christian, one needed to share a language. Victoria did not trust her Afrikaans to convey what she wanted. She feared that it would come out not as a plea, but as a demand.

She resolved on several occasions to seek advice from Sikhalo. For even he, the diehard Phola Park man, defender at all costs of the shack he had built with his own hands, found that his taste for this life was flagging.

We will leave soon, Sikhalo kept telling her. As soon as I find a quiet place in this land where I might earn a living.

But in truth she saw less and less of Sikhalo. On several occasions during the past two years, he had disappeared for more than a month at a time. She did not bother to ask him where he had been. The wages she was finally earning seemed to have freed him. He could roam in the knowledge that his children would not starve.

But even when he was in Phola Park he went out most nights and often did not return until dawn. She had lost count of the number of men who now regularly appeared at the shack to talk to her husband, and with whom he would disappear for hours on end. His circle of friends, it seemed, grew wider all the time.

One evening during the first week of April 1992, Sikhalo's younger sister came to the shack in Phola Park bearing news. Sikhalo was in jail in Bethlehem, she said. And so was Victoria's brother, Fusi. They were charged with killing a white policeman.

Victoria no longer recalls her thoughts or feelings when she heard the news. The arrest of her husband and brother were to dominate the next twenty years of her life. Between that moment and this stand so many memories and emotions; the evening it all began is shrouded by what came after.

Until her sister-in-law delivered the news she knew nothing of her husband's career as a soldier. In the following months, the pieces of his existence came to her in increments. She discovered that in the depth of night he had learnt to assemble an AK-47; that, under the instruction of his Mozambican friend Joe, he had practised his new craft by shooting at the glowing tip of a cigarette. She was told that he had learnt not to stand upright while discharging his weapon, but to crouch – and never to be still, but to empty his magazine while on the move.

These things she could readily comprehend. Her husband was a man of secrets, and none could be too dark or too terrible to believe. But that her younger brother Fusi was involved seemed to her incredible. Sikhalo had set him up. Sikhalo had somehow implicated Fusi in his business.

From the moment she had wed their son, the Ncalas had been bad news. First, her mother-in-law had driven her from the place of her birth. Now her husband had torn a hole into the bosom of her family. A bitterness entered her, a sense, in her deepest reaches, that she had been wronged.

Eight

In the early days at Phola Park, on her trips to fetch water from the hostel, Victoria would have encountered a young Mpondo man. He, too, queued at the tap in the mid-afternoons, precisely when Victoria was there. He was over six feet tall, his shoulders broad, his bearing strikingly straight, and in his face an eternal calmness, as if part of him was in another world. His name was Clement Ndabeni.

Why he spent his evenings in a hostel at the edge of Phola Park was a story he liked to tell. It seemed to come more from a fable than from the life of a man.

Like countless Mpondo boys, Clement had given up school at the end of Standard 6. Numerate enough to add and subtract, he had left the southeastern seaboard for Johannesburg to work in the mines. He was eighteen. The year was 1981.

His recruitment was a disappointment. Told that he was too young to work among the perils deep underground, he was given a job on the surface, a woman's job, to boot, sweeping and mopping and polishing floors.

Three months later, as he lay fast asleep on his bunk bed in his hostel room, he was woken by what seemed the start of the Armageddon the Jehovah's Witnesses of his childhood had described. A geyser, eight feet tall and as wide as a small room, had exploded with such force that it had broken from its moorings, torn a hole through the ceiling and plunged into the room next door.

He jumped up to find the man on the bunk above him dead, his chest crushed by a collapsing wall. Thankful that his ground-floor bunk had saved him, but conscious that masonry and brickwork were still falling, he climbed over the corpse and crawled through the air vent just beneath the ceiling. The drop was a good twelve feet and his leg buckled as he hit the ground. When he got up to run he fell over. And so he hopped on one leg into the night away from a building that would kill two more men before dawn.

The following day, several of Clement's fellow workers examined the vent through which he had escaped. They marvelled. It was so narrow that even the frame of a skinny child might get stuck. Men would be called from hostels nearby, strange men he had never met before, to compare the size of Clement to the size of the vent; they would cluck their tongues in wonder.

Only years later would he come to see divine intervention in his escape from death. For now, what struck him was the foolishness of the idea that the depths of a gold mine were too dangerous for a youth. The very next day he applied to work underground. Life on the surface, he pointed out, was not so safe after all.

He worked underground for the next four years. For nine months at a time he would descend each day into the farthest reaches of the earth. There he would work harder than he had imagined it was possible and in spaces far too cramped for a frame like his. For the remaining three months of each year he would retreat to Mpondoland and rest and drink beer and listen to the many stories his grandmother liked to tell.

By the winter of 1986 he had been working underground for fifty-one months. He was, he felt, as skilled and as knowledgeable as a gold miner could be. For some time now, he had been employed as the assistant to the technician responsible for the most delicate task of all – the laying of explosives and the management of the detonation. At first, Clement's job was merely to carry the white man's tools. He would accompany his boss to the rockface, watch him work, pass him one implement after the next, and then retreat with him to safety and await the blast.

But by now he could do the white man's job, all of it, unsupervised, and one morning in the first week of June 1986 this is what he was doing, laying the fuse, instructing the people who were preparing the explosion. Once the work was done, the men were rounded up and taken from the scene. Only when they were back at the station would the denotation begin. On this day Clement did something odd. He did not leave the scene of the coming blast with the other men. He took a shortcut, alone, through a series of tunnels so low that he would have to leopard-crawl. And his shortcut went not to the station where the other men would assemble, but straight to the lifts.

Among the many things the blast technician had taught him was the cartography of the mine. Up on the surface, on his hostel bed, he had studied the maps for hours on end. That he could at any moment place himself on those maps, that he knew, always, no matter where he was, several ways to the lift, to the station, to wherever he had to be next, was a source of pride. His own hubris had sent him on this shortcut. He was breaking blast scene rules. He did it because he knew he could; he could chart his own route and make it out alone.

Now, crawling along the tunnel, about two-thirds of the way to the lift, his lamp went out, leaving him in pitch darkness. He removed his hard hat, tapped the light, knocked it gently against the base of his palm; it would not turn back on. He unscrewed the covering and took out the bulb.

It fell from his hands. He is not sure why. Perhaps the morning's exertions had caused them to shake. Maybe the sudden darkness had drawn something unwelcome to the surface of his being and distracted him. He felt with his hands for the bulb on the invisible ground; he could not find it; he had heard it land just inches from his head, and now it was gone.

He found that he was weeping. Alone in the dark, lying flat on his stomach, his elbows nudging the tunnel walls – this seemed to him a pitiful way to die. The surface was three kilometres away. Up there, his crying caused not a ripple in the airways, not a breath in the air.

He had long given up, his mind lost to practical thoughts, when he felt between his fingers in the dirt something hard and small and round. He grasped it and with his other hand took hold of his headlamp; the moment he felt the bayonet clip into place the light went on. For all he was worth, he crawled, faster than he ever had before.

He was three or four metres short when the blast came. It threw him from the tunnel and knocked him out cold. When he came to, he saw many faces and watched their mouths move, but he could hear nothing. His knees were knocking together and as hard as he tried to stop them they persisted, as if possessed of a will of their own.

It was a Friday. His next shift duty was only on the Monday morning. That night, as he drifted off to sleep, the sound of the blast woke him. He lay awake and stared at the ceiling. The same happened on the Saturday night. Each time sleep came the explosion would chase on its heels. On Sunday morning, utterly exhausted, he packed his bag and left the mine, never to return. Avoiding public transport, for fear that a crowded taxi would feel too much like a tunnel, he walked all the way to Thokoza, some fifteen kilometres in all. There, he called on his paternal cousin, Sebenzile Ndabeni, who lived in Khutuza hostel next to Khalanyoni. It was mid-1986; the birth of Phola Park was less than a year away.

For a man who had just quit his job as a gold miner, Sebenzile's room in Khutuza hostel was a fortuitous destination. Clement's cousin was a salesman. And what he sold was sold best, it would turn out, by a man who knew the mines.

Sebenzile worked on a commission-based contract for Golden Products. Its owners were Israeli, and its factories, an ocean away, made three ranges of liquids and creams. The homecare range consisted of more than a dozen items that cleaned floors and woods and stoves. The skincare range boasted no fewer than ten creams, some for moisture, some to slow down ageing, others for the skin's general well-being. And the healthcare range stocked medicines for diabetes, for weak hearts, for those who felt sluggish or listless, and for many other ailments besides.

What mattered about Golden Products, though, was not just what it sold but how it sold. It enlisted hundreds of thousands of direct salespeople on contract across the world. There were no barriers to entry, no rules to determine how much or how little one worked. One sold as much as one could. And the company encouraged the enterprising and the charismatic to assemble large selling teams. Each team would be set a range of targets. Sell a hundred products in a week and the team would get a point; sell five hundred and it would be awarded five points. Each team member would receive a small bonus whenever a target was reached. But the team leader would receive a large bonus, and the greater the target reached, the larger the proportion of the profits the team leader accrued. And so if one could galvanise a team of fifty or a hundred or two hundred, there was real money to be made.

Sometime before Clement began working on the mines, Mpondo migrants and their families back home began consuming Golden Products in large quantities. Sales were especially buoyant in the household range. But customers were not using these products to clean their homes. From the pharmacy they would buy syringes and fill them with floor cleaner and carpet cleaner. They would discharge these liquids as deep inside their rectums as they would go.

The Israeli manufacturers were unlikely to have known that this was how their salespeople in the gold mines of South Africa would market their product. They probably had no idea that, in the countryside whence the gold miners came, emetics and suppositories were old and trusted medicines. Men would use Golden Products when they were constipated or when moving their bowels caused pain. Others would drink it in small doses when passing urine was uncomfortable. Traditional healers had begun administering it as part of a treatment to manage an assortment of venereal diseases.

And Clement Ndabeni, it turned out, was a gifted organiser of salesmen. He would walk into a mine hostel a stranger and garner the attention of an entire room. His speeches efficient and clear, his baritone resonant and true, he would extol the virtue of working in teams. With pencil and paper held aloft to show the calculations he had made, he would draw for the men the extra money they would make if they worked successfully together. And to show his intent, he would spend money. He would go to the hostel's butcher and buy the carcass of a sheep for the men he had just addressed. He would stay for hours eating and drinking and talking. He would spend the night. By the time he left in the morning, he was imprinted vividly in the minds of fifty men. And when they thought of him they would think that with hard work comes money.

During his first year in Thokoza, Clement Ndabeni and his cousin Sebenzile established teams on the platinum mines in Rustenburg and on the gold mines of the western Free State. He returned to his former employer on Johannesburg's East Rand and established teams there. In Thokoza itself, he would take his products door to door. And when he had visited every house and shack and backyard hovel in the entire township, he would knock door to door in neighbouring Katlehong.

Time may have swollen Clement's sense of his achievements – he remembers these as his halcyon days, days when the world bent happily to his will. His memories give off the fragrance of a dream.

But there is little doubt that Golden Products were delighted with their team leaders in the hostels and the mines. Apartheid had assembled hundreds of thousands of men in communal rooms, some with cracked skins, others with blocked bowels, still more with lesions on their genitals and stones in their kidneys. They were all poor and in search of money. That they had assembled themselves into great teams to sell cures for their own ills must have seemed too good to be true.

Golden Products treated Clement well. At least twice a month he would visit their distribution centre in Isando, east of Johannesburg, and it was not long before he knew everyone there by face and by name. In 1988 he was invited on a tour of the company's factory in Israel, a reward for all the points he had earned in the previous two years. But his beloved grandmother in Mpondoland was ill and he had to turn the offer down. Not that he had many regrets. His aims were considerably more ambitious than a place on a foreign tour. If he could assemble teams on a dozen mines and keep each of them going for five years, he would earn enough points, he believed, to be awarded share ownership in Golden Products. Each time the company distributed dividends, he would earn more than a mineworker might in five years.

For all that Clement's memories are sweet, Khutuza Hostel in Thokoza was not an easy place to live. One could not relax there, not when laughing and making merry, not even when sleeping. One lived in one's wariness as if it were a skin.

Clement had experienced nothing like Khutuza before. The mining compounds in which he had lived for the past five years were privately owned, their purpose to house mining companies' black employees. Khutuza was on public land and was run by a municipal government.

By 1986, the year in which Clement moved into Khutuza, the difference between these two sorts of institutions was very large indeed.

Johannesburg's municipal governments began building hostels for migrant workers in the 1910s in response to the demands of new industries for accommodation for their workers. These building programmes would continue, sporadically, in various parts of the city, for the next sixty years. They were a product of the philosophy of segregation and, later, of apartheid. Men from the countryside were to come to the city in their hundreds of thousands, not to live, but to work. If this were to be practicable, one would have to erect giant buildings to house them and giant bureaucracies to control their movement. They would be allowed to live nowhere but in the hostels and work nowhere but in the place of employment recorded in a passbook they carried at all times.

There were fleeting moments when successive governments imagined all black people in Johannesburg living this way, their labour acquired cheaply in the factories by day, their bodies rested in locked compounds by night. Certainly, this was what planners imagined when the first municipal hostel was built in 1913. It was a vision that flickered from time to time and appeared often to die. After all, to run a gold mine this way was one thing. But to lock every black soul across an entire city behind razor wire fences every night, to channel their movement during the course of every day: it took a taste for bureaucratic mania even to imagine this. Few of those who ran South Africa during the course of the twentieth century had much taste for it.

And yet, the vision would keep returning. As late as the 1970s, plans were afoot to tear down every private dwelling in the freehold township of Alexandra, home, then, to more than a hundred thousand people, and replace them entirely with hostels.

But as with most plans to manage human beings on a grand scale, these ones were practised mainly in the breach. In truth, millions of black South

Africans were to come to Johannesburg with neither the right stamp in their passbooks nor with any intention to live in a hostel; and countless employers, among them the municipal government itself, would employ them off the books.

By the early 1980s there were 51 000 municipal hostel beds scattered throughout Johannesburg. The black population of greater Johannesburg at the time was about a million strong. Little more than one in twenty of the city's black residents lived this way.

Khutuza, its neighbour Khalanyoni, and the other municipal hostels on Johannesburg's East Rand were built primarily to house workers employed in the area's metal foundries. And for much of their history, that is what they did. Men from the four corners of South Africa and beyond, between them the speakers of half a dozen tongues, would sleep in Khutuza and Khalanyoni side by side. They lived their lives in over-lapping associations. There were organisations in which the middle-aged and the elderly would stand as proxies for village authority back home, watching over the young men in their care. But men also joined a grow-ing metalworkers' union in the foundries and brought their working class politics into the hostel. And everyone, it seemed, was a member of a burial society, their membership always cosmopolitan – isiXhosa, isiZulu, Sepedi, Sesotho and Xitsonga-speaking men insuring one another against the costs of one another's deaths.

But by the time Clement moved there in 1986, a gulf had opened between the original intention behind the hostel's construction and its use. It still housed metal foundry workers, to be sure, but they now rep-resented half of the hostel's population at best. This was the year that apartheid's infamous influx control laws – which allowed black people from the countryside to live in the city only if they had bona fide work – were abolished. But in truth, the white regime's control of the movement of black people had long eroded. Between 1976 and 1986, Johannesburg's black population had almost doubled. Thousands upon thousands of new-comers did what Sikhalo and Victoria had done – packed themselves and their children into a single room or rented a shack in a stranger's back-yard. Or they invaded municipal land and fought bitterly all attempts to remove them.

Or, if they were young and single and male, and if they had a con-nection there, they came to the hostels. They would follow brothers and cousins and neighbours and kinsmen they knew only by name. They would rent a bed or even the narrow space between a bed and the floor. There were beds in Khutuza and Khalanyoni hired to one person at night and another during the day. The hostels were full, much too full, many of their new residents too young and too idle. By the time Clement got there, some forty per cent of hostel residents had no job.

With youth and idleness came disorder. Many residents of Khalanyoni remember the day the hostel committees permitted residents from Phola Park to collect water from the hostel taps. As nubile girls and young women moved in and out of the hostel grounds, an industry evolved around them. Men propositioned Phola Park women with marijuana and food. The enterprising offered to pimp women and split the proceeds with them. It is a wonder that Victoria recalls the taps as a place of gentle meditation for around her swirled a trade that would have troubled her Christian soul.

Although the municipality had lost control of the hostels it ostensi-bly managed, uniformed men nonetheless stormed the premises at will, sometimes in the dead of night, sometimes in the middle of the day, add-ing another dollop of havoc to the growing anarchy within. On the hoof, they would invent the laws they claimed were being broken. They were armed to the teeth and turned on anyone who was young and ragged and had uncombed hair.

Within weeks of arriving at Khutuza, Clement had bought himself a tattered copy of the New Testament and the dog collar of a priest. At the news that armed men had entered the building he would clip his dog collar to his throat, lay his bible beside him and close his eyes, his large hands folded together on his chest. The sight of this strapping priest, his sleeping face as serene as his body was strong, was like a plague cross on a front door. A policeman thought twice before disturbing a man who seemed to belong in a stained-glass scene.

The police aside, Clement and Sebenzile managed the chaos around them by turning their roommates into teams of salesmen. It did not take much to arrange. So many of these men were idle and hungry. That there might be a living to made, right here in the township in which they lived, was not a prospect to turn down.

From the hostel gates each day tens of men would stream, each with a range of Golden Products in his bag. They would fan out across Thokoza, some next door to Phola Park, others well beyond. It was in the shack settlements that business was best. For the people here were among the poorest, and it was the poor, it seemed, whose taste for medical adventure was greatest. The men in the Ndabenis' room divided the township into patches of sales turf, and everyone wanted a piece of Phola Park.

The Ndabenis used feasts to raise their men's spirits. Among the residents of their room was a butcher. He would lead a cow or two sheep into the hostel grounds and slaughter his animals in front of an assembled crowd. Together with three or four assistants, he would cut the beasts to pieces, and sell them room by room.

Clement and Sebenzile became his primary customers. Twice a week they would buy enough meat to feed thirty men. From the shebeen down the corridor they would buy beer. Their feasts became famous in Khutuza. In 2015, more than a quarter of century after Clement had lived there, I met a man who recalled the two big amaMpondo who sold Golden Products: they cooked enough food to feed a regiment, I was told; and their parties went until morning.

The Ndabenis did not confine their recruitment of salespeople to hostel residents. To the east of Thokoza was the township of Katlehong and east of that was Vosloorus. Several hundred thousand people lived within walking distance of the hostel. How many of them might be recruited to sell, the Ndabenis wondered. A thousand? There was much to be done.

By their reckoning, sales worked best through chains of familiarity. The customer should have some personal connection to the salesperson: a neighbour or a distant kinsman, for instance, or a niece of the man who lived in the next block. The salesperson, in turn, should like and trust his team leader – hence, the volumes of meat and alcohol the Ndabenis would buy and consume. And, finally, the team leader should be on excellent terms with the supplier. And so the twice-monthly trips to the depot in Isando.

The Ndabenis acquired a map of Thokoza, Katlehong and Vosloorus and divided it into workable zones. The place was big enough, they surmised, for a hundred sales teams, neighbour selling to neighbour as far as the eye could see. If this required the two men to spend each night of their lives at a different feast, so be it. There were worse ways, they reckoned, to pass the time.

In 1987, they set out systematically to recruit in all three townships and in the feasting and merriment that followed Clement Ndabeni found a wife. Her name was Zodwa Buthelezi. An isiZulu speaker from the town of Mtubatuba, up in the northern reaches of KwaZulu, she had, a year earlier, fallen gravely ill. Fearing that she might die, her relatives had sent her to the East Rand where her father was working. If she were indeed to die, it was thought, it had better be in her father's care; were she to perish in the care of others, questions about their intentions might linger forever.

Clement recruited her on their first encounter. Idle and living off her father's largesse, she was desperate for work. He left her that day with a range of products and a battery of advice on what sold best where.

She sold Golden Products for just two days for immediately upon meeting Clement she found work as a cleaner at Natalspruit Hospital, a giant institution serving all of the East Rand. And so what he acquired was not a saleswoman but a wife. On the day they married he left the hostel – they moved together to a house in the neighbouring township of Katlehong. Within a year they had a son.

No longer sharing a room with thirty men, no longer forced to be a sleeping priest when the police crashed through the door, Clement returned to Khutuza Hostel several times a week. The men there remained the lifeblood of his business and their continued productivity required his and Sebenzile's presence. Besides, he had left a piece of his soul in the hostel. Since 1981, he had known no other life but one shared with a room of men. The silence of his house and the company of his wife left him wanting. The twice-weekly feasts continued as before.

The way Clement tells it, the trouble came from out of the blue.

The usual Friday feast was underway; the hostel room was packed with meat and beer; a long night lay ahead. Five men walked in. Around their heads they wore red handkerchiefs and from their mouths came forth a demand: they had business, they said, with the man who sold meat. In their hands they carried knives and pangas. One of them was clutching a cutlass. Their intention, without doubt, was to kill.

The butcher was not there. He was back in Mpondoland for a funeral. Another was minding his business while he was gone.

The intruders seemed not to care. They would set upon the substitute butcher instead.

Sebenzile stood up. He and Clement were the leaders in the room, and if there were shoulders on which a burden should fall it was theirs. From the substitute butcher Sebenzile began buying meat, as much as he possibly could. If they were to see this man's pockets filling with money, he reasoned, they would rob him and spare his life.

There is a hole in Clement's tale for the next scene has Sebenzile and him running down the corridor and into the hostel grounds. Sebenzile has a handgun in his car; they want to get it and return to save the men in their room.

Out in the grounds what they discover is so horrible they do not at first take it in. The building is surrounded by men. There are perhaps as many as a hundred of them: around each of their heads a red handkerchief, in each of their hands a weapon. In harmony it dawns on both Ndabenis at the same time: every Zulu man's head is wrapped in red and everyone else is destined to die.

The Ndabenis are crawling through a hole on the perimeter of Khutuza Hostel. Over them stands a large man, his bulging belly naked, his flabby breasts streaked with sweat. He holds a panga aloft; it is clutched in both hands, ready to fall and crush and kill. The Ndabenis understand that the hole has been made for escaping Xhosa men to find. They have crawled like sheep into the mouth of an abattoir.

The fat man looks Clement briefly in the eye then turns and walks on, his attention on something far away. Clement understands that he has deliberately been spared. All the feasts the Ndabenis threw, all the laughter they shared – the fat man saw beneath his panga's blade not raw meat between shoulders but the back of a man he liked.

Clement places this moment in November 1990. It was in fact July; that is the month the Mpondo men fled Khutuza for their lives, never to return. Clement says that the Zulu men in the hostel were duped. The IFP

68

convinced them that Mandela was for Xhosa domination; if democracy came the Zulus would be humbled and shamed, perhaps even slaughtered.

Clement says that the leaders of the IFP were lying. His own wife, he points out, was Zulu. As a practical matter, how would Mandela give freedom to a man while slaughtering his wife? At the hospital, Zodwa had joined a trade union aligned to the ANC. She was Zulu and she was for freedom. She was Zulu and she would be voting for Mandela. Between her native tongue and her political loyalties there was no connection.

This Clement explains when he is asked. But at the kernel of his memories there are no ideas, there is only rage. The violence that descended destroyed his great plans. It was no longer possible to wander freely from door to door. The dream of a sales team on every block was gone.

More than that, more than the lost business and the ruined dreams, the men for whom the Ndabenis bought meat every night were now dead or bleeding or scattered and for their blood Clement wanted revenge. Warfare had come to him unbidden. And so a warrior he would become.

Nine

In September 1992, more than two years after Clement had fled Khutuza Hostel, a man called Robert McBride was released from prison. He was, at the time, for many white South Africans, the public face of evil. A soldier in Umkhonto we Sizwe, the armed wing of the ANC, he had in 1986 led an underground cell that chose to plant a bomb in a beachfront Durban bar. Three white women had died in the blast. McBride had been captured, tried and sentenced to death.

Now, six years later, he was among hundreds of ANC cadres released from prison as the old regime and the liberation movement bargained their way to a settlement. A month after he acquired his freedom, he was assigned by the ANC to the East Rand to represent the organisation, oddly enough, on the regional structures of a National Peace Accord, a multiparty initiative aimed at ending the violence that had erupted on the outskirts of Johannesburg and in the midlands of Natal.

What McBride saw on the East Rand shocked him to the core. The violence had spread across the entire area, but the epicentre was Thokoza and it was a Satanic horror, nothing less. The tit-for-tat of ethnic cleansing had rearranged the township's inhabitants. Those in shack settlements and township houses deemed to speak a rural-sounding isiZulu had fled to the IFP-dominated hostels. In turn, everyone within a wide radius of

Madala Hostel deemed Xhosa had been chased away. Between these two zones were large stretches of no-man's land, street after street of abandoned homes.

As if residents were not aware that no-go zones were dangerous, on the streets were grim reminders. The ambulance service had long ground to a halt and corpses lay untouched for days on end. Of all he witnessed, it was this, the rotting bodies, that upset McBride most, a breach in the rhythms of life that had left the dead untended.

As for the state of the war itself, the township was in a bloodied stalemate. Constrained only by the limits of their imaginations, each side used stealth and cunning to launch campaigns of slaughter on the other. Both sides aimed to maximise death. The IFP controlled a nearby railway station. Every few hours, the trains that rolled past Phola Park would spit volleys of lead across the shacks like horizontal rain.

If the war between the two sides was ghastly, the state of affairs inside the ANC-aligned forces raised the hair on the back of McBride's neck. SDUs had been established throughout the townships of the East Rand. To McBride they seemed an anarchy of militias, rogues and bands of armed men, each fighting one another and themselves. He tried to find out who was in control. The answer, it seemed, was whoever had the most guns. Mozambique's fifteen-year civil war was just ending and the hostels and shantytowns where Mozambicans settled were awash with automatic weapons for sale. In the SDUs, there were factions within factions and each was stocking its own armoury.

New members were not properly screened, McBride found. Among them were people who joined primarily for the opportunity to rob others at gunpoint. And the SDUs, he believed, were riddled with spies. A host of state agencies was active on the East Rand: the police's Internal Stability Unit, Military Intelligence, the infamous counterinsurgency unit, 32 Battalion. Each, he surmised, was running agents in the SDUs.

The SDU in Phola Park was by far the most effective. But, even here, the chaos was barely controlled. Among those in command were several members of Frelimo, their military training and their experience of warfare giving them authority. But McBride was wary of them. Some had lived until recently in the hostels, he discovered, and had probably helped the IFP before switching sides.

Most striking about the Phola Park SDU was the influence of the Xhosa from the Transkei. They ran their own units, which they called *amabhutho*, the Nguni word for a battle regiment. They even arranged for their own training – members of the *amabhutho* were periodically spirited off to the Transkei to be taught to shoot automatic weapons. Watching them march into battle for the first time was a sight McBride would not forget. Five hundred of them, each wrapped in a traditional blanket, each clutching a spear. Hidden somewhere in the innards of the swarm were five men armed with automatic weapons.

But the fierceness of their appearance was deceptive, McBride discovered, for the ones with the automatic weapons were unskilled in their use. They shot from their hips and they bellowed at the top of their lungs, as if noise were a substitute for poise.

Besides, the *amabhutho* were riddled with feuds brought from home. The amaBhaca fought with the amaMpondo, he discovered, and there were a host of other animosities and disgruntlements whose sources he hadn't the knowledge to divine.

Then there were the urban-born youth who would not deign to fall under the command of *amabhutho*. The blankets of the *amabhutho* stank of the bush, the young complained, and the bulletproof medicine with which their doctors doused them simply made them foolish. And so the youth formed their own SDU, which took commands from nobody. And nobody else took commands from the youth because they were young.

The Umkhonto we Sizwe command appointed McBride defence

co-ordinator for SDUs across the greater Johannesburg region. And so between his day job and his night-time work there emerged a rift. During working hours, he was a member of the National Peace Accord, his task to bring warring parties together. At night, his job was to arm and train the SDUs. He based himself in Phola Park. His task, as he saw it, was to get its ramshackle parts to obey a single code of conduct and to fall under a single command.

He immediately encountered fierce resistance. That he had military training meant little, that he was the most famous guerrilla fighter in the country even less.

We have been fighting, he was told. Where were you? Who are you to impose a code of conduct on us?

McBride recounted these memories at a faux oak table in a government office in Pretoria. Between the events of which he spoke and the present lay nearly a quarter century of living.

'We had to be in the frontline to earn credibility,' McBride said next. 'It wasn't always easy. It wasn't always nice. But it worked.'

That is one way we human beings recount our own acts of violence. The detail evaporates, the flesh of particular moments burns away.

The world McBride discovered is the one in which Clement lived for almost two years. Not that he would ever describe it the way McBride did. There is neither treachery nor infighting in his account of these times. There are no factions or divisions. The men alongside whom he fought were professional to a T. They were coiled and ready to fight, always, but only under the strictest discipline and on the instruction of their commander.

Clement must recall things this way – in public, at any rate. All these years later, he and his comrades desire to be remembered as soldiers, as men who put aside their lives, picked up weapons and fought for freedom.

They must be remembered thus because they wish to be recognised as veterans and earn the state compensation that is a veteran's due.

In Clement's recollections, he and his comrades performed their work in secrecy. To their spouses they would talk of urgent business trips and nights out with friends. Of their real vocation, their loved ones knew nothing.

Thus it was with Clement and his wife Zodwa. They lived together in their home in Katlehong. She worked at the hospital whenever the war raging around them subsided, leaving her son at a crèche across the road. He joined the Phola Park SDU and went to fight.

Clement's life selling Golden Products was done – the war had destroyed it in a swoop – but the fruit it bore would shape his life as a soldier. Selling had made him rich. In just a few years he had paid bridewealth for a wife, bought a house and acquired a bakkie with a white canopy. Now, in his life as a soldier, the bakkie took centre stage.

The army that had been cobbled together in Phola Park was deficient in war materiel. It had automatic weapons, to be sure, but almost nothing else. To transport its soldiers, it had to carjack vehicles, for it had none of its own. And with carjacking came gratuitous danger – to have its soldiers flash guns in broad daylight on Johannesburg's streets courted trouble.

And so Clement, owner of a large and reliable vehicle, became a specialist transporter of men and materiel. Much of his time he spent ferrying trainee fighters more than a thousand kilometres across the country. He would deposit them at a secret place in the Transkei where one-time members of the old Bantustan's army gave them basic military instruction. The training ground, remote and quiet and deep in the hills, was in the district of Port St Johns, where Clement had grown up. On home ground, he knew every path and every back road. And his local tongue put enquiring strangers at ease.

Among the tales Clement tells of this time is his first encounter with Donald Makhura. Clement was sitting in a deckchair in Phola Park outside the home of an SDU man named Sikhalo Ncala. There were just three of them when the evening began: Clement, Clement's cousin Sebenzile, and Sikhalo. They sat there a long time, Clement recalls, until long after the light had faded and the world around them had grown still. He remembers losing track of the conversation and staring out at the glow of a hundred wood fires, the only sign at this late hour that around him lived tens of thousands of human beings. He remembers thinking that he ought to get back to his wife in Katlehong, but that it was too late, that he was enjoying the stillness, and that he would probably stay here until dawn.

Two more men arrived, men he had not met before. One of them was wired and agitated and very alive. His name was Donald Makhura. It appeared that Sebenzile knew him well. Sebenzile knew everyone, it seemed.

From the moment he sat down, Donald and his stories took over the night. He was from Umkhonto we Sizwe in exile, it emerged; he was a professional guerrilla. Just weeks earlier, he had been living in an ANC camp in Angola. The moment news reached him of the war on the East Rand he decided to cross the border into South Africa to assist. His motivations were personal, he said, for he had spent a part of his childhood here in Thokoza, and the way the names of places and events rolled from his tongue this was no doubt true.

From what he had seen of the SDU it was in desperate need of professional assistance, he said. To look at you makeshift soldiers, you seem like grown men. But when you pick up an AK-47, he said, you become children.

With some theatre, he took from his bag a handkerchief and wrapped it tightly around his eyes. His hands swooped again into his bag and in the darkness of the night one could just make out that he was assembling

ONE DAY IN BETHLEHEM

an automatic weapon. His hands moved with dexterity and speed; he seemed to be conjuring his rifle from nothing. His eyes still blinded, he clicked the magazine into place, cocked the gun and pointed the barrel into the night sky. His weapon sat so very comfortably in his hands, so naturally, like a carpenter with his chisel, or a clerk with his pen. That he himself resembled a child when holding a gun now seemed to Clement not so absurd.

Donald Makhura had come to Thokoza to instruct the amateur soldiers of the SDU how to fight. From the start he wore on his sleeve the mystique of exile and the glorious name of the army that had trained him. With these he intended to summon the authority to lead.

As McBride would discover a few months later, the men of the SDU were none too impressed. They appreciated Makhura's expertise, to be sure, and they had respect for what he might have done in the past. But here and now, in the heat of battle, only the present counted and Makhura was put to a test.

Not long after he arrived, Clement said, Makhura dressed up late one afternoon in a sharp suit, a collared shirt and a tie. Tucked under his right arm was an old dictionary. He was going to reconnoitre, he announced, at the IFP's stronghold in Thokoza, Madala Hostel. Before departing on his mission, Makhura said, he wanted to practise his isiZulu. And from his tongue issued as pure and as rural an isiZulu as Clement had ever heard. In that moment he understood that Makhura truly was a remarkable man, a man of untold skill and talent, for he was a Sepedi speaker from the north of the country and had never stepped foot in KwaZulu or Natal in his life.

Dressed like a clerk, or perhaps a school teacher, Clement recalls, Makhura walked out of Phola Park and across the no-man's land that separated the warring territories. He walked right up to the gate of Madala Hostel and in his perfect isiZulu he talked his way in. Phola Park fighters are dirty and ragged, Clement said. One does not expect to see them in a suit and tie, let alone speaking as if they grew up in Nongoma or Ulundi. Makhura's disguise was so simple it beggared belief.

An hour later, Makhura left the hostel with a golden observation. Each car that drove to the entrance, he said, flashed its brights three times and then put on its right-hand indicator. The men staffing the entrance then opened the gate.

The following day, Makhura and four others, each armed with a rifle and a pile of loaded magazines, drove to Madala Hostel and were waved through the gates. Barely inside, they sprang from their car and slaughtered the men who had just let them in. They drove off in a hail of bullets but arrived back in Phola Park unscathed.

On 21 March 1992, Clement received news that his grandmother was ill. He phoned Zodwa at the hospital to tell her that he was leaving at once and did not know when he'd be back. Then he packed a bag and, in a state of heightened anxiety, drove across South Africa to Port St Johns, stopping only to refuel. It was very early when he arrived, about 3:00 a.m., and the world around him was sleeping. He sat in the driver's seat of his bakkie, he remembers, staring ahead of him, waiting for the dawn.

His grandmother, it transpired, was not as ill as he had feared. But she was in the hospital on the coastal road to Lusikisiki and he did not want to leave until she had been discharged. And so he visited her, dutifully, every day, bringing with him each time a meal cooked at home. And when he was not with his grandmother, he was in her village, sitting, talking, drinking with the old men and women who spent their days nursing stout beer.

He took in the stillness, the idleness, the absence of anything in particular to do next. And on the fourth or the fifth day, he came to grasp, quite suddenly, like an epiphany, that he was savouring the ebbing of his fear. He was fighting a war, after all, a business that put one forever on edge. For almost two years, he realised, he had woken each morning coiled, unrested, his slumber no reprieve from the fighting. Out here in the villages, he could hear himself exhale, note the pulse in his temple, feel the blood flow at a gentler pace through his veins.

He left Port St Johns late on the evening of 31 March. His grandmother had been home for three nights and there was no good reason to stay. Back on the East Rand the following afternoon, he discovered that his comrades had been anxiously awaiting his return. There was a mission to be performed, he was told; it had been placed on hold until his return. He had been assigned to drive and they had looked in vain for a substitute.

It was something new, something that the SDU had only begun performing in the past few months. The renown of the Phola Park unit's fighting men had spread by now and wherever fighting between IFP and ANC forces was raging – around the hostels in Soweto, for instance, and in the IFP strongholds in the midlands of Natal – embattled ANC forces were crying out for assistance.

The mission awaiting Clement's return was to Inanda, an IFP stronghold near the coast north of Durban. ANC forces were embattled there, Clement was told, and in desperate need of men and weapons.

He went home and slept for a few hours, then went to Phola Park to fetch his fighting crew. When his bakkie left the East Rand in the predawn hours of 2 April, it would hold eight men and ten AK-47s.

The men were Clement Ndabeni and his cousin Sebenzile; Sikhalo Ncala and Donald Makhura; Joe, the former Frelimo fighter who sold vegetables outside Sikhalo's shack; two more Transkei men named Mandla Fokazi and another known to his comrades only as McGregor. A man with the battle name Nozulu would serve as the commander of the operation. He had once been a soldier in the apartheid government's army.

Inanda was a six- or seven-hour journey from Phola Park. It would have been possible to drive the entire way in darkness, without stopping, but perhaps for the need briefly to refuel. The bakkie was full of AK-47s. One might imagine that the commander of the mission would insist that they travel quickly and by night.

And yet the men only left Phola Park a couple of hours before daylight. If they wanted to drive all the way in darkness, they would have to find somewhere discreet to keep their weapon-laden vehicle during the day. Why they left when they did, and why they stopped in Bethlehem, a one-hundred-and-fifty-kilometre detour off the highway from Johannesburg to Durban, is a matter of dispute.

According to Clement, he was the reason for the delay. He had just driven across the country when he was told of the mission, and the journey had exhausted him. He was in no condition to get back in his bakkie and drive for another six or seven hours. He had insisted on getting some rest. And since it was not possible to drive through the night, they would have to find somewhere for their vehicle to lie undetected during the day; Sikhalo's brother-in-law's place in Bethlehem seemed the best bet.

Later, I would be told of another reason for the delay: the men refused to leave until their herbalist had doctored them with *ntelezi*. Their vehicle would be full of weapons. On the freeway to Natal they may very well drive into a roadblock and have their vehicle searched by police. Their instructions were to surrender neither themselves nor their weapons, but to fight. They would not want to do that without war medicine. When the herbalist was late in coming, they insisted on waiting for him.

A third reason would be given for stopping in Bethlehem. Weeks earlier, Sikhalo had bought a dozen wheelbarrows from Sebenzile Ndabeni on credit. He had thought that he could resell them at a profit to friends in the construction industry, but he had had little luck. The repayment was late and Sebenzile was demanding with increasing fury that the debt be settled. Just a day earlier Sebenzile had told Sikhalo that if he was not repaid within twenty-four hours he was going to put Sikhalo in his grave.

Sikhalo had pleaded poverty. He had invited Sebenzile to ransack his home in search of cash. He would find none.

'Then you will borrow!' Sebenzile had said.

Sikhalo had racked his brain for an answer.

'The only person I know from whom I might borrow,' Sikhalo had said, 'is my brother-in-law, Amos Mofokeng, and he is in Bethlehem.'

'Then that is where we will go,' Sebenzile had said. 'You will come with us on our mission to Inanda as far as Bethlehem, we will get money from Amos Mofokeng, and then we will go on to Inanda and you will go home.'

And that is what transpired. All eight men and their armoury of weapons were to make a detour through Bethlehem so that Sikhalo could borrow money from his brother-in-law and pay Sebenzile for a dozen wheelbarrows.

Fusi Mofokeng was asleep in his bed when the eight men left Thokoza. His country's civil war came to him as he slept.

Part II

Ten

They were tried beneath the high, solemn dome of the sandstone courthouse in Bloemfontein. Day after day, from his place in the dock, Fusi Mofokeng would look up into the dome's inner cavern. When a thunderstorm broke – usually in the late afternoon, just as the day's session was drawing to a close – the rain would slam soundlessly against the dome's glass. Closing his eyes and listening to the silence, he would wonder how thick the glass must be to keep out all that noise. Six inches, perhaps? Maybe even more.

He would stare at the heavy chandeliers directly above him, at the plasterwork around the circumference of the dome and at the lion and the unicorn above the judge's bench. For years to come these objects would return to him when his mind drifted, bringing with them a sense of despair.

Of the trial itself, he remembers only fragments. As he recalls it now, his mind would drift for long stretches of time. He had nothing to do with the events of 2 April, after all; he protested his innocence by closing his ears.

Instead, he would write letters – to his mother, to Victoria, to his friend Sengata and his cousin Khulu. They were very formal, his letters, and they conveyed almost nothing at all. He wrote them in order to receive replies.

When they arrived, he would savour them. He would read them seven, eight, nine times in a row, the thud of repetition driving him back to the streets of Bethlehem. Once, he recalls, the judge stopped the proceedings and in exasperation admonished Accused Number Five to follow the trial.

He paid more attention, he recalls, to the five men next to him in the dock. Day in and day out they sat there, thigh by thigh, in the order in which they were accused. As they entered the court on the first morning of the trial, Fusi momentarily caught Tshokolo's eye and what he saw in that split second was a lostness so deep and irretrievable that he shuddered. He dared not look in Tshokolo's direction again for to share in that lostness was dangerous.

As Accused Number Five Fusi had Clement Ndabeni immediately to his right and Donald Makhura to his left. Before the morning of 2 April, he had known nothing of them. Now, a little more than half a year later, they were the most important men in his life. For in the preceding months, while awaiting trial in a Bloemfontein prison, it was these two men, Ndabeni and Makhura, who had made him feel safe.

In the prison courtyard to which they were admitted on their first day were groups of men with eyes so lifeless as to freeze Fusi in his tracks. When they looked at him, it was as if he were being hailed by the dead. Among them were men who might kill him and never think of it again, he thought. He felt an absence of safety so deep it shot electric arrows through the marrow of his bones.

But Ndabeni and Makhura were right behind him, and the moment they entered the courtyard, the faces of the cold men changed. Both emitted a fierceness as natural as the sweat that gleamed on their skins. Ndabeni was more a statue than a man, one that might emerge from a great firestorm unscathed. As for Makhura, from the very first he wielded a mesmerising charm. Out in the yard, Fusi watched a group of men gather around him, murderers, rapists and who knew what else, as if what he was to say next might alter their lives.

Now, in the courtroom, Donald Makhura was incessantly busy, scribbling notes and passing them to his counsel, whispering, his hand in front of his mouth, into the ear of his counsel's attorney. Fusi did not believe he had ever met a person so relentlessly alert; with Makhura's brain working at full throttle, he thought, perhaps we will all walk free.

He says that he paid little attention to the proceedings. But as we talk he stumbles upon scenes from the trial he has not remembered in years. He speaks of the two men who acted as counsel for the accused. There were two, he remembers, for between them the accused had two cases to answer. Clement Nbabeni was at the scene of the shootout opposite the Orsmond property on which Constable Oosthuizen had died. He, together with Fusi and Tshokolo Mokoena, were represented by a man called André Landman. Donald Makhura, Mandla Fokazi and Sikhalo Ncala had already left the scene by the time Oosthuizen was killed. They had shot and injured a farmer who had stopped them as they fled. The man representing Makhura and Fokazi was Paul Heymanns.

The moment he saw that their lawyers were white, Fusi believed their fate to be sealed. Why would white lawyers go out of their way to defend black men who had put a white constable in his grave? He was in an enemy's court, he believed; in the well where the lawyers performed there were no friends.

He remembers his surprise when it dawned on him, a day or two into the trial, that the two white men took their work very seriously indeed. There was, he recalls, a trial within a trial. He is vague about the matter at hand. It was a question of the conditions under which the police had extracted information from Donald Makhura.

Heymanns arrived in court one morning, Fusi recalls, in an animated state, his arms full of law books he had brought from home. He spread them before him, each thumbed and worn, and there they remained. In the hours that followed he cited from four or five or perhaps six of them, offering the judge references to cases and paragraph numbers. Something about the exchanges between lawyer and judge drew Fusi's attention to the spectacle. Heymanns was agitated and fierce and kept squeezing the lobe of his ear. It occurred to Fusi that this tall and broad and very confident man regarded the judge as an adversary and was throwing his very soul into the skirmish. Lawyer and judge, he saw, his heart leaping, were out to wound one another; and one of them was on the side of the accused.

Deep into the trial, a month, perhaps more, the state called Thabo Motaung to the witness stand. With all that had happened, Fusi had not thought of him since 2 April. He had arrived at the house shortly after the men from Phola Park, sent by Fusi's father because Fusi was ill and required assistance.

Now, on the witness stand, Thabo Motaung was saying that he had been party to a conspiracy; that he and Fusi Mofokeng and Tshokolo Mokoena had agreed to summon Sikhalo Ncala to Bethlehem; that Sikhalo would bring with him men and guns; that they would go to Ballyduff and rob the Orsmond family; that the Orsmonds had a great deal of money, enough to be split several ways.

The accused's counsel, Heymanns and Landman, jumped from their seats. Did the prosecutor at any point make the witness aware, Heymanns asked, that he was incriminating himself; had the witness been advised of the consequences of his testimony?

When his turn came to cross-examine Thabo Motaung, Landman asked him what he had done during the lunch recess the previous day.

Thabo replied that he did not have money to buy lunch.

'I put it to you,' Fusi recalls Landman saying, 'that you were seen at lunchtime yesterday with police detectives from Bethlehem. What were you discussing?'

Thabo bowed his head and said nothing.

As for Fusi, when he listened to Thabo's story he felt déjà vu, for he had heard the same tale from the lips of Steyn and Robertshaw. It was among the many stories they had told Fusi. They said that he had secretly left the country when he was sixteen and received military training from the ANC. They said that he was part of a team of PAC soldiers who went around killing white farmers. And they told him that he had brought the Phola Park men to Bethlehem to rob the Orsmonds. It seemed that they had chosen from among their stock of tales – how did they decide, he wondered: did they toss a coin? – and had landed on this one.

He wondered what had happened to take the story from their lips to the uncertain voice of Thabo Motaung. Had they gone to his house and thrown the furniture against the walls? Had they taken him to the police station and, in one of those windowless rooms, broken both of his arms, the desk sergeant on duty whistling a tune to block out the sound of his cries? Or had it proved unnecessary to use violence? Had they merely bamboozled him, as they had tried to bamboozle Fusi, telling him that if he did not regurgitate their story he would end up in jail?

In Fusi's memory, the judgment Judge Koos Malherbe read before pronouncing sentence was so long that it took much of a day to read. He sat in the dock straining to follow the Afrikaans for the judge read monotonously and swallowed his words, as if he were belting through a daily prayer. But he does recall the judge remarking on what Thabo had said. Counsel for the accused, the judge read, had brought to the attention of the court inconsistencies in the testimony of a key state witness, Thabo Motaung. The judge acknowledged that Thabo had not made for the best witness; but his testimony was consistent with the circumstantial evidence, the judge said, and that was enough. And besides, the reason Accused Numbers Two, Three, Four and Six had given for being in Bethlehem, namely, that Accused Number Two had come to borrow R300 from his brother-in-law, was implausible. Accused Number Two ran a prosperous construction business on Johannesburg's East Rand. Why would he travel 250 km to borrow R300?

On 15 December 1992, the judge found all six accused guilty of the murder of Constable Oosthuizen. They had not all been present at Oosthuizen's killing, the judge said, but they had all been party to the conspiracy to commit the crime that had led to the policeman's murder. It did not matter who had pulled the trigger, the judge said, or, indeed, that some of the accused had not been at the scene of the shooting; they were all guilty of murder by virtue of common purpose.

There was a long delay between the verdict and the passing of sentence. In early March 1993 Fusi was sentenced to life plus eighteen years.

On the evening after sentencing, the six convicted men – who had, throughout the course of their trial, been sharing a cell in a Bloemfontein prison – did not eat their dinner. They sat silently, their full plates in front of them, without exchanging a word. One by one they lay down on their mats to sleep.

Fusi settled on his mat and listened to the other men breathing and to the sounds of the prison beyond their cell. He felt a swelling in his throat and heard weeping; and he knew from the convulsions inside him that he was the one crying, although it seemed very much like someone else. He threw his blanket over his head and wept until his throat and his guts could take no more. But no sooner had he stilled his body than he felt unbearably thirsty. He got up and found his way to the basin.

He looked out of the window and watched the stars and imagined the world over which they shone. He saw rows of rooftops in Bohlokong, the starlight revealing their corrugated iron.

He understood that he had been sentenced to spend the rest of his life in prison. But he understood, too, that he would not be in prison for long. It was not in his destiny to be taken one night from his home, never to return. That that might be his story was inconceivable.

Eleven

usi Mofokeng came to my attention because he was taken from his life for nineteen years. If ever there was a person who did not author his fate, it is he. And yet, when he drifts unannounced into my thoughts, and an image of him forms idly in my mind, I see him at the moment he decided what would happen next.

He was fifteen years old. By all accounts, he was whimsical and shy, just as he is now. He was nonetheless possessed by a force of will that melted the future into a substance he could mould.

Fusi's mother was Maletsatsi Letia Mbele and she left his father when Fusi was in her womb. The nature of his offence lies buried in the vaults of Mbele history. It is too terrible to talk about, too ghastly to remember.

They were barely more than children when they met. The school in the valley where Oorsprong lay only went up to Standard 7 and Rose and Nono Mbele had wanted to educate their daughter as best they could. So they sent Maletsatsi to Bohlokong, the black township of Bethlehem, to live in an uncle's backyard, and registered her at the local school. Within months, she had conceived a child with another of her uncle's tenants,

Hlelle David Mofokeng. She was fifteen and he a year older. She dropped out of school, never to return.

There must have been something of much substance between Maletsatsi and David for they conceived five children over the following eight years. What it was that held them together is lost now, for the Mbele family has cursed David Mofokeng and has no good memories of him.

It was April 1967 when Maletsatsi left David Mofokeng. She considered sending her children to live at Oorsprong with Nono and Rose. But Victoria was six and Amos was four: both would soon have to attend school and they were too little to trek across the valley each morning. So she sent them to her sister on a farm at Afrikaskop, not far from Bethlehem, for the nearest school was a stone's throw from her sister's home. Two more of her children lay buried in Bohlokong's cemetery. With Fusi still growing inside her, she went to work in the kitchen of a white family on Johannesburg's East Rand.

Fusi spent the first few months of his life with his mother. And then he, too, went to Afrikaskop because Maletsatsi's employers would have him in their house no more.

He was to live there for three years; he believes that he was not yet four when his mother came late one night to Afrikaskop to take her children. Victoria and Amos were unhappy: they were not being treated right; the other children of the household were hurting them and they bore scratches and scars. She hoisted the little one onto her back, took each of her elder children by the hand, and walked out into the darkness.

The journey is among Fusi's earliest memories. He did not fear for himself, he recalls, for he was strapped to his mother and she was as solid as a being could be. It was Amos for whom he worried. They kept hearing baboons barking somewhere in the darkness and Amos, he felt, was drifting too far. At times, he disappeared almost entirely into the night, only the soles of his feet still casting a dim glow. Thinking that his brother would be swallowed by the dark, he began to cry.

ONE DAY IN BETHLEHEM

Early in the morning, dawn no more than a trace of dull orange on the horizon at their backs, a white man on a tractor stopped for them. He gave them a lift all the way to Oorsprong, a half-hour journey at least, who knows how much longer had they been forced to walk. And so it was on the back of a stranger's vehicle that Fusi crossed the threshold of what passed in his mother's family for an ancestral home.

His feelings about Oorsprong are wondrous. I drive him there and we walk through the fields where the Mbele home once stood and it is hard to describe what comes over him. The mountains and the sky and the yellow grass on the hills embrace him and he is much more than Fusi; he is old and silent and transcendent. I withdraw and watch and marvel; if you surrender to the calmness and allow its aura to touch you, the presence of a person in this state is wonderfully benign. When we drive away he is quiet, his body quite still, and it is the loveliest stillness for his soul has been washed. He seems to have made from Oorsprong a corner of his being that the world cannot touch.

He called Rose Mbele 'Mama', and when Maletsatsi visited at Easter and at Christmas, he addressed her as 'Sister'. Recalling this now, he is brushed by guilt and by sorrow. The course his life took caused his mother great pain and it stings him to think that already, when he was so young, he was hurting her.

I press him to remember Rose Mbele. The feelings he has for her are so tender; I want him to match them with scenes from the life they shared. But the image that keeps appearing in his mind is from the day of her death. He was six years old, he thinks. She was standing chopping vegetables and he was at her side and he watched the knife in her hand fall to the floor. And then Rose Mbele herself was on the floor, lying on her back, and blood was pouring from her nose and down her chin and onto her apron. He remembers being taken away to another tenant's home and then an ambulance arriving and carrying Rose Mbele away.

He was six. It was decided that his grandfather, Nono Mbele, was too old to look after him. Besides, it was time for him to go to school, and while the older children could now be expected to make the daily trek to the other side of the valley, he, it was felt, was too young.

And so he was shipped off again, this time to Thokoza at the edge of Johannesburg, to his uncle Jack Mbele and Jack's wife, Sylvia. The couple was famously childless. They had lost five infants over the previous decade and some wondered aloud what on earth had made providence so cruel. Sylvia, it was said, would be healed by the sound and the spirit of a young one in the house. Fusi was to be her compensation.

He was to spend nearly a decade in their home, and thus the better part of his childhood. And yet the time he was with them seems to have evacuated itself from his being. Whenever we sit down to talk of his past, his memories spool across this time, unable to stop and take the world in.

Periodically, I nudge him back to Thokoza. 'Tell me any story about it,' I say. 'Anything at all.'

He pauses a long while and thinks. And when he finally begins speaking it is about the holidays he spent at Oorsprong each April and December. He remembers, for instance, Madipela's grandson, Dirkie, who spoke almost no Sesotho and with whom he invented games without words. And he recalls the colossal task of making Madipela a dam. It was dug with a single tractor and scoop, he recalls, day in and day out, for weeks on end.

Once the dam was built, Fusi recalls, Madipela forbade her tenants to fish from it. And so she became saviour, not just to the rock rabbits in the fields, but to the fish in the water, and somebody among the tenants remarked that Madipela was the most jealous woman alive; were it in her means, she would count the stalks of grass in her fields and forbid anyone to pluck one from the ground.

We wander across Oorsprong and the stories pour from him. Yet when we walk the Thokoza street on which he lived, he is constipated, truly, his memories stolid and stubborn and jammed up inside. I wonder what coldness he encountered there for I know that his uncle Jack was a truck driver who spent weeks away from home, and that his aunt lived among the ghosts of the children she had lost.

In Thokoza, Fusi nurtured a secret. It was hatched in the days after the death of his grandfather, Nono Mbele.

Fusi was twelve. It was 1979. At Nono Mbele's funeral, in the tenants' graveyard at Oorsprong, Fusi's elder brother, Amos, put a hand on his shoulder and whispered in his ear.

'I have found our father, David Mofokeng,' Fusi recalls Amos saying.

Fusi no longer recalls whether he thought much about David Mofokeng before Amos whispered in his ear. But now that his existence had been drawn to his attention, his father consumed his thoughts.

Back in Thokoza, he tore a page from a school exercise book and wrote a letter, the very first he penned, oblivious that his life would make of him an inveterate writer of letters. It was addressed to Amos, who lived in Bethlehem, under the roof of yet another Mbele uncle, and it asked, simply, that Amos tell him more about his father.

The reply he received was more astonishing than he could have imagined. Amos had for more than a year been seeing their father in secret. And David Mofokeng, Amos wrote, had wept when his son presented himself. On the spot, he had invited Amos to live with him. And he believed that he would do it, Amos said; he would defy the Mbeles and live with David Mofokeng.

On his following visit to Oorsprong, Fusi did the long walk into Beth-lehem one morning and met his brother, Amos. They made their way through the streets of Bohlokong to a modest house where the door was opened by a visibly nervous man.

Fusi watched David Mofokeng as he moved about his house and he wished he had been able to observe him while he was still a stranger and not yet his father. What would he have looked like had he been just another man?

David now stood before his younger son; he stretched out his hand and offered him a watch. 'You are my child,' Fusi remembers him saying. 'You are my son and I love you.'

He does not remember which of the Mbeles first saw the watch and asked whence it came. But on hearing that it was a gift from David Mofokeng, each Mbele went into a fit of rage. It all came out, the years of unspoken recrimination against David Mofokeng. He had conceived five children with Maletsatsi and had contributed not a cent to the upbringing of any of them, Fusi was told. He had refused to pay bridewealth and marry her, rendering the children bastards. He was a drunk who barely managed to hold down a job. Nor could he keep his pants zipped, for when Fusi was in Maletsatsi's womb, another of David's children was growing in the belly of a stranger; two women were walking the streets of Bethlehem bearing a child of David Mofokeng.

When Maletsatsi discovered this terrible truth, Fusi was told, she con-fronted him in a rage and he beat her, beat her when she was pregnant with his own child. That was the day she left him. That was the day the Mbeles expunged him from their lives.

Fusi ingested this information and it sat inside him and what he thought and felt he cannot say. He did not lay eyes on David Mofokeng for another three years. But when he visited Bethlehem at Easter and Christmas he would see Amos and Amos would tell him that living with David Mofokeng was good.

In 1983 Maletsatsi took her fifteen-year-old son to a Home Affairs office to apply for an ID book. Only once they were standing in the queue did Fusi discover his mother's intention that his name be recorded as Fusi Mbele. He stood beside his mother saying nothing, a fierce resistance rising within him. As they moved closer to the front of the queue his resistance became a blanket refusal so powerful it seemed to come from a being much greater than he.

He told his mother quietly that his name was Fusi Mofokeng.

No son of mine, he recalls her saying, will be named Mofokeng, and the two of them faced one another down, moving all the while closer to the front. When they finally reached the official's desk, Fusi turned around and left.

Back home in his uncle Jack's house, Fusi composed another letter. This one, too, was to Amos. He asked his brother to ask David Mofokeng if he might also live under his roof.

Twelve

David Mofokeng was everything against which the Mbeles had warned. True, he held down a job, first as a driver for a butchery, then as a guard at an army camp. And, the occasional exception notwithstanding, he clocked in at work on time.

But at weekends he would drink his wages away.

There was seldom enough food in the house. Nor was there sufficient money to buy Fusi the clothes and books he needed for school. And on the rare occasions when David Mofokeng was flush and thinking of his boys, his purchases were extravagant and without sense. From out of the blue, for instance, David bought Fusi a car.

Once, when she was sure that David would not be home, Maletsatsi paid a visit to her sons. She examined the bare shelves in the kitchen cupboards and the sparseness of the utensils in the drawers. She made her way to the bedroom, opened the wardrobes and saw the state of her sons' clothes. And then she stood in the middle of David Mofokeng's house and wept.

At the end of 1986, less than three years after he had gone to live with his father, Fusi dropped out of school. He was only in Standard 7, a full three years from completing his secondary education. On the streets of Bohlokong the boys his age were wearing good jeans and shoes and they took trouble with their hair. His poverty, he knew, was like a cloak that made him invisible. If it went on much longer he might disappear completely. He left school to acquire enough money to remain in the world.

These were times when finding work was not so hard. Within weeks of leaving school, he had a job packing boxes at Checkers, the large supermarket in downtown Bethlehem. He thrived, and why would he not, this clever and quietly spoken boy, so very easy to be around. He was soon promoted to a job without definite boundaries for he learnt quickly to do everything on the supermarket floor: one day a cashier, the next a security guard patting down the male customers as they left the shop, the next a catalogue counter. Within months, he was earning the same salary as some of his white colleagues, a special black boy, efficient, well-spoken and keen to please.

Of his father Fusi refuses to speak ill. David Mofokeng was often sad, Fusi says. At times he would sit in his yard and stare for hours at nothing at all. Fusi would come out and join him and watch his father in wonder. His sorrow was bottomless, truly; there were no limits to his despair.

But these subdued states would seldom last. Without warning, David Mofokeng's temper would flare and it was as ferocious as his depression was dark. Once, Fusi recalls, he had to tear his father off Amos and sit him down and tell him that it was not right to unleash such violence on one's own son.

I ask of the resentment he must feel for his father, but he insists that there is none. I ask, too, whether he is ever harsh on his teenage self for abandoning so wilfully a safe Mbele home. He has no reason to be harsh on himself, he says, for he has no regrets. Were he sixteen again, he would move again into David Mofokeng's home.

And he begins to talk of his father in soft tones, on his face a whimsical smile. The car, he says, was a foolish gift, but that was how David expressed kindness, foolishly, and it was kindness nonetheless. And he remembers how each morning he would drive his father to work and watch him walk through the gates of the army camp; and he would not leave, he recalls, until his father had disappeared around a corner and was gone.

I am left wondering at the way Fusi remembers the past. His memory seems a magnet that attracts only love and kindness, as if the world is made of warmth and no more.

In any event, Fusi continues, life was pretty sweet once he began working, for the money was good and he was flush. And Amos, too, had work, as a cashier in a filling station just a few blocks from Checkers. The boys filled their home with groceries and fed their father square meals. It felt good to be looking after a living soul.

On weekends, the boys would leave David to himself and meet up with their cousin Khulu and their friend Sengata. They were always together, the four of them, each weekend, like clockwork, and what they did fell into two categories. They frequented the taverns of Bohlokong and Phuthaditjhaba, the capital of the nearby Bantustan of Qwaqwa, and got blind drunk. And they hunted women. Quite often they did both at the same time.

But to say that they were boys gallivanting does not do justice to what Fusi felt for his friends and, most especially, for Amos. His brother, he says, was clever and gentle and wise, and everybody he ever met knew this at once, as if there were an aura around him visible to all.

About Amos, he says, he felt a jealousy he has never felt for another soul. If they were drinking in a tavern and some drunk at the other end of the room had dark thoughts about his brother, Fusi would know; he would turn to the culprit and stare him down; and if anybody were ever to lay a hand on Amos, he would have torn the offender limb from limb.

That is how Fusi remembers. In feelings, not images. And such sweet feelings they are. There is Oorsprong – which overwhelms him with its stillness whenever he sets foot there. And Amos – who was almost god-like in the beauty of his soul. Even David – it is his kindness that comes to Fusi when he thinks of his father. As if his past were a place where it neither snowed nor stormed.

When I grow frustrated with his ethereal feelings, when I want very badly to attach them to stories, I invite him into my car and drive to a place from his past. Once we are walking in his footsteps, the stories come, and they are mainly about hunting girls.

Strolling with Fusi through the streets of Clarence, a pretty town at the edge of the mountains a half hour's drive from Bethlehem, a memory comes to him.

He was sixteen, he thinks. He and his cousin Khulu were interested in two girls they knew from school. Both girls lived in Clarence. One after-noon the two boys caught a red bus from Bethlehem to Clarence and they simply stood in its main street doing nothing in particular, for they dared not go to these girls' homes. They waited around like fools, full of excite-ment and without a plan. And lo and behold, they had been lingering for no more than an hour when the girl Fusi fancied walked down the road.

Her name was Cally, Fusi recalls, and he had no idea what to say to her. He walked her into town and bought her a cold drink and in an awkward moment told her he loved her, a clumsy communication of his intentions, he admits now. Sometime later, the following week, he thinks, they stole off from school together in the middle of the morning and made their way, hearts thumping in fear, to the Bethlehem golf course. Hardly anyone played golf in the mornings and in all those acres of land they could seek a place where a girl and a boy might disrobe.

One tale leads to another. His friend, Sengata, he remembers, met a girl who lived several hundred kilometres away, in a town called White

River at the edge of the great Blyde River Canyon. For many months, he and Fusi saved up to go there until finally, one Friday afternoon in the summer of 1989, Sengata asked his grandmother in passing if he could borrow her car, promising to bring it back later. The two of them drove north that evening and into the early hours of the morning, arriving in White River at dawn.

They had no idea where Sengata's girl lived, and so they parked their car outside the post office in what seemed to be the centre of the village. And they waited.

It was almost lunchtime when they caught sight of Sengata's girl, her hand locked into that of a scrawny young man. The Bethlehem boys debated whether to hide or to drive all the way home or to move on to another town. They decided instead simply to walk up to Sengata's girl and to ask her with whom she wished to spend the weekend, the boy at her side or the Bethlehem boys. They did this in front of the scrawny boy's face, all bravado and cool, and then turned on their heels and walked. By the time night fell she was with them in their car and they were driving out of town.

From Sengata I hear that the story is not complete. In his embarrassment Fusi had omitted that Sengata's girl brought a friend and there were four of them in the car. They went on a road trip visiting the Blyde River Canyon and the Kruger National Park, and since they hadn't enough money for a room they spent two nights in the car, one couple in the front, the other in the back.

I haven't the stomach to ask Fusi whether it was worth it. A poor boy like him, saving money for months, to get laid in the front seat of a small car. Clearly it was, for all these years later, both men glow with pleasure on telling the tale. They are middle-aged, now, and their youthful conquests seem to come from a dream.

That is how these times spill from Fusi's tongue – there were the girls and the camaraderie and there was good work and there were good clothes. By the beginning of April 1992, Fusi was seeing two girls, each behind the back of the other. Decades would pass before he learnt that he had fathered a child with a third. He was led through life by his young man's desire and his love of his friends and by the magic this love wove.

These were his very best years, his happiest by a long stretch, he insists, until Steyn and Robertshaw knocked down his front door and took him away. There is no place for unpleasantness before April 1992, no place, for instance, to explain why he and Amos now lived alone. He has not forgotten that they fled their father; it is just that he cannot remember feeling angry or sad.

Why should it not be this way? His life was stolen on 2 April. What happened changes everything that came before.

Thirteen

He was arrested in April and tried in November and in the period in between he fell ill. He lay on the floor of his cell in great pain. It was like nothing he had felt before, as if the flesh beneath his skin and the bones beneath his flesh had begun to melt and were running loose in his body. He was taken from prison to Pelonomi Hospital in Bloemfontein and remained there for more than a month.

About his illness he tells conflicting stories. The doctors found poison in his blood, he says, and he suspects that the police tried to kill him while he was in jail. But at other times he says he had been sick for a long time; that he was booked off work on 2 April because of a recurring illness; that he had searched far and wide for a cure.

I come to accept that this affliction is a territory not firmly nailed down. It lifts from its moorings and wanders and there are several places where it alights and calls home. In any case, it is not surprising that his memories of this time are unstable, for what happened while he was in Pelonomi Hospital was enough to scramble anyone's senses.

Twice a day, he recalls, he was permitted to leave his ward under armed guard and use a public telephone in the corridor. On a Saturday in late September, he phoned his aunt – his father's brother's wife. They spoke about nothing in particular, he recalls, and he was about to hang up when she threw a question into the conversation.

'Have they not told you about Amos?' she asked.

He was silent.

And she said it was not right that Fusi's mother had not told him; it was not good enough to say that he was too ill to handle the news. Amos had been dead three weeks now, she said; he had spent the weekend drinking in Phuthaditjhaba and on the road back to Bethlehem he had rolled his car and died. His funeral had been held the previous weekend; he was in the cemetery in Bohlokong.

He does not remember what happened after he put down the phone. He recalls sitting up in his bed that evening, several hours after receiving the news. He has no memory of how he got back to the ward. He understands that he has blacked out a chunk of that day, for, even now, these many years later, he must protect himself from what happened during those hours.

Amos had come to see him a week before he died. He had been very animated, Fusi recalls. He had leant forward in his chair next to Fusi's bed, gesticulating and talking and throwing up his hands; he was searching for the right lawyer, he had said; he was on Fusi's case; he was determined to do this thing right, to get Fusi out of jail.

And Fusi, who knew better than anyone his brother's propensity to drink, told Amos not to visit a Bloemfontein tavern after leaving the hospital but to drive straight home. I do not want you drunk on the road from Bloemfontein to Bethlehem, Fusi recalls saying. For the thought of a world without Amos was unbearable.

A month later Fusi was in the dock, the trial proceeding in another world, his eyes fixed to the letters he had received from home. Through those letters he returned to the streets of Bethlehem and Amos was on those streets; without Amos there were no streets in Bethlehem, no life, no people, nothing at all.

Fourteen

ometime in April 1992, Isaac Ganda, a veteran inmate at the
maximum-security prison at Grootvlei, opened the newspaper to
find a photograph of six men spread across the centrefold. They
were accused of killing a young white police constable on the outskirts of
Bethlehem. The picture had been taken at the town's Magistrate's Court.
In the accompanying article Ganda read that at least one of the men was
a guerrilla trained in exile by the ANC.

Any case involving armed insurgents interested Ganda. A guerrilla
himself, auto-invented and self-trained, he was humbled in the pictorial
presence of the real McCoy. Scanning the faces in the photograph, he
tried to guess which of them was the soldier. Can you tell by the look in
a man's eyes, he wondered.

It was the least soldier-like among them who captured his attention.
He counted the names in the caption, left to right, one, two, three: Simon
Mofokeng. He was very young, just a baby, really. Amazingly, he was
smiling for the camera, the expression on his face mildly pleased, as if he
were attending a wedding. His hair was long, almost an afro, and Isaac
Ganda smiled with affection, for he did not need to see the rest of the boy
to know that he wore shoes he could not afford.

Isaac Ganda took in the pretty face and the careful hair and a bolt of sadness shot through him. This was just a boy; how would he survive what lay in store?

And he saw in a flash that if the boy was to be saved it was he, Isaac Ganda, who would do the saving. Now just a poor-quality image on newsprint, the boy in the photograph was moving steadily towards him, would be right here beside him, in the flesh, in a matter of months. For the case would go from the Magistrate's Court in Bethlehem to the Free State Supreme Court in Bloemfontein. And as sure as he was sitting reading the newspaper, all six would be convicted, for black men are not set free when a white cop has been killed with an AK-47. They would probably begin serving their sentences right here, in the maximum-security prison at Grootvlei.

From that day forth, Isaac Ganda scanned the paper for the Bethlehem Six. He monitored the progress of their trial. On the day after they were sentenced, he worked the channels the accretion of his years inside had opened and asked whether any of them would be joining him in his section.

Ganda had been in Grootvlei for more than nine years. He had spent the last four of those in the prison's School Section, where inmates who were studying were held. Ganda himself had not studied in more than three decades. He was in the School Section because he taught maths and science. As with his soldiering, he was a self-invented instructor, but in his teaching his felt considerably more confident than in his soldiering, for while the latter landed him constantly in prison, those he taught almost always passed their exams, at least if they had aptitude and discipline.

Fusi Mofokeng and Donald Makhura arrived in the School Section of the maximum-security prison at Grootvlei in March 1993. Tshokolo Mokoena opted not to go to study and Isaac Ganda met him only fleetingly in the prison courtyard from time to time. The remainder of the Bethlehem Six Ganda would never lay eyes on for they were transferred to other prisons immediately after sentencing.

Makhura was a man the likes of whom Ganda had never seen. The sheer volume of his activities was overwhelming. He was writing some sort of book, about what Ganda was not quite sure. He was also preparing assiduously for his appeal; and beyond his appeal, a demand for amnesty from a truth commission that had yet to be established. In Makhura's mind, so Ganda surmised, three or four possible futures beckoned, and Makhura divided his time between preparing for each.

Beyond anticipating these futures, Makhura was investing considerable energy in the present. He was attempting to enlist the leaders of the three great prison gangs, the 26s, the 27s and the 28s, to rise up and seize the prison. About this project Ganda had mixed feelings. Indeed, about Makhura in general he was not sure what to think. He was a well-trained soldier and he was clever. But his temper was short and his thinking unpredictable and about him was a constant sense of impending trouble.

As for young Mofokeng, here was a disturbing sight. In his years behind bars, Ganda had met many men the day after they had been sentenced to serve life. Men responded to this prospect in all sorts of ways. Some were too bewildered for normal human intercourse; you would look into their eyes to find that they were not there. Weeks or even months would pass before body and soul reunited; that was when the time for talking had arrived.

Others greeted the news with rage. You could tell at once by the way the body moved under the fluorescent lights. Were you to brush shoulders with that body, or poke it or nudge it, or lay a gentle hand on the forearm, it would lunge at you and tear you to pieces. To such men you offered distance; if you were to talk to them at all you did so from beyond an arm's length.

Fusi Mofokeng's response to his sentence was in its own league. About him was an aura of what could only be described as serenity. He was quietly spoken and polite and taken to smiling. Were one to grab his wrist and take his pulse, Ganda surmised, it would read a cool fifty-five. Fusi Mofokeng arrived in prison behaving as if he were going home in a few days.

Isaac Ganda, who knew what it was to brush with madness, worried a great deal about Fusi Mofokeng. What would happen to the boy on the day he understood he was not going home? How does one prepare him for that?

The best medicine, Isaac Ganda believed, was something consuming, something that would take years to complete. If Fusi Mofokeng was in a make-believe land it was best to fill his head with a task that would out-last his delusion. He interviewed the youngster at length, discovered that he only had a Standard 7, and announced that under his, Isaac Ganda's, stewardship, the boy would finish secondary school, an endeavour that would take a good five years, maybe more.

The School Section of Grootvlei was a world within a world. While the gangs controlled the rest of the prison, the School Section was filled with revolutionaries of various stripes.

There were, for instance, Velile Mxosana and Lebohang May, both members of the armed wing of the PAC. In 1992 they had responded to their organisation's call to attack apartheid installations by firing on a police station in Bloemfontein with automatic weapons. They were caught the next day. Then there was Abel Choane, like Makhura a member of the ANC's armed wing. He had been stopped at a roadblock transporting a dozen AK-47s from Bloemfontein to the Eastern Cape.

And there was Isaac Ganda himself, his revolutionary credentials much harder to pin down. Forty-seven years old on the day Fusi met him, he had been convicted for armed robbery three times over the past quarter of a century. From the beginning, he says, his aim was to overthrow the apartheid state. But as a lone maverick, without formal training or membership of an organisation, he was restricted by his very limited means. He robbed to acquire funds, he said, for building an army costs money. But he never got beyond his fundraising activities for they kept landing him in jail.

The revolutionaries of the School Section were interested in the outside world to the point of obsession. It was 1993 – the exiled liberation movements had been home for three years; now, they were negotiating the terms of a new dispensation with the apartheid regime. The three years of transition had thus far claimed many thousands of lives and the men in the School Section had come from that violence.

From his sister Victoria, Fusi received a tape recorder. And from the last of his savings, Isaac Ganda bought an old television set. One of the PAC soldiers had a radio. With these three devices, the School Section resolved to record South Africa's transition to democracy.

The negotiations between the government and its opponents were taking place at a convention centre next to Johannesburg's international airport. Plenary sessions of the negotiations were broadcast live across the nation. At the start of each plenary, the men of the School Section would gather around the radio or the TV and Fusi would turn on his recorder. Talking was forbidden while the recorder ran and anyone who coughed or cleared his throat would be slapped across the back of the head.

History was being made, out at Johannesburg's airport, and these men wanted to bathe in it, to use it as a balm for their souls. They believed that their freedom was bound to it. For each of them regarded himself as a political prisoner and each expected indemnity or amnesty from a future truth commission of which people spoke.

Periodically, officials from their respective organisations – the PAC and the ANC – would come to visit. And these officials, too, would talk of amnesties and indemnities and the prospect of a truth commission. Indeed, these officials kept assuring them that their time behind bars would be brief.

And so the men of the School Section wanted very much for the negotiations to end well; were they to be abandoned or derailed, were the country to descend into war, were the apartheid regime to drive the liberation movements back underground, they, the men of the School Section, would remain behind bars.

And the more they talked of their impending freedom, the more the white warders who ran the prison loathed them. Isaac Ganda had been permitted to bring his television set into the prison for educational purposes. Now that it was being used to watch the transition to democracy it was confiscated. Ganda screamed blue murder. He wrote a raft of complaints. He threatened to go on a hunger strike. The head of the section replied that he would enjoy watching Ganda starve.

When the television set went, the revolutionaries recorded the negotiations on the radio. Its electric cables were promptly confiscated. If you want to listen to politics, the men of the School Section were told, you must do so with your own batteries.

Isaac Ganda watched Fusi Mofokeng partake in this recording of events. And he understood that for Fusi it was a magic ritual; he was jumping into the history of his times in order to steer it from the inside. For were the proceedings broadcast on the radio to end in amnesty or indemnity or a truth commission – these prospects were spoken of interchangeably and had become a three-headed beast – they would take Fusi Mofokeng back to the streets of Bethlehem where he would resume his young man's life with his cousin Khulu and his friend Sengata and with the girls who were drawn to his pretty face and his careful hair.

Isaac Ganda himself was sceptical. The eccentricity of his own position made him wary. Donald Makhura could stand up before some tribunal or commission and prove himself to be a member of Umkhonto we Sizwe. Velile Mxosana and Lebohang May could vouch that they were members of the PAC's armed wing. What could Isaac Ganda say about himself?

Examined from the outside, his actions resembled those of a common criminal. He had held up a petrol attendant with a knife and emptied his cash register. He had terrified a shop attendant and run off with his takings. How could he show some commission what these actions actually meant and whence they arose? What would he say? That he was the son of labour tenants from the Bothaville district of the northwestern Free State? That as a boy he had witnessed his family's eviction from their land without cause? That the Gandas had scattered under the weight of this hammer blow? That the injustice to which he and his family were subjected had invaded his soul? That with the best will in the world he could not ignore the power of what he felt deep inside? That he could not in a thousand lifetimes bring himself to work for a white man? That all of this happened long ago, while the liberation movements' armed forces were still inaccessible in their distant exile? That becoming a lone bandit was the best he could do in constrained circumstances?

He knew that this would not fly. When he observed the others gather around his television to steer the course of events, he did so through a pane of glass. He was among them, but he was alone. He was happy, but he also felt a sadness too dark and hollow to share.

And when he thought of his plight, he thought, too, of Fusi Mofokeng. Like Ganda, Fusi was not a soldier. What exactly would he say when standing before the wise men of some commission?

And so he was gratified to see that Fusi had not put all his eggs in one basket. In addition to watching the negotiations on television, Fusi had appealed against his conviction. And when he heard nothing about it for months on end, he wrote to the court. And when it did not reply, he wrote to the Minister of Justice asking him to intervene.

He wrote, too, to the man who had acted as his lawyer during the trial, André Landman. And when Landman replied that he could not help, Fusi wrote to Makhura and Fokazi's lawyer, Paul Heymanns, the man who had walked into court one morning laden with the law books he had brought from home. And when Heymanns did not reply, Fusi wrote to him again.

Eventually, the Minister of Justice replied to Fusi and said that he had written personally to the Legal Aid Board to find a lawyer to handle the appeal. And, in due course, a certain Advocate De Vries wrote to announce that he was Fusi's new lawyer. Advocate De Vries lived far away, in the town of Aliwal North. He would not come all the way to Bloemfontein, he wrote; he would conduct his relationship with his client by correspondence.

Fusi shared the news with Isaac Ganda who took one sniff at the situation and did not care for its odour. Should Fusi place his fate in the hands of a strange man from a strange town, a man who would never meet his client face to face?

Fusi and Isaac Ganda read and reread De Vries's letters. They handed them on to Donald Makhura, who read them too.

All three men came to one conclusion. The more arrows in Fusi's quiver, the better. Let us shoot this one off. The situation is hardly perfect; De Vries is invisible and has no face and why does he not have the time to meet his client? But if you shoot enough arrows from your quiver, one of them will find its target. What is there to lose?

Fifteen

On 10 May 1994 the men of the School Section gathered around Isaac Ganda's television set, recently reacquired. During the course of the day they watched power change hands between the apartheid regime and Nelson Mandela's incoming government.

Mythical figures filed one by one across the screen – Zambia's Kenneth Kaunda flitting his famous white handkerchief; Britain's Prince Philip, as stiff and as foolish as his braided uniform; Yasser Arafat in his checked headwear.

When Fidel Castro appeared, the men of the School Section stood to their feet and burst into song. His uniform crisp, his cap snug, he was a guerrilla's guerrilla, his presence, just paces from Mandela proof, if any, that these were revolutionary times.

Mandela spoke stiffly from a prepared speech. When he was done he stood stock-still and grave as the old regime's fighter jets saluted him from the sky. The prisoners watched in silence and in awe, unable to match this strange spectacle to words.

The ceremony over, the television belting out adverts for footwear and cold drinks, they wandered around in bewilderment, hugging one another and shaking hands.

The following morning news passed swiftly from cell to cell: on the flagpole in the courtyard the old national flag was gone – in its stead, the corpse of a rat. The head warder of the School Section, Mr Engels, looked smug that morning and the prisoners assumed that this was his greeting to the new president.

And so there they were, the men of the School Section and their captors, one group drunk with expectation, the other stupefied by dread.

The first thing that happened was more humdrum than either had contemplated.

Mandela's Cabinet filled with the faces of black men and women. Within months, the new Minister of Correctional Services, Sipho Mzimela, toured the Free State's prisons. After visiting Ramkraal, the awaiting-trial facility outside Bloemfontein where Fusi and his co-accused had been held during their trial, he declared it unfit for human beings and ordered its immediate closure.

The old apartheid bureaucrats scrambled to accommodate the will of their new boss. In haste, they arranged to transfer Ramkraal's entire population to Grootvlei. To make space for the new arrivals, some of the prison's current population would have to be moved. At a stroke, the men of the School Section were to be dispersed to prisons across the country.

The first consequence for Fusi of the coming of democracy was not impending freedom but the threat of great danger. Sheltered until now from the wrath of his country's prisons by the men of the School Section, he was on the brink of exposure to the unknown.

What happened next saved him from hell. He wonders sometimes whether God guided his way – this is one among many of the things he both believes and does not believe to be true.

The way he remembers it now, the men of the School Section were offered several maximum-security prisons from which to choose. There was Goedemoed in Aliwal North, Groenpunt in Sasolburg, Leeuwkop outside Johannesburg, and Barberton way out in the northeast of the country. He did not want to go to any of these places. They were all maximum-security facilities and the men they housed were creatures of prison. They had years left to serve and did not care for their freedom. They raped and stabbed and killed and they felt neither remorse nor fear. Goedemoed, in particular, had the most terrible reputation. Fusi had heard of prisoners slicing open their stomachs with razor blades to avoid entering its doors.

As much as the violence of these places, he feared their distance from Bethlehem. Grootvlei was far enough – a long and expensive taxi ride. Were he banished to Barberton or Aliwal North he would slip from the grasp of those he loved and he feared that he would drift from their minds.

When asked where he wanted to go he said Kroonstad Prison; it was less than two hours from Bethlehem by car. This was not possible, he was told; Kroonstad was a medium-security facility and as a man in the early phase of a life sentence for murder he could not go there.

The way he recalls it now, the trucks were lined up in the courtyard leaving for various prisons and he simply climbed on board the one bound for Kroonstad. It occurred to him as he sat there, the truck's engine idling, that Grootvlei Prison still held R50 in his name to spend at the tuck shop. He dared not ask for his money lest he draw attention to himself. Best that they keep it, he thought.

On arrival at Kroonstad he was taken immediately to the observation cells, a limbo in which one is classified and assigned to a section. It was only a matter of time before his presence at Kroonstad was deemed a mistake.

He remained in observation for six weeks. Others came and were classified and assigned. But Fusi they neither sent to a section at Kroonstad nor banished to another prison. He simply waited in his purgatory day after day. He believes that they did not know what to do with him. His prison card described him as a murderer two years into his sentence. Yet to the warder in charge he put on display the full ensemble of his innocence: his soft-spoken voice, the sincerity in his eyes, the stillness that drifts from his aura, causing those in his presence to slow down.

He no longer remembers the name of the warder over whom he cast his spell. But he recalls the man saying: 'I can vouch for him, this one; he is harmless. He would not squash a cockroach with his boot or swat a fly.'

And with these words it was determined that he could stay. He could stay in Kroonstad, a medium-security prison, close to his mother, close to his sister, Victoria. Between it and a maximum-security prison was the widest of gulfs. Among the prisoners here were murderers and rapists and men who had committed atrocities behind bars; but they were on the brink of release now, and they thought twice before forfeiting their freedom. The gangs were shadows of themselves. Robbed of the will to draw blood, they were nothing, just groups of sorry men and their arcane rituals. In their stead was a thriving soccer league, a brass band, a large section for study and a social worker who ran workshops to manage anger.

He felt, as he settled in, that he was living a triumph. He had had the gumption to get on a Kroonstad-bound truck. And at the end of the journey, in the observation cells, standing on the threshold between doom and salvation, he had learnt to exercise his greatest power. For it was here, in a quiet room, one on one, that he could expose another to his being and illustrate the truth: that he was not meant to be in jail, that something had gone horribly wrong.

He wanted very much to resume his studies. But the School Section at Kroonstad was full, he discovered, and he would have to wait. It would not take long, he assured himself; the traffic in and out of this place was dense. Each day, it seemed, somebody was ending his sentence.

But as he waited, he wondered how anyone might study here, for it was a great, open prison, more than a thousand inmates wandering its halls. The noise was persistent and deafening. It was one thing that a person could never be alone; with eighteen men sharing a cell, somebody was always watching you. In time, he thought, he could learn to live with that. But to be unable to flush the noise from one's head and hear nothing, that seemed a greater invasion; how could one sustain a conversation with oneself in this din?

A couple of weeks in, he strained hard to remember what it was to hear silence. Even when he woke in the dead of night there was noise – each hacking cough, each snort, each cry from a dream, bounced from surface to surface before settling in the rafters above. A thousand men sleeping, he thought, make enough of a racket to wake the dead.

But if the noise oppressed him, the sights lifted his spirits. Grootvlei had been sealed off from the world; between its inhabitants and the outside stood a great wall. Even the dismal prison yard was invisible from the cells, for the windows butted up against the ceiling.

Here at Kroonstad, however, the windows were no higher than his chest, and between the prison and the world was just a barbed-wired fence. Each moment of each day, one could see and hear the outside. One needed only to lift one's head and look.

At night, he would lie on his back and close his eyes and listen to the vehicles on the Viljoenskroon road. And if he could not sleep, he would turn onto his stomach and look out. There were car lights. There was the boop-booping of passing trucks. An image of each truck driver formed in his mind. Some were old and a little rotund like his uncle Jack. Others were young and wore cut-off sleeves, their shoulders strong and lean. And if the truck in his sights was heading southeast, he would go along for the ride. For perhaps it would leave the Kroonstad highway and head down the R76 to Steynsrus, then make its way to Senekal, just a stone's throw from his beloved Oorsprong.

He counted the steps he'd take to get to the Vijoenskroon road. Seventy? Surely less than a hundred. In his mind he would stand in the tramlines on the road's verge. He would put his thumb in the air and a truck would stop and he would explain to the driver that although he had no money he would pay on the other side. And the driver would look this stranger up and down and then nod to the passenger seat; for between free people there was an implicit understanding.

He had not been in Kroonstad long when he was summoned from his cell and told that his father's brothers had come to see him. He knew at once that something was wrong for it was not a visiting day; he was taken to the administrative wing of the building and led to a quiet office where his uncles were waiting. They had come all this way, they said, their voices hushed, their tone stiff, for such matters could not be conveyed by phone. David Mofokeng had fallen ill some three weeks earlier and had been taken to hospital where his health only declined. He had died the previous day and was to be buried the following weekend.

Fusi could barely absorb this weighty news, for sitting between his uncles, his head bowed, his hands clasped together, was Thabo Motaung.

All these years later, his father's death sits lightly with him. Even at the time, he thinks now, the news sounded familiar the moment he heard it, for it seemed that David Mofokeng had been dying for a long time.

He thought of the enquiries he'd need to make and the forms he'd need to fill in to request to attend David's funeral. He knew in advance that his request would be denied and, in this moment, he felt great sadness for David Mofokeng. His one son was dead, the other in prison, and whether anyone at the graveside would grieve Fusi could not say.

These thoughts could hardly settle for in front of him sat Thabo Motaung. The harsh truth was that David had died and was thus a man of the past, while he, Fusi, was alive and in the midst of a great struggle. He wanted very much to know what the young man before him would say.

Thabo stared at his chest and mumbled, his hands quivering. He began to speak, but so softly and with such reluctance that Fusi could not make out what he was saying. It was only when Fusi spoke to him in tones that were quiet and patient and without menace that Thabo lifted his face and in a frail but clear voice said that he was sorry; he had made this trip with Fusi's uncles, he said, because Fusi was in prison and it was his, Thabo's, fault.

If Fusi felt anger, he does not recall it now. The boy was squirming, he says, as if Fusi's presence had trapped him like an animal in a net. If the encounter were to last, he would have to put Thabo at ease. And so he spoke in his softest voice. And he said plainly that he was not angry. After all, he told Thabo, he knew all too well how the security police turned the screws. He himself so very nearly agreed to become a state witness. That he had not was sheer luck. Could he blame another for doing what he himself had almost done?

As Thabo relaxed, so he began to speak more freely. The security police had put him under such strain, he said. Mapalala and others came several times to the house. They told him that he was implicated in a terrible crime and that only his testimony against his friends could save him. He had left Bethlehem and gone to Phuthaditjhaba, hoping that the police would not follow.

On discovering that he was gone, they began working on his elder sister, the matriarch of the Motaung household. They would give the family R75 000 if her brother were to testify, they said. The Motaungs were poor and R75 000 was a lot of money and it was not long before Thabo's sister came to Phuthaditjhaba to tell him that he was obliged for the sake of the family to testify. Before he knew it, he was filling in a form, he said, the pressure from these police officers and from his sister and from his family at large reigning over him.

Fusi listened quietly and said he understood. And Fusi's uncle, Lefo, chimed in. You are young and inexperienced, he said to Thabo. And forces much more powerful than you were at work. It is all very much understandable.

Fusi wrote to Donald Makhura, who was being held at the maximum-security facility at Leeuwkop. Makhura was the intellectual among them, the one who knew the world. He, too, would have a sense of what to do.

Makhura replied at once. Thabo Motaung was in grave danger, he wrote. For when the police got wind that he was recanting his testimony and revealing that they had offered him a bribe, they would silence him. And by that, Makhura wrote, I mean that they will eliminate him. He must get out of town immediately. And then he must write an affidavit describing exactly what had happened between him and the police.

Fusi read the letter carefully several times. He did not know what an affidavit was, let alone how Thabo might go about writing one.

And so he wrote for advice to a lawyer named Essa Moosa. He had met Moosa two years earlier, when he was still at Grootvlei. Moosa had been travelling the country on behalf of the ANC's legal department seeing scores of prisoners who had committed crimes in the organisation's name. Now Fusi wrote to Moosa to tell him that the chief witness in his trial had come to confess that his evidence was a lie. I ask you humbly for your expert advice, Fusi wrote. I have been advised that the witness must write an affidavit. What is an affidavit?

Several weeks later, Moosa's reply reached Fusi. It had come via fax to the head of Kroonstad Medium A Prison. From there it had gone to the head of Fusi's section, and then finally to Fusi. Who knew for how long it had lain around?

'Affidavit' was just a fancy word, Moosa wrote. In clear and simple language Thabo should write down everything he had said to Fusi. Then he should walk into a police station, any police station, and sign his statement before a commissioner of oaths. Moosa included in his letter a sample affidavit, the details of some other, unrelated case filling its pages, to show Fusi what an affidavit looked like.

On Thabo's next visit to Kroonstad we will do this, Fusi had thought to himself. The police station is not so far from the prison. He can take this sample affidavit with him to the station and write one of his own.

From the payphone in the corridor, Fusi called his uncle Lefo. Tell Thabo he must come back, he said. As quickly as he can. He has an opportunity to rectify his mistake.

Instead, it was Uncle Lefo himself who came. He took the sample affidavit and promised that he would go to Thabo, explain to him how the document was to be written and drive him to a police station a safe distance from Bethlehem.

Lefo left for home and Fusi waited. And the waiting proved insufferable. By now he was in the School Section. But what with the noise of the prison and the presence of Thabo Motaung in his mind he battled to pay attention to his books. Beyond the School Section, the prison was awash with activity. The inmates had formed several soccer clubs and when a game was about to begin the prison came to a standstill. For days before and after, inmates spoke of little else.

Fusi could absorb none of this. He was living in a future that came to him in flashes – an affidavit, a day in court, the first night back in Bethlehem. He was both here in Kroonstad and not here at all. The gap between the place of his body and the place of his mind was hard to bear. At times the pain was physical, as if his head had been split open like a nut.

Several weeks after Lefo's visit, Fusi received news on the phone from a cousin that Thabo Motaung was gravely ill; that he was lying in Pelonomi Hospital in Bloemfontein; that he was expected soon to die.

There and then, on the payphone in the corridor, Fusi begged his cousin to go immediately to Pelonomi. Perhaps Thabo had written that affidavit; perhaps he had it there with him in his hospital bed.

Two days later, Fusi's cousin relayed on the phone the most dispiriting news. He had driven to Bloemfontein as Fusi had requested. On arriving at the hospital he was told that the man he had come to see, Thabo Motaung, had died in the early hours of the morning.

When Fusi heard the news he thought immediately of Donald Makhura and his warning. On his last visit to Kroonstad, which, after all, was not that long ago, Thabo had had flesh on his bones and the glow of health on his skin. There had been nothing wrong with him, nothing at all.

A sequence formed in Fusi's mind, a definite series of events starting with Thabo's visit to Kroonstad and ending in his death, his affidavit uncomposed and unsigned. Thabo Motaung had been killed.

Fusi could not prove it. Of course he could not. Those with power leave no traces, or at least not the sort a hapless prisoner might find.

He wrote to the Motaungs. He told them that the death of their son and their brother was suspicious and that they must do all in their power to investigate it. They must find police officers loyal to the country's new democratic order, police officers who would not fear going after their colleagues. From the Motaungs he received no reply.

As for his uncle, Lefo, on his next visit he could only shrug and murmur uselessly that the boy had fallen ill and died and that Fusi should leave him to rest.

Sixteen

No sooner had Fusi absorbed the fact of Thabo's death than a flag of hope was raised. In December 1995 the High Court in Bloemfontein requested that Fusi be moved, temporarily, back to Grootvlei. Advocate De Vries, his hitherto invisible lawyer, wanted to talk to him.

It made sense that De Vries would want to meet him there, Fusi remembers thinking. For during all this time Tshokolo had remained at Grootvlei and the lawyer would of course want to talk to his two clients together.

Fusi was taken from Kroonstad in the back of a prison van, a toothbrush, soap and a change of underwear in his bag. He would stay at Grootvlei for two nights at most, he was told.

These many years later, he has no memory of De Vries's face or body. Whether he was bearded or clean-shaven, tall or short, fat or thin, Fusi cannot say. He is now just 'De Vries', a name attached to no particular being.

The lawyer consulted his clients over the course of two mornings. Fusi told him of Thabo's confession, of the race to get him to sign an affidavit, and of his suspicious death. He recalls De Vries taking notes and nodding his head, his thoughts inscrutable.

One wonders why Fusi did not push him further. He had taken such decisive action in the wake of Thabo's revelations. He had written at once to Donald Makhura, then to Essa Moosa; he had summoned his uncle Lefo to receive the sample affidavit; by remote control he had guided his cousin to Pelonomi Hospital to extract the document from the dying Thabo. Why did he not similarly press his lawyer? Why did he not suggest, for instance, that De Vries get an affidavit from his uncle Lefo, testifying to Thabo's confession?

For all his determination, Fusi was, after all, uneducated, young and black; perhaps in the face of this white man, his loftiness written all over his mien, Fusi shrank into the meekness of his station. He watched his lawyer taking notes and when the meeting was done he had no inkling of what De Vries might do next.

Remembering the consultations now, it is Tshokolo who captures Fusi's imagination. His friend's eyes were dead, he recalls, his speech slurred. Whether he understood anything De Vries and Fusi were saying was hard to tell. Within minutes, it was Fusi alone to whom De Vries spoke. And in the back of his mind it occurred to him that while he, Fusi, was sometimes lucky and sometimes not, Tshokolo seemed destined to have no luck at all.

When the meetings with De Vries were over Fusi discovered that his move back to Kroonstad had been blocked. The warder overseeing his transfer must have been unusually thorough and unwelcomingly diligent; when he saw that Fusi was less than three years into a life sentence for murder, he refused to sign the transfer papers. A man at that stage of that sentence is not a medium-security prisoner and cannot be accepted into a medium-security prison.

Fusi had to call De Vries back to the prison, and he, in turn, had to speak to the head of Grootvlei, who was persuaded to make a call to the head of Kroonstad. Fusi watched in great anxiety as these important men went about determining his future; he hoped and he prayed that between them they would muster sufficient concern to help him.

He waited. A day came and went. Then another. It struck him that he hadn't the wherewithal to describe to those ignorant of the experience what it was to be a prisoner. You pack a bag because you have been summoned to consult with your lawyer; it does not occur to you that you might never come back, that a wary bureaucrat, for whom your existence is as light as the dust on his shoes, might alter your fate.

Finally, on the third day, he was returned to Kroonstad. And he was surprised to discover that it felt like coming home. The thought of it angered him. If you take everything away from a human being and leave him with the barest of bones, he is grateful for each scrap you throw his way.

Settling back into his Kroonstad routine, it struck him for the first time that he did not know when the court was to hear his appeal. In a week? Six weeks? De Vries had not said. He wrote to his lawyer and heard nothing. Weeks went by and he wrote again. He waited another month and wrote once more.

By March 1996, a full three months had gone by and his memory of his lawyer had grown dim. He would wake in the night with the horrible feeling that there was no De Vries, that there had been no consultation in Grootvlei Prison, that he had invented it all in his sleep. He would turn on his stomach and look out the window and stare at the lights on the Viljoenskroon road. Only once he was fully awake did he reacquire the certainty that his appeal against his conviction was real.

In the end, he learnt of his fate in the most dreadful fashion. From out of the blue one morning, a warder came to him clutching a copy of the Afrikaans-language daily, *Beeld*.

'You are in here,' the warder said, and stabbed a finger at a small head-line at the bottom of an inside page.

Fusi remembers very clearly the words he read: '*Twee mans van Bethle-hem se appèl slaag nie.*' ('Two Bethlehem men fail on appeal.')

He is not very good at recalling anger. When I ask what he felt he is mute. In lieu of remembering what was happening inside him he says only that now, two decades later, he still has not heard from De Vries.

He remembers returning to his cell and firing off a series of letters. He wrote to Paul Heymanns for there was a time when Heymanns responded to his correspondence. For good measure, he wrote once more to André Landman, hardly expecting a reply. He wrote to the Human Rights Commission – it was a long, careful letter beginning with the morning of 2 April 1992, when Sikhalo Ncala had knocked on his door.

He was desperate, truly. He recalled his discussions back at Grootvlei with Isaac Ganda and Donald Makhura. They had counted the many arrows in his quiver, so satisfied that they were men who were clever and wise to the world. Well, he was shooting off these arrows one by one and his quiver was now almost empty.

He was a prisoner, after all. He controlled nothing. The world was a lumbering beast, passing him by as he rattled the bars of his cage. He could shout in his loudest voice and it would not hear. He could pick up a stone and hurl it and watch it hit its mark behind the beast's ear. It would stop and stare down at him for a brief moment before turning and resuming its course.

From the Human Rights Commission he received a reply. South Africa's Truth and Reconciliation Commission (TRC) had just opened for business, it said, and Fusi should write to them at once.

He wrote immediately to the TRC and it was not long before they replied. They told him of the workings of their Amnesty Committee and encouraged him to apply to be heard there. The Committee would hold hearings in Kroonstad, they wrote, and that was where he could tell the Committee and the world what had happened.

But no sooner had this been set in stone than it was undone. For the TRC's investigators now discovered that they had been working separately on the cases of Donald Makhura, Clement Ndabeni, Mandla Fokazi and Sikhalo Ncala, and that all of these cases should be combined as one. The matter would be delayed, perhaps for as long as a year or two, so that this disparate investigative work could come together.

He wrote once more to the Legal Aid Board telling them that his appeal had failed. He had been told by those who knew the law, he wrote, that he could directly petition South Africa's highest court, the Supreme Court of Appeal. The Legal Aid Board's reply was slow, but it came. He was to be assigned another lawyer.

Throughout the course of their association, he never met his new lawyer. Indeed, he had assumed that this person was a man; it was only years later, his case now in the hands of diligent lawyers, that he discovered that she was a woman. In any event, she did not bother to show him the petition she filed on his behalf. A prison warder brought him the last page to sign; that is all he saw of it.

Once more, he waited. He wrote to the new lawyer and heard nothing. He wrote to De Vries who did not reply. He wrote to them both again. And then again.

In October 1997, more than a year after the new lawyer had taken his case, he received news, finally, from the Supreme Court of Appeal, that his petition had failed. With the court's letter came a copy of the original document Fusi's lawyer had submitted, the one he had signed but not seen. He read it very slowly, over the course of an afternoon.

That night, the words he had read robbed him of his sleep. The language was hard to follow, the style a formal legalese. He was not sure that he had understood. Early the following morning, he began reading it again. Still, he was not certain that he really grasped what he had read. He gave the petition to a fellow prisoner, a former prosecutor in disgrace for having committed fraud. Now, this man, who knew as well as anybody how to read a document of this ilk, took it to his cell and returned with it the following day.

The news he brought was precisely what Fusi had feared. The petition appealed against the charge of murder, not against the charge of conspiracy to rob. There was no mention of Thabo Motaung's shaky testimony, no word of his subsequent confession, nor of the strange circumstances of his death. In the petition the Supreme Court of Appeal had read, a petition Fusi had been made to sign without reading, he and Tshokolo did not dispute that they had brought the Thokoza men to town to rob the Orsmonds.

He considered writing to his lawyer to tell her that she had failed him. He considered, too, writing directly to the court to say that his lawyer had made a mistake; that a prisoner is not free to conduct his appeal as best he can; that he is like a marooned man throwing a bottled message into the ocean. But it occurred to him that this letter, should he write it, would constitute yet another message in another bottle, cast out into a world that was busy and harried.

There and then, he made a decision. The most important task before him, he resolved, was to complete his education. He was writing letters in his third language about a legal system he did not understand. He must learn English well enough for his letters to reflect what was in his heart.

He must learn to master the law. Perhaps with these skills under his belt, his letters would be become powerful; perhaps, then, somebody would read them.

Seventeen

In the midst of this drama, he began a relationship with a woman. Her name was D. She was an inmate at Kroonstad's correctional facility for women.

From her letters, it appears that in December 1997, from a telephone in the corridor in the male prison, Fusi told her that he loved her. He had neither met her face to face, nor seen her picture.

In lieu of having anything to say about his looks, she complimented his handwriting. 'It is beautiful,' she wrote. 'Your fingers are like a computer.'

Only her letters remain. What he said to her one must guess from her replies. But he clearly wrote a great deal at first for there are times when she is replying to his letters every couple of weeks.

With her pen, she made a world in which they lived together. 'If only they allowed us to come and wash your clothes,' she declared, 'I would keep coming to wash your dirty clothes and wash them and iron them carefully.'

Three months into their liaison, she chided him, gently, for still not sending a photograph. 'It is not urgent,' she wrote. 'I will wait for you.'

And she instructed him to listen to her favourite songs in order that he might join her in spirit. 'Said I Loved You … But I Lied' by Michael Bolton, 'Whatever You Want' by Tina Turner, 'Un-break My Heart' by Toni Braxton.

A month later, they tried but failed to talk on the phone. It was so very difficult to arrange. The public phones in their respective prisons served hundreds of prisoners – they could arrange a date and a time, but only luck could decide whether both phones would be free. In the physical world, they lived within a couple of hundred metres of one another. Were they free, the journey from his room to hers would make for the briefest evening stroll.

Finally, in March 1998, they managed to speak again and, in the wake of this excitement, her letters were charged. 'Darling,' she wrote. 'On Saturday I slept so well because I heard your voice on the phone. I slept so well that I had inappropriate dreams ... I had to wake up in the middle of the night to go bath.'

The following month, she made love to him again. 'If only they would allow us to be together,' she said, 'I would leave you in a state.'

There was a long silence. From her next reply it appeared that Fusi was in some turmoil and had spoken to her with candour. She expressed disappointment that he no longer wrote to her erotically. 'I understand that you have a problem having many sexual feelings,' she wrote. But perhaps she did not, for in the next paragraph she scolded him again for not sending photographs and declared that 'the thing that strengthens love between two people is sex'.

'I don't know how I will handle myself when we meet properly,' she wrote. 'I don't know where we will find a place to go crazy.'

A month later he repeated that having sex with one another via their pens was damaging him. 'I understand,' she replied. 'I have the same problem. I take your letters and I start to read them. Afterwards, my feelings for you grow and I get turned on by you.' She advised him to deal with the situation as she did: 'What I do when I have this problem is that I take my bible and read it for a while, then I pray a lot and then I feel much better.'

By August, she was furious with him. They had just spoken on the phone for the first time in months and the conversation had not gone well. She scolded him for not writing; he protested that he had sent many letters, but that they clearly had not reached her. One needed either to use the postal system, it seems, one's letters stamped and sent out to the post office, only to come straight back to the prison in the mail; or one smuggled letters via a warder. Fusi, it appeared, had been using the second method and it was not working.

They made up. Her letters grew warm again. But, even now, there was anguish and a hint of betrayal.

'Darling,' she wrote. 'Somehow, somewhere, you hurt me, I mean regarding the photograph. I feel left out because I only know your voice but not your face! But you know both my voice and what I look like. Please, darling, try everything in your power to let me know you, since you promised me Heaven & Earth regarding your photo, but I realize you can't keep your promises.'

There was silence again, for another two months, and it appears that in the interim Fusi sent a letter in which he gave anger free rein. She had taken too long, it appears, to reply to an earlier letter, one that was especially revealing.

'Darling,' she wrote, 'you know what? These letters look like they stir trouble between us, and I don't like it when you get hurt. And Darling what I can tell you is that on the day I received your letter, I respond on the same day. It's just that the post is not very reliable, and Love I don't like the way you write, scolding me, and my heart really becomes sore. Please stop scolding me for no reason.'

It appears that she heard nothing from Fusi again. For this is the last of D's letters in his possession.

Fusi and I are driving on the open highway somewhere in the eastern Free State when I tell him that I have read D's letters. He winces, just momentarily, then looks at his hands.

'That was really quite silly,' he says. 'That was nothing, really. Just a ... How many letters of hers did you find? If I remember correctly, there were two.'

'There were in fact nineteen,' I reply.

He raises his eyebrows. 'As many as that? That surprises me.'

We drive in silence for a while.

'To me they are so very important,' I say. 'It is so hard to recover what someone really felt long ago. They are evidence of some of what you were feeling.'

He glances warily at me. 'They are not important. I barely remember them. I keep them because I keep all the letters I received during that time.'

I let it pass for it seems stubborn to persist. But for me Manana's letters are heart-wrenching. Six years before their correspondence began he spent his weekends drinking beer and pursuing women. Now, through D, he relearnt what he could afford to imagine and what he could not, and the strictures turned out to be awfully narrow: even to have sex via pen and paper was too much of a risk.

I try to convey what I am thinking. 'I am amazed at the discipline you were forced to exercise over yourself,' I say. 'You could not even afford for your daydreams to surprise you. Because they might take you somewhere dangerous, somewhere from which you might not return with your sanity intact.'

He likes what I am saying, I think, for now he is leaning back in the passenger seat, his hands no longer fidgeting.

'In my mind I decided I could only afford to think of my mother and my sister,' he says finally. 'It was important to think only of them. Everyone else might forget me.'

For a long time, neither of us says anything. Victoria wrote to him dutifully several times a year. Her letters are steady and formal and Christian
and they are full of woe. She salutes God, she lists the things she must
suffer, and she signs off. She writes again a couple of months later and it
is more of the same.

'This time of D,' he finally says, 'it was the time just before we were due
to appear at the TRC. After waiting for such a long time it was all happening. It was being arranged for Ncala and Makhura and Clement Ndabeni
and the others to come to Kroonstad. We would be reunited. We were
told that we would all spend one night together at Kroonstad and then be
taken to Welkom the next morning for our hearing. And then it was just
a matter of waiting a little longer to be free.'

Eighteen

That he was running late was not Booker Mohlaba's fault. The case documents had been couriered to him only the previous day and he could hardly walk into a hearing knowing nothing. He woke early and began reading. After skimming an English-language summary of the trial judgment and a couple of other documents he realised that the hearing was about to begin and that he must go.

From the papers it seemed a straightforward case. A group of eight SDU comrades from Phola Park, among them trained MK guerrillas, had been sent on a mission somewhere in Natal, their bakkie loaded with weapons. They got as far as Bethlehem in the eastern Free State where two police officers stopped them. The men killed one and wounded the other and then scattered in different directions. In flight, three of them ran across land belonging to a white farmer who made the mistake of trying to apprehend them. One of them shot the farmer in the stomach.

Booker Mohlaba was dealing with an untold number of amnesty applications. His law firm, Koopedi, Mohlaba & Moshoana, was among those retained by the ANC to represent the many hundreds of people who claimed to have committed crimes in the course of furthering the organisation's aims. The work was all-consuming; he was at it night and day. And it wasn't especially satisfying. It did not, he felt, deepen his knowledge of the law. From the vantage point of his development as a craftsman and a practitioner, it was dead time. But the contract with the ANC was large and that was important to his firm. And, besides, there was satisfaction to be had in helping prisoners who deserved to be free.

It was rushed work. The volume was simply too great to consult before-hand with every client or even to read all the papers through. Indeed, the hearing involving these men who had met trouble in Bethlehem was one of three he would need to attend to in Welkom over the following days. But Booker Mohlaba had by now learnt to get to the heart of a matter with speed. This case, from what he had seen of the papers, seemed a cinch.

The hearing was being held in a community hall in Thabong, the black township attached to Welkom. It was one of those flat, beige public con-structions that could be a school or a community centre. Inside was a stage and a long, wide gallery filled with plastic chairs. It was already half-full when Booker Mohlaba arrived.

He presented himself to the three commissioners hearing the case, apologised for his lateness, and begged their permission to wait a little longer so that he might consult with his clients. He was led across a court-yard to a small room where they were waiting for him.

There were supposed to be six, but only four had made it. This was not unusual. Getting prisoners to their hearings was not, in Mohlaba's experi-ence, a job Correctional Services performed very well. Four was enough; the case, in his view, could proceed.

The moment he sat down with his clients it was clear that the one to talk to was Donald Makhura. Of the four, it was he who could com-municate the facts of the case with clarity; it was he who could join the dots. Time was short. Efficiency was what mattered. He gave Makhura the floor.

Makhura spoke and Mohlaba took notes and as he listened so the image of the case that had formed in his mind earlier in the morning fell apart. When Makhura finished speaking, Mohlaba put his pen down carefully next to his yellow legal pad and addressed the man called Fusi Mofokeng.

'It is your testimony that you and Tshokolo Mokoena were not members of the ANC?' he asked.

'We were not.'

'It is your testimony that you had nothing to do with the operation these men were on?'

'We knew nothing at all of their operation. We were not even informed that they were SDU members.'

'It is just that one of them was your brother-in-law? He stopped at your house with the others simply because he was your brother-in-law and then he moved on?'

'That is correct,' Mofokeng said.

'May I ask,' Mohlaba continued, 'have you appealed your conviction?'

'Mokoena and I appealed and lost,' Mofokeng said. 'Then we petitioned the Supreme Court of Appeal directly and they did not accept to hear our case.'

Nobody can know what Booker Mohlaba felt in this moment, not even he, for it was long ago. He had by now met many people applying for amnesty and the great majority, in his experience, did not understand the process. But this case took the cake. Why had nobody told Mofokeng until now that he had no business applying for amnesty? Why was it left to Booker Molhaba, here and now, after 9:00 a.m. on the morning of the hearing, the commissioners growing annoyed at the continued delay?

One came here to tell the truth about one's crime and to provide evidence that it was undertaken to further a political organisation's aims. If the committee accepted one's evidence one would be granted amnesty and walk free. One could not come here to declare one's innocence. The only institution in the country that could free you because you were not guilty was a court of appeal. Mofokeng had gone there and failed.

In a few minutes, three men would stand up and say that they had committed murder. In exchange for their story, they were sure to get amnesty for their case was clear-cut. This man's story was that he and his friend Tshokolo had committed no crime. In exchange for *that* tale he would remain in jail another decade or more.

Way back, many months ago, if Mofokeng and Mokoena had been properly informed, they might have had a choice. They might have decided to say that they were involved in the crime and thus walked free with the others. But the time for that was past. They had told their story and it made their application for amnesty senseless.

In a quiet and steady voice, Booker Mohlaba advised Fusi Mofokeng to withdraw his application. He described in the crispest language why it could not succeed.

At first Mofokeng did not absorb what his lawyer was saying. He asked if he could try to find other words, words he might better understand. And so Mohlaba explained again that if he had committed no crime he had no grounds on which to apply for amnesty.

For a long time, Mofokeng stared at his lawyer. Then he finally spoke. He had been waiting six years now, he said, to tell the world, in words of his own choosing, the true story of what had happened on 2 April 1992. No matter that his application was withdrawn, he wanted to address the truth commission, and the audience that had gathered in the hall, and the camera that would film his testimony. It was, he said, so very important that he be permitted to speak.

Nineteen

The isiXhosa–English interpreter had not yet arrived when the applicants entered the hall; and so Applicants One and Two, Thozamile Clement Ndabeni and Mandla Wellington Fokazi, both native isiXhosa speakers, could not yet read their statements.

Donald Makhura thus spoke first. He testified in English, with great command, as if he talked every week to halls filled with large audiences and cameras and judges. He had fled South Africa in the heat of the insurrections against apartheid, he began, in 1986, when he was twenty-two years old. In exile he joined the ANC and received military training in its camps in Angola.

On 27 February 1992, he continued, at the height of the violence between the ANC and Inkatha, he sneaked back into South Africa with the express purpose of assisting the civilian SDUs that had formed to fight Inkatha. In Phola Park, he made contact with the SDUs and began to fight with them side by side. Not yet five weeks back inside the country, an SDU commander, Sebenzile Ndabeni, asked him to join a mission to assist allied forces in Natal. That was why he was in the back of a bakkie with seven other men and five AK-47 assault rifles early on the morning of 2 April.

En route to Natal, Makhura continued, Sebenzile informed him that they would be making a stop in Bethlehem, a Free State town of which Makhura knew nothing. Sikhalo Ncala, Sebenzile said, was in the vehicle, not because he was coming along to Natal to fight, but because he owed Sebenzile money. Bethlehem was his hometown. He would find money there to give to Sebenzile and then go back to Phola Park while the others continued to Natal.

They stayed all day in a house in Bohlokong, Bethlehem's black township, Makhura continued. It was late afternoon before they made off again, stopping at a petrol station in the centre of town where Sikhalo picked up money from his brother-in-law. Sikhalo got back into the bakkie, but just to see the driver to the highway to Natal, for Sikhalo was the only one among them who knew Bethlehem and its roads.

They had just reached the highway when trouble began. Sebenzile had grown angry with Sikhalo, very angry, for Sikhalo had only given him half the money he owed. Those in the vehicle who knew Sebenzile well feared what he may do next. Mandla Fokazi took charge. He grabbed Sikhalo by the hand and led him out of the car and he ordered Donald Makhura to get out too. Fokazi and Makhura were to escort Sikhalo away from the angry Sebenzile, steer him back towards Bohlokong, where he would be safe, and then return to the vehicle. They made their way down one of the roads that leads off the highway.

Walking alongside Fokazi and Sikhalo, Makhura heard from somewhere behind him the unmistakable sound of an AK-47 discharging a volley of bullets. All three men knew at once that their comrades had run into trouble, that the security forces would soon be out in large numbers, and that they needed to hide themselves. Sikhalo pointed out a shortcut to Bohlokong through an adjacent farm.

It so happened that the owner of the farm, a white man called Bruce Collie, was returning from the bank where he had withdrawn a sum of cash to pay his workers their weekly wages. Four of his farmhands were in the back of his bakkie. Seeing three strange black men trespassing on his land, he pulled up next to them, ordered them into the back of his bakkie and drove promptly towards the Bethlehem police station.

Makhura and his two comrades were panicked now for the police station was the last place in Bethlehem they wanted to visit. Fokazi drew his gun and shot into the air. Collie stopped his vehicle and got out, his own firearm now drawn. Makhura shot him twice in the stomach and ran.

In their flight, Makhura and Fokazi lost Sikhalo, the only one among them who knew his way around these parts. After a few false starts, they found their way to Bohlokong, these two strange and suspicious-looking men, the streets now swarming with soldiers and police and rumours of what had happened. They sought shelter in a stranger's house who welcomed them in and promptly called the authorities.

He did not add, but his co-applicants all knew, that within an hour of his arrest Makhura, battered and bleeding, had led the police to Fusi Mofokeng's house. He knew neither the address, nor how to get there, but he remembered that a green Peugeot was parked in the driveway across the road. For fear that they would beat him to death if he did not speak, he described the Peugeot to the police.

Following Makhura's testimony, the evidence leader, Mr Zuko Mapoma, stood to cross-examine him. Why was Makhura applying for amnesty for murder, Mapoma asked, if he was not even at the scene when his comrades shot the young constable, Oosthuizen?

'Sir,' Makhura answered. 'From Phola Park the mission was to go and defend people in Natal. There was an outstanding order that … at no stage must anyone, the Security Forces or whoever, must take weapons from us. For the reason of common purpose I knew that those weapons were going to be involved in war … a political mission was put on our shoulder. I am aware that I did not participate in actually pulling the trigger when the police died but since I loaded those arms, since I loaded the magazines, since I was with my comrades, all of them and since I knew where we were going and I was lastly charged with the very same murder, because of common purpose I'm applying [for] amnesty even for those murders, Sir, for that murder I mean.'

Satisfied, the evidence leader, Mapoma, began another line of questioning. The trial court, he said, had found that Makhura and his comrades had conspired to rob the property outside which the shootout had occurred, a farm belonging to a Mr Orsmond.

'Well, Sir,' Makhura answered, 'I must answer that at length. Highly trained members of the ANC like us couldn't just go to one man to rob him … We couldn't carry five AK-47s and ten magazines to go and rob one man, Sir. It is not correct, Sir, that we were intending to rob anyone.'

The three commissioners began asking questions; to the audience in the hall their concerns must have seemed obscure. The chair of the committee, Judge Selwyn Miller, wanted to know from Makhura whether the bonnet of the vehicle was open when he, Ncala and Fokazi walked away from it.

'I did not notice,' Makhura replied.

'But did the vehicle have mechanical problems?' Miller persisted.

He thought it may have had, Makhura said, and advised Miller to save his question for the driver of the vehicle, Clement Ndabeni.

The isiXhosa–English interpreter had now arrived and Mandla Fokazi took the stand. He confirmed Makhura's story about the mission to Natal, the detour to Bethlehem, the trouble between Sebenzile Ndabeni and Sikhalo Ncala, the incident with the white farmer, Bruce Collie.

When he had completed his recollections of what happened in

Bethlehem, Booker Mohlaba asked Fokazi if he had anything to add in aid of his amnesty application.

'Yes, there is something that I would like to add concerning asking for forgiveness to the people, to the families of the victims because the victims were still young. The deceased and the one who survived, I would like to apologise to their families because this is painful, nobody would enjoy this. I would like to ask for forgiveness for my involvement in this case and to the people of South Africa at large.

'And to my, the family of my co-accused I would like to ask for forgiveness because now in this country there is democracy and I would like to build the nation, to build South Africa in a democratic country. So I would like to ask for forgiveness with my whole heart, thank you.'

Once Fokazi had completed his statement, Miller asked him if he knew Tshokolo Mokoena.

'I met him when we were arrested,' Fokazi replied.

'And the fourth applicant, Fusi Simon Mofokeng?'

'I met him on 2 April because we went to his place. I saw him there in his home.'

'You had never met him before 2 April?'

'I had not.'

Miller asked him to comment on Thabo Motaung's testimony at the trial. Did Fokazi and his comrades come to Bethlehem to rob a white man called Orsmond?

'I deny that, Chairperson,' Fokazi replied. 'I don't know Thabo ... He was used ... All he was saying was a lie. We were not there to rob. We had weapons so that we could fight.

'Thabo made a confession ... He was going to try to help us to get out of jail ... I said to my co-accused it is better to hide this boy because if the police were aware that he was giving out such information they would take him out of the way. Then Fusi Mofokeng told me that he was out of the way. So I don't know about this robbery.'

Once more, Miller turned to the question of the car and its mechanical problems.

'Did the driver at any point open the bonnet?' Miller asked.

Fokazi gave the most confusing reply, saying both that he had and had not seen the car bonnet being opened. In any event, he continued, we had a brake fluid problem and so the driver must have opened the bonnet.

Miller did not pursue the matter further.

Clement Ndabeni took the stand. After Ncala and the two others left the vehicle on the side of the Natal highway, he said, he and his comrades waited for Fokazi and Makhura to return. Clement's short-tempered cousin, Sebenzile Ndabeni, soon grew tired of waiting and demanded that they go looking for them. Clement obeyed. He turned the vehicle around and went in search of the others.

But no sooner had they begun their search for their comrades, Ndabeni said, than his brakes began to fail. He stopped the car and opened the bonnet while the others fanned out to look for Fokazi and Makhura. They drove around some more and, finding nothing, decided to abandon their comrades and continue on the journey to Natal.

'I made a U-turn to go back. We saw a police van. I slowed down because I wanted to see which road [it] would take. We then realised that it was coming towards us. I was in the front seat together with Joe. Joe then said that these people are coming towards us so I must take off the number plates and put on the other ones because we had spare number plates. While I was doing that they came and blocked the car.

'I went out of the car. They [addressed me but they were] speaking Afrikaans. I couldn't understand them. I lifted my hands and they shot at that time, they shot twice. Then the people at the back of the bakkie started shooting at the police. The police were running and one of them fell.'

Mohlaba asked Ndabeni if he had anything to add.

'I would like to say to the South Africans, I ask for forgiveness and I ask for forgiveness to the families of the police who died and to the people who were with us, I would like to ask for forgiveness to their families and to the families of the police and the families of the deceased that were with us and South Africa at large.'

Ndabeni's was an odd story and the commissioners had a number of questions. About the number plates in particular they seemed bemused. You are in a car full of weapons and a police vehicle is approaching. Why, of all things, change your number plates?

When one had weapons in one's possession, Ndabeni replied, one was supposed to use false plates. He had meant to put them on much earlier, he said, but he kept delaying.

That did not quite answer their inquiry, but the commissioners let it pass. The evidence leader asked several other questions, and, once again, the audience must have found their intent obscure.

Was the car stationary or moving when the police arrived? he asked.

The car was moving, Ndabeni replied. He was trying to get away.

And then the chair, Selwyn Miller, returned to the question of the bonnet and when exactly it was opened.

Ndabeni said that the vehicle had brake fluid trouble and that he had opened the bonnet shortly before encountering the police but had then closed it again.

Miller then wanted to know whether at any stage Ndabeni had taken the car along gravel roads. Ndabeni was puzzled and asked for the question to be repeated. He thought about it and said no.

One of the commissioners asked what had become of the other members of the party once the exchange of gunfire ceased. He and his comrades had scattered, Ndabeni explained. He got back in the bakkie and in a flash decided to head for the border with Lesotho. But he was tailed and shot at and abandoned his vehicle and fled on foot. He eventually managed to hide by burying himself and his assault rifle in a dam. He lay there face up in mud for more than two days, he said, before finally deciding that it was safe to emerge. But no sooner had he stood up straight than a joint police–army patrol spotted him. There and then, he was heavily beaten and feared for his life.

Two more of their party, Sebenzile and a man known only by his battle name, McGregor, were gunned down by police on the afternoon of the shooting. The police had shown him Sebenzile's body in the morgue, Clement said; it was riddled with bullet holes, too many to count.

As for McGregor, Clement continued, the security police had buried him in an unmarked grave somewhere near Bethlehem. To this day, his family was searching for his remains so that he might be laid to rest under the gaze of his ancestors.

And, of course, Clement continued, Makhura, Ncala and Fokazi were all captured in Bohlokong; and Fusi and Tshokolo, too, although they had nothing to do with the whole business.

The two remaining members of the party, Clement concluded, their battle names Joe and Nozulu respectively, escaped that day. Joe turned up later in Thokoza and was shot dead there two years later in an incident unrelated to the events of 2 April. As for Nozulu, he was never seen again.

It was almost lunchtime when Fusi Mofokeng took the stand. His application for amnesty now withdrawn, he was testifying merely as a witness.

146

At the back of the stage on which he sat were curtained wings and a small dressing room and a back entrance through which actors and performers might come and go. That morning, the prison van transporting him and his co-applicants to the venue had parked up against the back of the building behind the stage. On the short trip from the vehicle to the back entrance – five or six paces in all – he had seen three snipers staring down at him from the roof of the community hall, each armed with an automatic weapon. Of all he had seen since the day of his arrest, this struck him as among the strangest. Over the past six years, so little trouble had been taken with him. So many officials had ignored him or failed to answer his letters. And yet here, at the site of the hearing he thought was to free him, escape surely the furthest notion from his mind, his captors had arranged for heavily armed men to shoot him should he attempt flight.

Now, on the stage, a microphone and a glass of water on the desk before him, a set of headphones wrapped around his head, he prepared to speak. Under the stage lights, in front of the large audience, Booker Mohlaba led Fusi straight to the question of Thabo Motaung.

In his native Sesotho he spoke softly of Thabo's confession; of the flurry of measures he took to turn that confession into an affidavit; of his rushed efforts, conducted from a prison payphone, to get to Thabo to sign the document before his death.

'Were you ever involved in planning a robbery with Wellington Fokazi and them?' Mohlaba asked.

'There was nowhere in my life where I planned something which was against the law,' Fusi replied. 'Even Fokazi and the others, I saw them for the first time in Bethlehem when they were together with my brother-in-law. I haven't planned anything which was against the law.'

'So, in short,' Mohlaba said, 'you are telling this Committee that you were falsely implicated and convicted and [are] subsequently serving a prison term for something which you did not do?'

'That is correct. Even after I was imprisoned I made means so that I should be released from prison because I was arrested and convicted with people I did not know. I don't even know the victims they've killed.'

His testimony complete, the evidence leader briefly confused Fusi with a Simon Mofokeng who was standing trial for another murder; when he discovered that he was mistaken, he offered no further questions and sat down.

Judge Selwyn Miller had questions for Fusi Mofokeng. Fusi claimed that Thabo Motaung had died in 1995. But in his amnesty application, dated 1996, he wrote that Motaung was prepared to testify to the Amnesty Committee to his innocence. When, precisely, did Motaung die, Miller asked.

Fusi Mofokeng apologised for his mistake. He had filled in so many forms during that period, he said.

'I did not know where to write. I tried all corners ...'

Miller did not pursue the matter any further. His fellow commissioners had no questions. And so it was over. Fusi could not have been on the stage more than ten or fifteen minutes, this momentous public appearance, among the milestones in his life's journey, swallowed up in the course of a hasty hearing.

The last witness to testify was the father of the young constable who had died, Cornelius Oosthuizen. He began softly, the gentleness of his voice at first masking his gathering fury.

'Accused Number Three, Thozamile, says that the vehicle was not at a standstill, he was busy driving after he changed his number plates,' Oosthuizen said. 'As far as the information is concerned which was given to us the parents, the vehicle stood at one place the whole time and the people phoned the police and said that there were suspicious-looking people standing there the whole day. He also alleges that the police shot at them but I was informed that my son did not even have a weapon on him ...

'He also said that they never drove on a gravel road. [W]here my son was shot was about five kilometres away from the tar road, so they had to drive on a gravel road.'

He paused and gripped the glass of water at his side.

'From these accused I would like to know, and I want to look them in the eye and ask them: Do you know what you have done to us? A child, he was not even twenty-one years old and a person who did everything for the interests of this country, who went out without a firearm to you, he did not have a chance to say one word to you but you immediately started shooting at these two children and now you come and you make this kind of talk and you're not telling the truth. Do you know how that feels, do you know what you are doing to us? Me and my wife were at the point of a divorce. It's nothing to lose a parent but to lose a child is very hard. And if it was in the interest of this country I still could have accepted it but it was not in the interest of our country, it was robbery. It doesn't matter what you say today but what I've inferred it's about robbery and I accept it as robbery.'

He took another gulp of water, put the glass down and shook his head.

'And I want to ask you this,' he continued. 'Did you find peace with God, with our God who gave us this country and who gave us this life? We are not justified to take life. What are you going to do when you leave here? Are you going to continue breaking down this country or are you going to stand together with us so that we can build up this country? That is my question to you. I can forgive you with my mouth but in my heart I cannot do that.

'As far as my information is concerned you were not telling the truth, you only spoke in such a way in order to free yourselves. That is all, Chairperson, that I would like to say.'

The chairperson asked his fellow commissioners if they had questions. They did not. Oosthuizen was thanked and dismissed.

Now, Booker Mohlaba made his final submission. As he saw it, he had just one task – to show that the robbery story was implausible. A condition of amnesty was the making of a full confession. If the robbery story were correct his clients would have been shown not to have told the full truth about their crime.

By now he knew that his work would be easy. The commissioners had not bothered to ask Oosthuizen a single question. They did not want to know why he came to believe that the men who killed his son had been hanging around the Orsmond property all day. They didn't ask him where he had heard that the police were on the scene because fearful people had called them. They must have taken these statements as the rantings of grief. And the commissioners had interrogated the testimony of Fusi Mofokeng with so little enthusiasm that they must surely have accepted what he said.

Mohlaba's argument was simple.

'If these applicants here have in fact conspired to go and rob the farmer,' he said, 'it would have been easier for them to come and justify that and say for instance: "Yes, it was our mission to go and rob this farmer so that we can acquire money to further the interest of the organisation." They don't come to this Committee and say that and that would be a very easy lie which would go undetected, but they insist, Mr Chairman, that they were not involved there.'

Mohlaba was right. Had his clients testified that they planned to rob a farmer in order to buy war materiel, they would have received amnesty. And if this was indeed so, why would Mofokeng and Mokoena have lied when the truth would have freed them? The hapless Mofokeng and Mokoena were evidence that all five of his clients were being honest.

Mohlaba, of course, knew better than anyone that many of his clients did not understand the amnesty process. Just that morning he had sat staring at Fusi Mofokeng, wishing that the man across the table could only reverse time.

The hearing was adjourned and immediately several people made their way to Fusi Mofokeng. They were full of sympathy and advice and offers of assistance. An important official at the truth commission, the man who had led the evidence during the hearing, told Fusi that the Commission would write a formal recommendation to the Department of Justice that Fusi's matter be taken up urgently. The Justice minister himself, and the director-general of the department, would both be alerted to the situation. They would be urged to alert the President of the Republic who had the power to grant Fusi a pardon.

One of the three amnesty committee commissioners, Mr Tsotsi, also approached Fusi. He would personally write to the Minister of Justice, he said, for something surely had to be done.

Booker Mohlaba took Fusi aside. It was no use going back to court, he explained. Fusi's petition to appeal had been refused and that was the end of the matter. The only route to freedom now was to petition the Department of Justice, just as the truth commission officials had said. The ANC had set up a Truth Desk, Mohlaba continued. And his law partner was involved in the running of that Truth Desk. He would inform the ANC of Fusi's situation and the matter would be taken up. It would be taken to the Minister of Justice.

By nightfall Fusi was back in his cell in Kroonstad. He was feeling okay. Certainly, Mohlaba's revelation had shocked him. But that was hours ago. Indeed, it seemed a lifetime ago. So much had happened in between.

He had sat on a stage and told South Africa's Truth and Reconciliation Commission his story. And the three commissioners appeared to have believed him. The questions they asked him had been practically irrelevant and were soon cleared up. The Oosthuizen father aside, nobody had contested his story.

Yes, mistakes had been made. De Vries and Ederling had messed up his appeal. And he had been misinformed about the nature of the truth commission. But he had spoken into the record and he had been believed. Powerful people had witnessed his testimony. They had undertaken to take his case to the highest officers in the land. His innocence had finally been proven.

Twenty

O n Saturdays Fusi and his mother spoke on the phone. Stilted, laboured, heavily edited, their conversations were the highlight of his week. He knew that his suffering infected her and must thus be concealed. And so he was all high spirits, full of the plans he had hatched and the letters he had written, as if he could blow a brisk wind that might catch her sail.

In exchange for this labour he received her voice; for beneath its incessant complaints about his suffering and hers, was its love. He imbibed it slowly, luxuriously, making the phone call linger. When their conversation lapsed into silence, he would wait, the receiver pressed against his ear. Sometimes, many long seconds would go by. And then one of them would resume speaking.

On a Saturday at the end of July 1999 she told him, in the course of their regular conversation, that Sikhalo was out of prison, that somebody had seen him on the streets of Bethlehem. His heart went cold. His first course of action was to slam down the phone lest he transmit his distress along the wires connecting them.

He stood there staring blankly ahead of him. His fingers were shaking and his brow was wet and when he brushed it with his sleeve another layer of sweat formed. In a flash, it occurred to him that his life was destined to change during Saturday phone calls, for he was thinking of Amos and the news of his death.

Eight months had passed since the truth commission hearing; he had not once in that time imagined that his co-accused would be released without him. Important men had heard him speak. The most powerful organisations in the country had vowed to help him. The ANC's Truth Desk was to go to the Justice department and the truth commission itself was to make a submission. He had simply assumed that, when the time came to release the others, his and Tshokolo's names would be added to the list.

He contacted Booker Mohlaba and begged him to do something. Mohlaba replied that he could not act unless instructed by the ANC. And who exactly at the ANC would instruct you if you were to be instructed, Fusi asked. A woman called Patience Molekane, Booker said; it was she who ran the ANC's Truth Desk.

And so Fusi phoned Patience Molekane who confirmed that all the others were free; just Fusi and Tshokolo, she said, were still in jail. She would instruct Booker Mohlaba's firm to return to the case.

The following Monday he phoned Booker Mohlaba who said that he had not heard a word from Patience and thus could not do anything. And so he called Patience who was now, it seemed, never available; when he finally managed to speak to her, more than three weeks later, she said that she had instructed Booker Mohlaba long ago and did not understand why he could not proceed.

He wrote to the secretary-general of the ANC, and received no reply. He wrote to her twice more and heard nothing. He wrote to Booker Mohlaba and to Patience Molekane; he received no reply. He wrote to the man who had led the TRC's evidence, the one who had vowed to take the matter to the Justice department. He received no reply.

He entered an area of darkness. Looking back now, he cannot see himself; he cannot know what he thought or felt. He can only describe what others observed when they saw him – they saw a man who was crying inside, he reports, a man who perhaps was even dying.

His eyebrows rise in surprise when he says this, as if they must have been talking about somebody else. He believes them, for they are better witnesses than he, but he is nonetheless astonished.

I ask him to try to remember something of that darkness, and he says, only, that when you are in prison, you think a lot about all sorts of things, but primarily about moments in your past. Some of them come to you over and again.

For instance, he says, there was his first sighting of the ocean. He was twelve or thirteen, a schoolboy in Thokoza. They went in five buses on an educational outing to the coastal city of Durban. They were to visit the harbour, the aquarium, the snake park. They were to go to the beach.

They were approaching the hamlet of Umgababa, he says, when he first sighted the sea. It was cloudy above, the day a dull grey, and he could not tell where the sky stopped and the ocean began. This confusion unsettled him for he wanted his eyes to see with certainty what was before him; he did not like that they were an untrusty guide.

Then they were on the beach and the expanse of water before him was astonishingly wide. All of this is just the surface, he thought to himself, the rest invisible. He tried to comprehend the vastness inside. And he thought of himself somewhere in those depths. The ocean seemed to want him and he believed that it had the power to take him; were he to go in and swim the waves would wrap themselves around him and pull him out.

He crouched at the edge of the ocean and touched it with his fingers. The water rushed through them and his fear was confirmed; this great mass was alive and powerful and its vocation was to take you away.

Why this memory kept returning during his dark time he does not know; perhaps, he speculates, because the sea is the opposite of a prison cell.

Out of the blue one morning, the prison's head of social work, Mr Gerrit Steyn, approached him.

'You look strange,' Fusi recalls him saying. 'Why are you angry?'

Fusi looked back in astonishment. He knew Mr Steyn a little; he knew him to be kindly and polite, but that is all.

'There is nothing wrong,' he replied.

'No,' Steyn said. 'I see you,' and with those enigmatic words he told Fusi to report to his office the following morning.

The next day, behind the social worker's closed door, Fusi told his story, slowly, over the course of much of the morning. He had told it so often by now. Sikhalo's knock on the door on the morning of 2 April; the security police breaking down the same door that night. The story seemed to die as it left his tongue.

For a long time, Steyn listened without saying a word. He would not interrupt, Fusi realised, until the story was done. And as he grasped that he could speak for as long as he liked, his tale took on a life of its own. He spoke of his mother, of Victoria and of the death of Amos Mofokeng. He spoke of the letters he had written, of the string of lawyers who had failed him. He spoke of the TRC and his certainty that it had been a triumph, that he and Tshokolo were bound to be released with the others.

Finally, he was quiet. A silence followed, and when Steyn finally began to talk the words he uttered were shocking.

'You are boiling with anger,' Fusi recalls him saying. 'And you are depressed. You are depressed because you do not accept what has happened to you. What is going on in your heart is making you ill.' Then he paused, for what he was to say next was very grave indeed. 'If you do not accept what has happened to you, you will die.'

Fusi looked back at Steyn in disbelief. The social worker's words danced around his mind like electric charges. Nobody had ever spoken to him like this before; nobody had addressed him so bluntly and directly about what was in his heart.

Before he could offer a response, Steyn was speaking again. He offered there and then to help Fusi, not just with his emotions and his spirit, but practically. When you need to send a fax to your lawyer, I will do it for you, Steyn said. When you need to see a lawyer, I will book you out of prison and take you in my car. When you need to talk to a loved one, I will make sure you have a phone at your disposal. When you need to eat decent food, I will bring groceries for you.

These many years later, Fusi marvels at Gerrit Steyn. It is not just that he picked Fusi out from a thousand prisoners and saw into his soul; it is that he appeared to believe Fusi's story the moment he heard it. Why did he know it to be true from the start? To Steyn he attributed spiritual powers. He was a deeply religious man, Fusi observed. Perhaps his gift to see through one's skin came from God.

And from Steyn he learnt that one does not judge a person by his race. A son of labour tenants in the eastern Free State, Fusi knew as well as any living soul white people's disregard for black well-being. What had Robertshaw and Johannes Steyn hurled at him day after day if not hatred? And yet here was an Afrikaner, a son of the Free State soil, who carried under his white skin God's power and compassion.

Fusi began working for Steyn, at first just as a cleaner, but, soon as much more. Steyn was interested, primarily, in inmates' anger. But he did not have the language to do his work. His native Afrikaans was fluent, of course, and his English was proficient. But the majority of inmates were Sesotho speakers and to ask them to examine their depths in a borrowed tongue was clearly no good.

And so Fusi became Steyn's interpreter. Groups of inmates, sometimes as many as a dozen, would gather around the social worker; you are all human, he would say, and therefore you all feel anger. He compared human beings to animals. A person with the characteristics of a lion wants to be feared by everyone, he said. A tortoise is the opposite of a lion; when there is violence he hides in his shell. The owl is a very clever person. When the sparks fly, he can intervene in a way that changes the whole situation.

Steyn's purpose was not to make everyone into an owl, Fusi recalls, only to show how different people behave in different situations. He did not want to change inmates into what they were not, but to have them understand better who they were. And so when conflict flared, they might pause and see themselves from a distance before deciding what to do next.

Through Steyn's courses, Fusi learnt much about himself. He was too soft, he realised, too submissive and too eager to please. If a person had no toiletries, for instance, Fusi would offer his own just to make that person happy. But then how would he himself wash? He could not make everyone happy. He must see to himself first.

Soon, he was facilitating workshops himself while Steyn looked on in silence. To his surprise, he found he could command a room. Indeed, he could draw his audience much closer than Steyn himself ever might. He was black and an inmate, Steyn white and a warder; Fusi could speak from his heart in Sesotho, Steyn only in Afrikaans. From these workshops he grew to understand that there was power within him; that tough men, men grown hard and difficult and ungovernable, might leave his presence thinking about him; might wake up the following morning still thinking about him.

But what he learnt from Steyn, above all else, came from their first morning together. It was so simple and yet an utter revelation. It was so easy to follow when one thought about it, so hard when one's feelings reigned. The past lay in the past; it had already happened; it was fact; to fight it was to smash one's head against a rock. If he could understand that, truly, he could be free of the most horrible burden, free from the fierce anger he had not even known he harboured, free to act, free to do his utmost to get himself out of prison.

It was nothing less than an epiphany and at times he felt he had been reborn. But it was also such slippery knowledge; he was liable to forget it in a flash. He learnt through bitter experience that he must not think of Robertshaw or Johannes Steyn or Mapalala; they were dripping in acid and should he allow them under his skin they would burn a hole through him.

He fought against fighting them. But how can one fight against fighting? Sometimes the things Gerrit Steyn had taught him seemed impossible to learn.

I write to Gerrit Steyn.

'Fusi has told me about the enormously important role you played in his life when he was incarcerated in Kroonstad,' I say. 'He told me how you helped him to understand that he was depressed, to manage his anger and to accept what had happened to him.'

I ask if we can meet.

He replies less than an hour later.

'I really appreciate Fusi's acknowledgement of what I cannot even recall,' he writes. 'What made Fusi survive is for sure not coming from the environment he found himself within (and me being part of it) but from an inner driven force to overcome the lowest form of injustice you can possibly face …

'You know his story very well. He never compromised his integrity – and eventually received his freedom without admitting to a crime he never committed. For sure an amazing path of endurance.

'Yes, for sure he was strengthened by a God Almighty who was also despised for the values He believed in! Dear Jonny, please respect my wish to remain a non-mentionable part of Fusi's path to freedom. This is really a matter between him and God. Please exclude me.'

I write to ask him to reconsider and he does not reply. A year later, I write again, and the following year, again.

Twenty-one

My name is Thabang Mokotedi. I am a schoolteacher by training, but life zigzags, for sure. I have worked for sixteen years now, not in a school, but in a prison. Funny, isn't it? My father was a prison warder. I did not choose to follow him but I have. We both ended up inside this world unto itself, this prison-world, first the father, then the son.

I did not know it straight away, but the time I met Fusi Mofokeng, in 1999, was his darkest time ever, so dark that nobody can see in there.

Let me say that it was not such an easy time for me either. I had been working for two years at a high school in Edenville, teaching maths and science. It was my first job after finishing teacher training college. You will not have heard of Edenville. It is tiny. You cannot even buy the Sunday newspapers there. You have to wait for Monday when people who were away for the weekend come back.

I am a social person. I need company. I wanted to go back to Kroonstad where I was born and raised and knew the people in the street.

The dice rolls. It happened that the only job going there for a schoolteacher was to teach high school classes as well as Adult Basic Education and Training to inmates at the Correctional Services facility. So I applied for that job and I got it. It was quite a shock. Your father worked in a prison but that does not prepare you. He leaves that place behind when he comes home and even though he is sitting at the table with you, you cannot see what he has seen. Prison is a world of its own. Some of those inmates, you look at them, you are not feeling okay. I was thinking to myself, how do I deal with this? How do I work here?

I was the first qualified educator to work in that prison. This was not so long after the end of apartheid. To have a prison with black section heads, it was still quite new. To have a qualified educator to work full-time with the inmates, it was new. There were not so many rules on how to deal with this situation.

The first time I saw Fusi, I remember it so well. He was sitting alone. And the next day again, he was alone. And the next day. It was bothering me a lot.

I went to the head of School Section, Mr Dan Mohanoe, and I said to him: 'There is an offender who does not mix with others. It is like he is crying.'

Immediately, he said: 'It is Fusi.'

'Who is he?' I asked.

He invited me to sit and relayed the whole story. 'That offender told me that he did not commit the crime,' Mr Mohanoe said. 'I believe him.'

'Come on,' I replied. 'Nobody in here has committed a crime.'

Mr Mohanoe shook his head: 'I've spent a lot of time with him. He does not behave like other offenders. He is telling the truth.'

Slowly, I started interacting with him. There was opportunity because he was my student. He was still busy with his high school studies. We saw each other every day. It was not easy to ask what he was here for. I had to nudge a little here and there. He would tell me about the TRC.

'Do you follow it?' he would ask. 'I have testified there.'

He never forced his story onto me. I came and got it from him. To tell you the truth, when I heard it the first time, I had my reservations. More than reservations, to be honest. I did not believe him. Flatly. An offender tells you that the police framed him … It's not so original, is it?

But, you know, I was bothered by the fact that I did not believe him. Why? Because of the way he was relating the story. A person's face tells you so much. The story came straight out of the textbook of lying. But the man telling the story did not seem like a liar at all.

Eventually, what clinched it, he said to me: 'Do you have access to the Internet?' And he gave me the TRC case number and asked me, very nicely, mind you, to go and check for myself. So I go home, I find the TRC's report on the web, and it is exactly as he said. Exactly.

Once I believed him, our connection was at another level. From now on, in my eyes, he was the offender who was not an offender, a man who should not be wearing those overalls. And that is what he craved. He was hungry for me to see him through those eyes. It seemed to be what he needed more than anything, more than food, even. He was so grateful that I had come to see him that way.

Now that I had taken his story as true, we were free to talk about many things, some of them deep matters. All these years later, there are things he said to me that I remember like yesterday.

Once, I said, 'Fusi, where do you think you would be today if you had not gone to prison?'

And he said: 'You know, Mr Mokotedi, I am not happy in prison. It is hurting. But somehow, I want to think that I was meant to be here.'

And he told me how he had money on the outside because he was working at Checkers and with his money he had gone a bit wild. He was smoking and drinking every weekend. He was chasing the women. And the ones with whom he was going wild on the weekend, now they were dying one after the other, while here he was in prison being preserved.

'If I was on the outside maybe I'd be dead by now,' he said. 'This is a bad place, but good things come out of it. I have changed.'

Another time, he put it much more heavily than that. 'A lot of people were sacrificed during the time Christ was in this world,' he said to me. 'People were just killed innocently. God was aware. Maybe what happened to me He meant it to happen, maybe to try to keep me away from certain things outside. Maybe I would be sick, maybe dead. There is HIV out there. There is violence. Maybe in a strange way I am here because God loves me.'

And then he said to me, 'Maybe I am just believing that story to motivate myself. But I can tell you, it helps.'

But I am mixing things up now. In the end I knew Fusi for twelve years in prison. And the way you remember, you take something someone said in 1999 and something they said in 2008, and you remember them like they were on the same day. The thing about God putting him inside to protect him, it came much later, after the tremendous ways in which Mr Steyn, the social worker, helped him. But that is a story I cannot tell as I was not there.

I can tell you only that I came to see Fusi Mofokeng almost like a brother. When he completed his secondary schooling I immediately encouraged him to qualify as an Adult Basic Education instructor. He did. He and six others. After they qualified they worked with me side by side. These were mainly good men. Five of them are now outside and prospering. We lost only two to further crimes. Five out of seven; you know the re-offending rate in this country? Five out of seven: it is not bad.

In 2003, I was transferred to the juvenile section. There were no tutors there. I asked for three prisoners who could help me.

'I hope you are not looking for Fusi,' Mr Mohanoe said.

'Well, no, but if you can spare him.'

So every morning I went out of my way to pick up Fusi and the other two. And that is where I saw another side of Fusi. Juveniles are wild, wild, wild. Fusi handled them so very nice. They did not make him sweat.

They did not make him uncomfortable. One thing I have learnt from Fusi, that guy has so much patience.

Man, I used to complain. I used to say out loud that I wish I was back among the adult offenders.

'Adult offenders come to class to learn,' I'd say. 'These kids, you wake up early in the morning to teach them, you have stayed up late preparing lessons for them, and they don't care, they want to play.'

And Fusi would smile and say: 'Yes, they are behaving like children in any normal school.'

To see him with the juveniles, it made me happy and sad. Sad because I thought to myself: this man should be a father. This prison sentence of his, it offends against nature. There are kids who have not been born because he is here. It is wrong at a very deep level.

But then another part of me was happy. He had been deprived of his own children, but he had these juveniles. At least he had a taste.

Now, it seems I have forgotten to tell a story. It is from before the time Fusi was working with the juveniles. It is from the time he was still doing his secondary schooling, I think.

He and two others came to me. They said they could not study in this prison. It was just too noisy. They had a proposal: 'Can we appeal to the offenders in this section to be quiet every day from 5:00 p.m. until 7:00 p.m.? Can we appeal that for those hours nobody plays music? Nobody shouts? It doesn't need to be like a vow of silence. If offenders want to talk to a person they must go and stand next to him so that there is no need to shout.'

So we tried it. We gathered the whole section and said please, let us make these two hours study hours. I remember looking at the faces and thinking, shit, this cannot work. They will especially be noisy from 5:00 p.m. just because we told them not to.

The next day at 5:00 p.m., the music stops. First one turns off his music, then another, then another. There is silence. I have never heard silence in this prison before.

Somebody breaks the quiet, shouting to his friend at the other end of the section. One of the offenders intervenes: 'Haai! Shut up! It's study time.' And then there is quiet again. This time it holds. The section is mellow. It's a different place. Everything has changed.

I must not single out Fusi because there were three of them that made this appeal. But looking back now, I think, aha, Fusi Mofokeng, the quiet man, the man who never in twelve years raised his voice, bringing his silence to the prison.

Twenty-two

That Gerrit Steyn believed him, that Thabang Mokotedi believed him, that Dan Mohanoe believed him – these men lifted Fusi from his place of darkness and carried him back into the world. Once more, he felt inside him the wherewithal to fight.

He understood that writing to Patience Molekane, Booker Mohlaba or the TRC was a waste of ink. And so he wrote instead to the Legal Aid Board in Kroonstad. His English was so much better than when he first began writing of his plight. He felt, for the first time, that what was on the page bore some connection to what was in his heart.

His efforts bore fruit, it seemed, for the Legal Aid Board requested to see him, not in Kroonstad Prison, but in their offices in town. And so in the company of a corrections officer he did the short journey into the centre of Kroonstad. The official he met there, he recalls, was astonished by his letter. 'If any of this is true,' he remembers the official saying, 'you should have a lawyer.'

Once again, then, he found himself in the hands of a strange white lawyer. This one, though, was a pleasant surprise. He resembled neither the distracted De Vries nor the invisible Ederling. His name was Terence van Rensburg. He was kindly and attentive and extremely serious. And in the gulf of language and custom separating lawyer from client stood Mr

Gerrit Steyn, who began to talk weekly to Van Rensburg on the phone, the clipped Afrikaans that passed between them transmitting the sense that something was being done.

To Fusi, Van Rensburg said that there was just one remaining legal avenue to explore – a very strange statute on the books, he said, one that was rarely used. It was called Section 327 of the Criminal Procedure Act. It was for convicted felons who had reached the end of the road, their appeal against their conviction lost in the highest court. Under Section 327, a person could petition the Justice department to say that new evidence had come to light since his appeal had been lost; the Justice department could ask the High Court to hear this new evidence; if it was found to be credible, the case could then be taken to the President of the Republic at whose discretion the prisoner might receive a pardon.

If the findings of the truth commission did not constitute new evidence, Van Rensburg asked, his palms turned to the heavens, what did?

Van Rensburg wrote to the Department of Justice advising that he wished to write a Section 327 petition; the same letter requested that the truth commission make available to him the statements lodged in Fusi's amnesty hearing. The truth commission did not produce the statements. Van Rensburg asked that the High Court be requested to furnish him with the transcript of the original trial. The court did not.

Almost a year after he had taken on the case, Van Rensburg finally lodged a petition with the Justice department, but without either a transcript of the trial or the statements that had been submitted to the Amnesty Committee. From its reply, it was apparent that the officials at the Justice department had not understood the bare rudiments of the case. The petition had no merit, a Justice department official wrote to Van Rensburg, for the fact that Mokoena and Mofokeng where not at the scene of the crime did not constitute new evidence.

Van Rensburg wrote once more to the Department of Justice and Fusi himself wrote too. Time and again, they received the same formulaic reply, each an echo of the last: 'Your case is being considered.' Finally a letter arrived showing signs that it had been written by a human being who had paid some attention to the matter. The author of the correspondence was none other than the director-general of the Justice department.

'I have tried to locate your file but all in vain,' he wrote. 'I would like to suggest to you that you send us new documentation pertaining to your petition. The matter will receive the necessary as soon as the documents are received.'

Van Rensburg had been working on the case for more than two years when Fusi received this reply. The Legal Aid Board had long stopped paying for Van Rensburg's time and he was working for Fusi for free. But even he, now, gave up, for he had bills to pay and mouths to feed and the prospect of starting a hopeless campaign all over again was more than he could bear.

It was 2002 when Van Rensburg threw in the towel, almost four years since Fusi's appearance at the truth commission. If this dispiriting business had taken place in the wake of the TRC hearing, it would have crushed him. But he had grown a shell now and under it was a man who simply kept working. The schoolteacher and the social worker had resurrected from his depths the steeliest will.

From out of the blue, sometime in 2004, he requested a transfer from Kroonstad to a new, privately run correctional facility in Bloemfontein called Mangaung. Tshokolo was there. After working alone year upon year he now decided that he could go no further without consulting the man who shared his fate.

He wonders, in retrospect, whether he did not have an ulterior motive. Perhaps he moved prisons simply because he could; he wanted to wake each morning to the knowledge that he was where he was because of a decision *he* had made. It was 2004. He had been in Kroonstad nine years, much of it waiting for letters to be answered, for lawyers to make contact, for others to act. He needed to act himself.

Mangaung, it turned out, was an awful place. It was run on a set of bureaucratic rules so rigid and senseless as to defy belief. Any action one could think of required filling in an application form and all application forms were summarily lost. It seemed a place designed to break one's will. He resolved after just a week that he should return to Kroonstad as soon as he could. And it struck him for the first time in quite some while that he was lucky, lucky to have Kroonstad, where there were warders who cared for him and work that stirred his soul.

Despite the poor conditions, Tshokolo was in much better spirits than at any previous time since their arrest. The vacant expression that had unnerved Fusi in the dock all those years ago was gone. Indeed, his friend seemed positively self-possessed. He could chat away for hours, unself-consciously, as if they were back in Bethlehem, side by side on upturned crates, with all the time in the world. Perhaps human beings can get used to anything, Fusi thought to himself; the passing of the days files slowly away at the catastrophe until it is a catastrophe no more.

They spoke at length of what to do next. It was better to abandon all attempts to rouse the criminal justice system from its disinterest, they resolved. For Fusi to batter himself against it yet again was to risk his sanity. Instead, they decided, they should simply tell the world what had happened. And to do that, they reasoned, Fusi had to leave the Free State, which, after all, was at the periphery of the world. He should move instead to the heart of things, to a prison in Johannesburg, where the great engine of the national media roared.

He had tried at various times to attract the media's attention. Whenever relatives came to see him, they would leave clutching a letter he had written, their instructions to give it to a journalist. He had written personally to Mr Vusi Mona, the editor of *City Press*, the Sunday newspaper read across the nation by the new black elite. Mr Mona had forwarded Fusi's letter to his newspaper's Bloemfontein desk and a lowly reporter there had written a news story one paragraph long. The Free State was useless to them. They needed to conduct the loud voices in the big city to sing.

The obvious place to go was the massive correctional facility at Leeuwkop, north of Johannesburg, and Fusi began to prepare himself mentally to live there. It would take a lot of work. Transferring from one Free State prison to another was simple enough. But asking to go to a prison in another province was irregular and would raise questions. He could not orchestrate such a move from Mangaung, where the warders were strangers and would not lift a finger to help. He would have to arrange the move from Kroonstad where the likes of Thabang Mokotedi and Gerrit Steyn would pull the strings that had to be pulled.

No sooner had he resolved to move to Leeuwkop than his preparations were thrown off course by an unwelcome piece of news; from Victoria he learnt that his mother, Maletsatsi Letia Mbele, was in hospital with pneumonia.

The news felled him. In the wake of Victoria's phone call he lay down on his bed, his intention to gather his thoughts, only to find that he had no desire to get up. To be vertical again, to walk the corridors and interact with the people around him seemed the heaviest labour. That his mother's illness affected him so came as an unwelcome shock. He did not like to surprise himself like this.

During the years of his incarceration he had seen her no more than a dozen times. The journey from Bethlehem to Kroonstad was not cheap and she was dirt poor. Sometimes, she would voice her intent to borrow money to come and see him and he would refuse. That his fate caused her pain was bad enough; it should not, he believed, leave her without good food or new clothes.

Her visits were momentous occasions, draining, terrifying and life-giving. From the moment she announced that she was coming, the thought that the journey might kill her filled him with dread. Seeing her imprisoned son was dreadful, after all. Shaken by the experience, might she not wander afterwards into the streets of Kroonstad and be run down by a car? He demanded that she be accompanied on her visits by a young relative, one who was alert and strong.

Two weeks passed before she was well enough to speak to him on the phone. Her voice was so eerily thin, as if the flesh had been sucked out of it, leaving just a spindly frame. She was a large woman, strong and loud; he wondered at the power of the illness that had so diminished her.

They began speaking regularly and with the passage of time her voice grew stronger. But the idea that she might die was now trapped in his mind, pacing his head like a restless beast, and when he listened to her speak he sometimes felt that her words came from another world.

The wheels grind slowly in prison. It was May 2006, the beginning of a cold Free State winter, when Fusi's transfer back to Kroonstad was finally approved. From there he would move to Leeuwkop in Johannesburg, but not before he had seen his mother in the flesh once more. Getting to Johannesburg was beyond her means, for sure, and who knew how long he might have to remain there?

In the end, he waited seven months. And before it had even begun, her visit was an ordeal. She had arranged for a relative to take her in his car. But the road from Bethlehem to Kroonstad was under construction, it turned out, and they had to begin their journey heading south, to Senekal, while Kroonstad lay to the northwest. No sooner had they reached Senekal than their car broke down, leaving them stranded more than a hundred kilometres from their destination.

By the time his mother arrived, visiting day was over, the prison locked down. He does not remember which warder was on duty, but the situation was treated with the kindness it deserved; an administrative office was given over to the meeting between the prisoner and his mother; night was falling, but they were offered as much time as they liked.

He was shocked when he saw her. A big, strong woman, she was thinner than he could have imagined. And no sooner had he sat down than she was crying. She fished in her bag for a handkerchief and wiped her eyes and her face. Then she folded it and put it aside and grabbed his wrists in her hands.

When I ask what they spoke of he tells me that it wasn't the words that mattered. She would complain of his suffering and of her own suffering and he would reassure her that he had influential warders on his side.

Far more important than her words, he tells me, was the grip of her hands on his wrists. He imagined those hands out in the world, swinging at her sides as she walked. And he saw them bunching into fists. From Victoria he knew of her growing anger and her newly acquired taste for violence. When she had seen Sikhalo on the streets of Bethlehem after his release from prison, she had threatened to tear him limb from limb. He had had the audacity, she shouted, not just to cheat on her daughter and neglect his children; he had also ruined the life of her last surviving son.

Nor had her fury for David Mofokeng abated. It in fact appeared to have grown in the years since his passing. She had always enjoyed lager beer. But now, Victoria reported, she had acquired a taste for homemade sorghum brews and was drinking heavily. When she was drunk, she cursed men who lied and cheated. And if there was a man in the vicinity who reminded her of David Mofokeng, she would challenge him to fight.

As much as Fusi was preoccupied by her anger, he was consumed, too, by what she had suffered for her children.

When her father, Nono Mbele, had died in 1979, she had given up her job in a white family's kitchen to return to Oorsprong. Nono was the last Mbele on the property; had another not come to replace him the family would have lost the one place in the world that counted for a home.

And so once more she was working for Madipela for a pittance. And when David Mofokeng proved unable to feed and clothe Amos, despite the fact that the boy lived under his roof, she began working in the evenings, too. Having laboured all day for Madipela, she would come into Bohlokong as the sun was going down to sell chickens and vegetables to people returning from work.

It was an impossible life and within two years she had given up Oorsprong. She sensed, in any case, that remaining was futile. Across the Free State farmers were ridding themselves of their labour tenants. On the next-door farm and the farm next door to that the tenants had all been evicted or had left, their homes empty and crumbling, the families that once lived there now scattered. In their stead contract labourers were employed, people who would arrive in the mornings and leave in the evenings with their wages in their pockets. And so she fled this sense of impending doom in search of a house of her own, one her children might inherit when she died.

It was a quest that took almost two decades to fulfil. First she rented a house in Phuthaditjhaba. Then, after Fusi was jailed and Amos killed, she rented the very house in which they had lived, sleeping in the bedroom in which they had slept, eating at the kitchen table at which they had taken their meals. I do not know why she chose to move there or what it meant to her to live among her sons' ghosts. When I ask Fusi and Victoria they both shrug and tell me that there is no answer to my question.

The coming of democracy finally brought Maletsatsi a home of her own. A beneficiary of the new government's programme to house the poor, she was given title deed to a tiny new house in the middle of Bohlokong. That is the house to which she returned after visiting her son in Kroonstad's prison in December 2006, the same house in which I first sat down with Fusi and Tshokolo, six and a half years later, to hear their tale.

Maletsatsi had not been able to save her elder son from death or her younger son from prison. Nor could she rescue her daughter from a bitter marriage. But she had given her two surviving children a property that would be theirs for as long as they lived.

The day after his mother's visit, Fusi began to set in motion the plan that would take him to Leeuwkop. It was an enormous ordeal. As a prisoner whose home address was in the Free State, he had no right to transfer to a Johannesburg prison. And so he had to persuade a warder to doctor his prison file, erasing his address in Bohlokong and adding his uncle's address in Thokoza.

No sooner was that done than he ran into resistance; the head of the prison refused point blank to sign his transfer request. He had become vital to the anger programmes he was facilitating and to the adult literacy classes he was running and the prison head simply did not want to lose him. Who on earth would speak to prisoners about their anger, the prison head asked. What would happen to this prison if the programme ceased? It amused Fusi to think that he had become indispensable.

He appealed to the prison head's boss, the area commissioner, who listened carefully to his story and took detailed notes and ruled, finally, that he could go just as long as he undertook to come back the moment his business in Leeuwkop was done. And so it was settled: he would go.

The first of July 2007 was a Sunday and thus a visiting day. Shortly after lunch, just when it seemed that he would have no visitors, Fusi was informed that two people had come to see him. On arrival in the visiting area he found Modieah, one of his former girlfriends, who had recently written from out of the blue. She had come with Amos's son, Thapelo, she told Fusi, but he had left his ID document at home and had not been permitted to enter the prison.

In a fit of anger, Fusi stormed out to confront the head of the prison.

'It is my nephew I want to see,' he recalls complaining, 'not a girlfriend from long ago.'

And so the prisoner was assuaged, the rules bent. He returned to the visiting area in time to see Thapelo, who so uncannily resembled his dead father Amos that Fusi flinched when he saw the boy make his way into the room. His eyes were swollen, his cheeks wet with tears.

Fusi took one look at him and understood that Maletsatsi Letia Mbele was dead.

Within an hour, he had lodged an application to attend her funeral. And when it was declined he found that he was in a state of panic. He imagined her being lowered into the ground, her grave filled up and sealed, her body lost to him forever. The thought was intolerable.

By now he had learnt some ingenuity. If he could not attend her funeral, he could, at the very least, sit with her corpse. He applied immediately for a temporary transfer to the small correctional facility in Bethlehem; once there, he reasoned, he could negotiate with the authorities to take him around the block to the morgue. The only question was whether the wheels might turn fast enough; the funeral was to take place on 14 July.

In the end, it happened in the nick of time. He was transferred to

Bethlehem not twenty-four hours before her burial and was permitted to go immediately to the morgue.

His uncle Jack Mbele and his aunt Sylvia were there when he arrived. Had he come just five or ten minutes later, they would have been gone. When Jack Mbele saw his nephew, his legs in chains, a guard at each side, he flew into a rage. Fusi could not possibly present himself to his mother in this state, he shouted; such a scene offended against God and against nature; it was simply intolerable.

Fusi had never seen his uncle this way, and it occurred to him that, in the face of death, nobody was who they seemed to be. Everything was out of place. Who knew what might happen next?

What with the frantic transfer and his uncle's rage, he found, when he was finally alone with her corpse, that he had not prepared for this moment. No sooner had he taken in the sight of her than he was weeping as he had not wept during his fifteen years in prison. His body shook and rattled as if it were in the grip of a giant pair of hands. It had come from nowhere, this weeping; that such torrents of feeling had lain buried within him was astonishing; he wondered if he'd ever summon the self-control to leave this room.

She was not an old woman. She was only in her sixties when she had fallen ill and died. From the bottom of his heart he knew that his arrest and imprisonment had killed her. And yet whether his tears were for himself or for her he did not know. Was he distraught because his fate had caused a person to die of suffering? Or was it that a woman who had loved him so deeply as to suffer to death was no longer there for him? The world seemed awfully empty. He had fought so hard for so long to be free. Would his freedom matter if she was not there to witness it?

It was the craziest question. But sitting there beside her corpse, it seemed the most sensible question in the world. And what the answer might be he did not know.

He needed to master his feelings, he realised. He needed to retrieve the wisdom of Gerrit Steyn's greatest lesson. Fate had decreed that he would not bury his mother. He must accept what was not in his control. To go insane now, after these years of endurance, over a matter beyond his grasp, was not acceptable. God's children do not destroy themselves thus.

Twenty-three

Within three months of his mother's death, he was in Leeuwkop. It was an astonishingly risky move. His Kroonstad life was padded by warders who cared for him and work that moved him. He was abandoning all of that for who knew what. Leeuwkop had a fierce reputation.

But his resolve to move was only quickened by his mother's passing. To stop fighting was to curl up like a foetus and wait to be nourished. If he were to do that, he would surely die. He was an orphan, not an unborn child. To live he had to act. If that meant going to the most notorious prison in the country, so be it.

In the end he was pleasantly surprised. Leeuwkop's grim reputation, he soon learnt, arose from its prison for new arrivals, a veritable rail station of Gauteng's underworld, its violence so notorious that inmates called it Beirut. The medium-security prison, where Fusi was interned, was an altogether more peaceful place. And not only that: Fusi was assigned immediately to the section of the prison reserved for inmates who were studying. It was quiet. He was surrounded by men who were nothing less than gracious. And for the first time since his conviction he had a cell of his own.

It was a revelation. He only dimly remembered what it was to spend untold hours alone. During the first days he would hold himself still and listen to the silence. Instead, sounds he had not listened to in years would fill his ears: the creasing of his sleeve as he moved his arm; the beating of his pulse in his temple. He felt he was living in a cocoon.

From time to time, a gangster was thrown into the single cells as punishment and Fusi would be reminded of the chaos in the prison next door. Warders would beat the offending inmate with batons and spray pepper spray into his eyes; they would strip him and turn fire extinguishers on his body, the force strong enough to throw a grown man across the floor. His cell ankle deep in water, his discarded clothes sodden, he would spend the night wet, naked and exposed.

Fusi knew that what he witnessed was against policy and against law. But what was written on paper and what happened in the great world behind bars were not the same. He was a veteran now. The prison's rhythms beat in time with his pulse. He thought of life after his release. He wondered whether he had the power to convey to those on the outside what it was like in here.

The way he tells the story of his time in Leeuwkop, it is hard to believe that he was there for more than two years. Only when he is talking of something else and mentions Leeuwkop in passing does one sense how much happened during this time: the untold number of letters he wrote; the red herrings he chased; the tricksters who promised to help him and did not; the scores of fellow inmates he seduced with the story of his innocence; the one-sentence reply he received from Archbishop Desmond Tutu, regretting that the Archbishop could not assist; the visiting politicians and officials and ANC party members whose help he tried to enlist.

All of this vanishes when he tells his Leeuwkop tale. The whole two years is reduced to one event and its aftermath.

It was an evening in August 2009. From a cell down the corridor a prisoner called Barnard shouted to him.

'Fusi! Switch on your wireless. Go to 702. What they are talking about is for you.'

He turned on his radio to find that a white man was being interviewed. His name was Jacques Pauw. He was the director of the Wits Justice Project at the University of the Witwatersrand's School of Journalism. Its mission was to uncover miscarriages of justice.

Fusi had not heard of Jacques Pauw. But as he listened he discovered that Pauw was famous. Among his many books was one called *In the Heart of the Whore: The Story of Apartheid's Death Squads*, about the secret assassination unit the apartheid regime had run during its final years in power. Pauw's trade was to find the truth. He was famous because he knew how to take the heaviest and best-kept secrets from their place of concealment and expose them to the light. Now he was saying that it was not uncommon for the justice system to get things horribly wrong, that there were innocent people in jail all over the country and that the work of his project was to prove their innocence.

What he felt was akin to a religious experience. It was as if Jacques Pauw were addressing him alone, for, truly, the words may have been coming from the radio but it was as if they were whispered into Fusi's ear. When Barnard had shouted for him to listen, other inmates had done the same. And so had the warders on duty. By the time the interview was over, the whole section was shouting for Fusi to write to Jacques Pauw. For he was known by now as the innocent one, the one who had only come to Leeuwkop to tell the world that he had committed no crime.

It was late. To the warders on duty he asked if he could leave on his light beyond the permitted time. Caught up in the spirit of things, they agreed.

He wrote through the night. By now he had told his story countless times. He had indeed been practising the telling of it for much of his adult life. But never before had it seemed quite as urgent to get it just right. When day broke he had written more than forty pages.

Among the prisoners in the section was a man called Miles Ramon. He had a typewriter in his cell. Early in the morning, Fusi's handwritten letter was passed to Ramon and he was urged to type it as fast as he could.

Ramon was not sure how to spell the name of the man to whom the letter was addressed.

'I am not certain,' Fusi remembers saying to Ramon. 'It sounded like "Jack Paw".'

The moment Ramon was done, the clean, typed copy of Fusi's letter was handed to the head of the prison who duly faxed it to the Wits Justice Project. Eighteen hours had passed since Fusi had turned on his radio and heard the voice of Jacques Pauw.

The letter was faxed on a Wednesday. On the following Saturday morning, Pauw came to Leeuwkop to see Fusi.

Fusi was taken aback by the sight of Jacques Pauw. The checked shirt, the casual jacket, the plump, red-faced middle age: he looked the epitome of a police detective. Had he announced himself as a colleague of Steyn and Robertshaw, Fusi would not have been surprised. And he was so very suspicious. He spoke in the quietest voice and told Fusi that it was best to conceal from the warders that he was a journalist. Fusi tried to explain that by now the warders were on his side; they were positively willing his success. Pauw frowned doubtfully, Fusi recalls, warning that one can never be too careful.

Over the years, Fusi had gathered in three files every correspondence he had ever received concerning his case. Together they amounted to hundreds of sheets of paper. Now, he asked a warder if he could go back to his cell to retrieve them. On his return, he handed them to Jacques Pauw who looked through them briefly before asking if he could take them away to make copies. Fusi immediately agreed. He trusted Pauw without reservation.

The following Wednesday Fusi phoned Pauw on his cell phone to discover that he was in Kroonstad and had just met with Tshokolo Mokoena. On the Saturday Fusi phoned him again and this time he was in Bethlehem sitting beside Fusi's uncle, Lefo, the one who had brought Thabo Motaung to give his confession. Just hours earlier, Pauw said, he had met with Steyn and Mapalala and both had been hostile in the extreme.

Ten days had passed since Barnard had told Fusi to turn on his radio. He had made more progress in this time than in the past seventeen years.

Then Pauw fell silent and for a while Fusi wondered whether he, too, had forgotten. His suspicions deepened when he received a visit from another person at the Wits Justice Project to say that Pauw had now moved on but that Fusi should be reassured: the project remained committed wholeheartedly to his case.

And then from out of the blue Pauw contacted Fusi on a Sunday morning in late October. His altered circumstances had in fact worked well, he said, as he was now head of investigations at Media24, the group that owned *City Press*; in today's very edition of the newspaper, he continued, he had published a story on Fusi and Tshokolo.

Fusi went immediately to a warder in his section and demanded a copy of *City Press*. By evening he had read the story Pauw had written and it was good, very good.

'On the surface,' Pauw's story began, 'Fusi Mofokeng and Tshokolo Mokoena look like just another two orange-clothed jailbirds incarcerated in a high-security prison. Both have been convicted of murder and are serving life sentences. Both claim they had nothing to do with a shooting in which a policeman died and two others were wounded. While many convicts claim that they're not guilty, the difference is that Mofokeng and Mokoena might be right. They are almost certainly innocent and have spent the past 17 years in prison for a crime they did not commit.

'Over the years the two have petitioned everyone from the state president to Desmond Tutu, the Human Rights Commission, the African National Congress (ANC), the public protector and the Department of Justice – all of whom have either not bothered to respond or said they couldn't help. Yet evidence has existed for the last 14 years that security policemen might have bribed Mofokeng's childhood friend to implicate them in murder, attempted murder and conspiracy to commit robbery. Both men have lost everything.'

Unlike the previous pieces that had been published on his case, bitty, scrappy, one-paragraph notices, hardly likely to be read, let alone comprehended, this one went on to tell a tale Fusi recognised as his own.

It was his and Tshokolo's story, finally, proper and true.

The very next day he received an urgent communication from Booker Mohlaba. He had been at home reading the newspaper, Booker said, when he turned the page to find Fusi's picture, exactly as he had last seen him eleven years earlier, earphones around his head, a microphone and a glass of water on the table in front of him. He had nearly fallen off his chair. Why are you still in prison, he asked, aghast. Please tell me how I can help.

Fusi swallowed his anger and answered politely that the Wits Justice Project had taken him on as a client and that he had the help he needed.

Booker Mohlaba's response was just the beginning. Fusi phoned a relative in Bohlokong that evening and was told that the whole township was talking about him. People dimly remembered that two local boys had been sent to prison many years earlier but had long forgotten why. They were astounded to hear that they had been in jail all this time. It had been seventeen years; an entire generation had died and a new one had been born; most of the kids who filled the schools had not yet been conceived when these two men last walked the streets of Bohlokong. Could they really have been in prison all this time?

An ANC branch in Bohlokong passed around a petition which more than a thousand souls soon signed. It was sent to South Africa's newly installed president, Jacob Zuma, and it asked that he consider pardoning these men who had committed no crime.

The matter came to the attention of the premier of the Free State, Mr Ace Magashule, who phoned the mayor of Bethlehem to ask if he knew of the injustice his two constituents were suffering. The mayor was indeed aware of the case, but he'd always assumed that the TRC had given these men amnesty in 1999. Everyone, it seemed, once knew of Fusi and Tshokolo; when jolted into remembering each thought that they had forgotten only because the men had long been free.

Mr Magashule instructed the mayor to have Fusi brought back from Leeuwkop to Kroonstad. The matter would be fought and won in the Free State, the premier said, and that is where the two imprisoned men should be.

The man who had taken over from Jacques Pauw at the Wits Justice Project, another prominent journalist called Jeremy Gordin, lobbied a host of politicians about Fusi and Tshokolo's case. Among them was Mr Archibold Jomo Nyambi, chairperson of the Petitions Committee of the National Council of Provinces, the upper chamber of South Africa's Parliament. When it crossed his desk, the story fired Nyambi's imagination. He arranged at once for a delegation to visit Fusi and Tshokolo in Kroonstad. The two prisoners found, much to their astonishment, seven suited members of their country's Parliament gathered around a wide table in the administrative wing of the prison, waiting to see them.

Resting on the table was a sheaf of papers the parliamentarians had brought with them. It was a complete collection of all the official correspondence Fusi had received during his eighteen years in prison, the same collection he had handed to Jacques Pauw. The parliamentarians were convinced that a great injustice had transpired; they committed themselves to working with the Department of Correctional Services, the Department of Justice and the Presidency to ensure that Fusi and Tshokolo were freed as soon as humanly possible. It was March 2010. The Soccer World Cup, which South Africa was hosting, and about which much of the country was speaking, was due to begin on 11 June. You will be out in time for the tournament, the parliamentarians swore; you will watch at home with your families.

It took much longer than that. As much as the Petitions Committee was moved by the prisoners' stories, none of its members quite knew how to get them released. They called a public hearing on the matter. The state attorney's office was represented there, as well the Department of Justice, the Department of Correctional Services and Parliament's legal office. But for all the collective wisdom in the room, nobody, it seemed, had the expertise to free Fusi and Tshokolo from prison.

They could not get amnesty, after all, for they had committed no crime. And the Supreme Court of Appeal had long ago turned down their application to hear their case. In South African law, that was the end of the matter; it could go no further. The possibility of a presidential pardon was raised, but a senior law advisor testified that the men would be required to apologise to qualify for a pardon and they could hardly be asked to do that. When the hearing adjourned the committee was none the wiser about what to do.

It was September 2010 before a way to free them was finally conceived. A prisoner by the name of Paul van Vuren had taken a case to the Constitutional Court arguing that he ought to be released on bail. In the years since the end of apartheid, prison sentences had, ironically enough, been stiffened. A person sentenced to life had to serve a mandatory twenty years before being considered for parole. Van Vuren had been sentenced in the late apartheid era when a lifer could be considered for parole after fifteen years. He argued that the new parole stipulation ought not to be applied retrospectively; that, having served more than fifteen years, he should be eligible to be free.

The court ruled in his favour and Van Vuren duly applied for parole. After a psychological examination he was deemed unfit for life on the outside and confined to prison indefinitely. He remains there as I write these lines. But for Fusi and Tshokolo, the court's judgment meant that they could walk free. They too had been sentenced in the late apartheid period and they had now been in jail for more than eighteen years. Suddenly, overnight, they were eligible for parole.

Fusi and Tshokolo were released from jail nineteen years to the day after Steyn and Robertshaw took them from their homes. Technically, two convicted men were being released on parole. But in substance what awaited them was a ceremony celebrating the freedom of two innocent men. As they left Kroonstad Prison, the inmates sang in unison to salute their impending freedom. Outside, the warders formed a gauntlet that Fusi and Tshokolo walked in their borrowed suits. Thabang Mokotedi was waiting in the driver's seat of the state vehicle. They climbed into the back and he drove them to Bethlehem as if he were a chauffeur.

Awaiting them in Bethlehem were cameras and journalists and rafts of officials. And when they walked free they were joined by the people who had helped them: Jeremy Gordin, who had fought tooth and nail; Jomo Nyambi, who had rallied his committee to their plight. Many senior officials in the municipal administration were there. By nightfall Fusi and

Tshokolo had been promised free homes, courtesy of the state, as well as full-time work at the municipality. They had had their adult lives stolen, after all, and tomorrow morning they would be starting anew.

Fusi's abiding memories of that day are of sadness. The handshakes, the back-thumping, the encouraging smiles – he observed them as if through a pane of glass. Many of the people who came to greet him were utterly strange. They embraced him like long-lost friends but he had no idea who they were. Others he recognised faintly; they had faces he once knew but had now almost forgotten. He struggled to recall their names.

What he felt, above all, were the absences. When he last walked these streets his mother and his brother had walked them, too. He did not truly believe that they were gone. Had he entered his mother's home to find Maletsatsi Mbele and Amos Mofokeng sitting on the couch, he would not have been remotely surprised. They belonged in the only world he knew; without them the world he knew was no more.

That night, he went to bed in the house his mother had acquired while he was in prison. It had not been built when he last lived in this town and it left him feeling strange. Early the next morning he crept out of the house, its other occupants still sleeping, and walked gingerly down the empty street; on either side were houses he did not recognise. Beyond them, to the north, lay a dense shack settlement where before there had just been a vacant field.

Bohlokong, he realised, was at least twice as big as when he had last walked its streets, perhaps even bigger. Entire neighbourhoods stood on ground he remembered as empty veld; shack settlements now circled the periphery of the township where before there had been nothing. Where had all these people come from, he wondered.

It did not take long to find an answer. They were *his people*, all of them;

they were his parents' and his grandparents' people; they had come from the white-owned farms, tens of thousands of them.

In his mind, and in the minds of many around him, a simple explanation emerged. Fearing the rights that democracy would bring their tenants, white farmers evacuated their land, issuing one eviction notice upon the next. And so people descended en masse upon the towns, but there was nothing for them there.

As he began to move about Bohlokong, what he saw disturbed him. People with hunger in their eyes, others with the vacant stare of souls that had died. He did not recall seeing such people before. Nor did he recall so much idleness; he could have sworn that when he last walked these streets, they were empty on weekdays, the adults at work, the children at school. Now, wherever he looked, there were people without purpose.

He kept these thoughts to himself. A parliamentary committee composed largely of members of the ruling ANC had done so much to free Tshokolo and him. The provincial premier, a senior ANC figure, had taken a personal interest in their case. And the mayor of Bethlehem, also from the ANC, had promised Tshokolo and him houses and jobs. One does not repay such kindness by talking darkly of what one has discovered beyond the prison gates. One does not embarrass one's benefactors by announcing that the world over which they preside leaves one feeling sad.

For many weeks after his release, he struggled to sleep. He listened to the noises coming from outside, and although they were the same as the previous night and the night before that, they still felt unfamiliar. When he drifted off to sleep, he would sometimes find in his dreams that he had wandered off into the night and was walking through streets he had never seen before.

To make this place home, he knew, would take a colossal effort; as much as he had been through inside the prison walls, a great task, perhaps the greatest of all, lay ahead.

Twenty-four

Take the N7 freeway north from Cape Town and within half an hour you are in fields of grapes and wheat. The valleys are shallow and serene, rather than beautiful, places of pleasing stillness. At the small rural town of Malmesbury you turn right onto a quiet district road; after twenty kilometres, you are in the hamlet of Riebeek-Kasteel. Jacques Pauw lives there. I go to see him on a sweltering day in 2013 just before Christmas. Fusi has been out of prison almost twenty months.

Jacques Pauw invites me into his home, an antique Boland house with stripped wooden floors and wooden frames and pressed ceilings. It is quite lovely. He is middle-aged, chubby and barefoot and he is courteous to a T. There is a domestic worker shuffling about the house whom he asks in a soft voice to bring us something cold to drink. Across a wide table under a cool awning, he tells me how he came to know of Fusi Mofokeng.

In 2009, when he still headed the Wits Justice Project, Pauw begins, he wrote a double-page spread for the *Mail & Guardian*, a national weekly, about prisoners waiting eternally for their trials. Some had been incarcerated ten years, some fourteen, their cases forever postponed.

Following the article's publication, Pauw continues, the domestic worker now come and gone, the drinks she has brought sitting on the table before us, he received an e-mail from an official at the Department of Home Affairs. His name was Donald Makhura. He wanted to talk about two innocent men serving life sentences for murder.

Pauw went that very week to see Makhura in his government office in Pretoria. From the start, he says, the Home Affairs man had about him an air of conspiracy; they could not possibly talk at his office, he said, for the walls had ears, and he dragged Pauw off to a branch of a steakhouse chain in the nearby suburb of Brooklyn.

In the car, Pauw asked Makhura, by way of small talk, what he did at the Department of Home Affairs. His answer was vague. He wore a khaki uniform and carried a large briefcase. At the steakhouse he put the briefcase on the table between them and opened it, making sure that Pauw had sight of the pistol that lay atop a pile of files. He rummaged through the files and retrieved a short document which he handed to Pauw; it was a summary of the judgment that had convicted the Bethlehem men of murder. While Pauw paged through it, Makhura told him of the Bethlehem shootings, of the trial and of the amnesty hearing that had left two innocent men in prison.

The moment he was released in 1999, Makhura said, he mustered whatever he could to get the innocent ones freed. He raised the matter with senior ANC figures, including Winnie Mandela. He visited the ANC's headquarters in Johannesburg where he tried to get an audience with anyone possessed of sufficient clout to do something. His attempts were rebuffed. Nobody was interested.

When Fusi managed to acquire the services of a lawyer, a man by the name of Van Rensburg, Makhura drove to Kroonstad to see him. Van Rensburg, too, could do nothing; the Justice department barely responded to his stream of communication.

Pauw was immediately hooked – these two innocent and invisible men, the political establishment unwilling, it seemed, even to register their existence; this dodgy character from Home Affairs the only one to remember them, knocking on one door after another.

He went out to seek help. He approached the Wits Law Clinic, which took up cases pro bono, but was told that they did not do this sort of work. He spoke to Winnie Mandela, who said she was outraged, but did nothing. He contacted the respective premiers of Gauteng and Mpumalanga; they were also outraged, but did nothing. He tracked down the man who had led the TRC's evidence at the amnesty hearing in Welkom. He was now a member of Parliament. He vaguely remembered the case and said he would take it up; he did not.

Pauw finally returned to an experienced lawyer at the Wits Law Clinic and pleaded with him to take the case. 'This isn't going to happen,' he recalls the lawyer saying. 'Nobody is going to reopen this case for you. The best you can do is make a huge stink and embarrass enough people for these guys to get early parole.'

Makhura had not even been certain where the two men were incarcerated. He thought that one was in Kroonstad and the other in Leeuwkop, but he could not swear to it. And so Pauw drove instead to Bethlehem in the Free State to the house in which Fusi had been arrested in 1992. He was pleasantly surprised to find a close relative of Fusi's living there, who directed him to Leeuwkop. And that is where he went next. He and Fusi met twice, Pauw says, on two successive Saturday mornings in September 2009.

Pauw was astonished by Fusi Mofokeng. He seemed preternaturally calm and so very mild. He appeared to possess not a jot of anger. When Pauw announced his business Mofokeng got a warder to escort him back to his cell and returned shortly with a massive sheaf of documents. Throughout the conversation that followed he referred to them in extraordinary detail; he clearly carried an intricate index to them in his head and in a flash Pauw saw the years of obsession that had collated them.

Pauw recalls speaking to the prisoner frankly. 'I have it on the best authority that this case simply will not be reopened,' he remembers saying. 'If we apply enough pressure, maybe you can get early parole.'

Mofokeng listened carefully, he said, and nodded and smiled affably, and as Pauw stared back at him he was as certain as he was of anything that the man opposite him was not a criminal. True, they all say they have committed no crime, but this man so obviously did not belong in a prison.

He was nonetheless coping remarkably well, it seemed. Leeuwkop was a veritable gulag, a truly shocking place, but Mofokeng seemed as at home there as a person could be. He greeted the other prisoners with decorum and grace and when Pauw remarked on this Mofokeng told him he was chairman of an inmate soccer club and well known throughout the prison. And he clearly had excellent relationships with the warders. When he had asked an official if he could return to his cell to get his legal documents, the exchange between prisoner and warder had about it an air of comfortable civility.

As their meeting progressed, Pauw recalls, both men grew increasingly excited, Pauw because he had found an innocent man, Mofokeng because Pauw was listening with such intent. By the end of the meeting, Mofokeng's hopes had scaled too high. He had found the saviour he'd been looking for, he announced. His case would finally be reopened. No, Pauw pleaded, the best you can hope for is early parole. Keep fighting. Keep writing letters. They will all help.

As Pauw was leaving, the prisoner pulled out yet another document, this one a social worker's report on Mofokeng. He insisted that Pauw read it; it was a document, it appeared, of which he felt very proud. Pauw skimmed it, just to be polite, then returned it.

'And Tshokolo Mokoena?' I ask.

'I went to see him in Kroonstad. We really did not communicate very well. It was through a pane of glass. It was difficult. It made more sense to focus on Fusi.'

'Did you not receive a letter from Fusi,' I ask, 'right at the beginning, before you met him? Was it not a letter from him that took you to Leeuwkop?'

'No,' Pauw replies. 'Donald Makhura told me about him.'

'That's strange,' I say, 'because Fusi heard you talking on the radio about the work of the Wits Justice Project. He was so excited that he stayed up through the night drafting a letter to you.'

'I didn't ever get that letter.'

I tell Pauw of how things looked from Fusi's vantage point: hearing Pauw on the radio; the feverish correspondence summoning Pauw to Leeuwkop; the story in *City Press* finally alerting the world to Fusi's plight; the petition of an ANC branch in Bethlehem; the visit of the Petitions Committee of the National Council of Provinces.

Pauw frowns as he takes this in. 'Well, I didn't know about the Bethlehem petition,' he says. 'So maybe a corner of the world was actually alerted. But from my perspective, the whole thing was very disappointing. Nobody was interested. I battled to get *City Press* to run the story at all. When they did, they buried it on page eleven or something. It was just such a foreign concept that innocent people can be in prison for murder.'

'The publicity from the *City Press* piece wasn't the trigger?' I ask.

'No, I don't think so. When I left the Wits Justice Project, my successor, Jeremy Gordin, contacted everyone he could think of. That's how the National Council of Provinces got involved, I think. Jeremy contacted them and the story captured the imagination of the chair of the Petitions Committee. But few other people's imaginations were stirred, I can tell you. I found the whole business frustrating.'

Pauw's own imagination, it seems, drew him back to Donald Makhura. They met again on several occasions at the Brooklyn branch of the steakhouse. Each time, Makhura would order a cheese steak and an Amstel beer and he would eat and drink at a snail's crawl, their lunchtime meeting dragging through the late afternoon. Always, his briefcase would lie open on the table, his firearm resting on a pile of documents.

Pauw was by now head of investigations at South Africa's largest media company, Media24, and Makhura wanted to discuss matters he thought might interest the journalist. He was involved in a large investigation, he said, together with the police and the revenue service, of a criminal syndicate based in Pakistan. Makhura, as a Home Affairs official, was interested in the syndicate's use of fraudulent passports. And he took from his briefcase the police docket of the Pakistani syndicate case and allegedly offered to sell it to Pauw.

'He never got as far as naming his price,' Pauw recalls. 'I said to him: "It's a criminal offence to buy a police docket. Media24 can't do that."'

'He was enraged. I could not believe how angry he became. He was absolutely furious with me for not buying his docket. He got a very unpleasant look in his eyes and just stared at me.

'At one point, I said: "You are a Home Affairs official. Do you realise that I could write about you trying to sell a docket?"

'"You wouldn't dare," he said quietly. And he looked at me with those eyes.'

Makhura recovered quickly from his anger, it seems, for he contacted Pauw again soon afterwards. This time he was excited and chatty and over lunch he handed the journalist his memoir and instructed him to read it. When you are finished, he told Pauw, you will want to write a book about me. You will not believe the life I have had.

That was the last time they saw one another at the steakhouse in

Brooklyn. The next Pauw heard of Makhura he was in prison accused of gunning down his own daughter and her boyfriend.

'I went to see him in lock-up in Pretoria Central,' Pauw says. 'It was a horrible experience. There was a throng of visitors. We spoke through a pane of glass. His girlfriend was there to see him too and a small child. It was truly awful.'

Through the glass, the journalist told the murder suspect that he wanted to write a newspaper story about him and asked permission to quote from his memoir. Makhura agreed, at least at first, but later sent Pauw angry missives through intermediaries telling him to use nothing.

'He is not a stupid man by any means,' Pauw tells me. 'But those eyes of his. When he was angry he would look at me with those eyes. Here's a man given a second chance – gets amnesty for murder and lands a good job. And he fucked it up. At those awful lunch meetings we had, he was always after a little extra. I would pay for his steak and his Amstels, but then he would ask for an extra few hundred bucks.'

'Why did he kill his daughter?' I ask.

'Nobody knows. It happened outside his ex-wife's house in Mamelodi. He was often seen in the neighbourhood spying on her house. At some point, the daughter refused to continue to see him because of his violent past. There was huge anger building up in the man. He was probably prowling and saw his daughter kissing her boyfriend in the car and simply shot them.

'Donald underwent very tough military training in Angola. It would be interesting to know what this did to him psychologically. I think it damaged him a great deal.'

As I drive back past Malmesbury, Jacques Pauw's story has taken over the farmland and made it strange. The wheat and the grapevines seem too brightly lit, the valleys unnaturally still. Fusi and I have spent months journeying through his past, and we have, it appears, wandered onto the most delicate terrain.

Fusi's is a tale one resists. One listens intently and thinks one has taken in the depth of it, but it is not so. For one does not want to walk in his shoes.

To narrow your whole life – no, more than your life, the very essence of your being, the very purpose of your every moment – into a quest to be heard. To have nothing come back but the sound of your own pleas. It is a primal scene, truly. It is lodged so deep under the crust we show the world that we encounter it only in the most horrible dreams.

In the story he has told, there is justice and redemption. Of his many hundreds of letters, written over countless years, one is answered. He has been shouting to the world. And now, almost too late, it hears.

Sitting up through the night, poring over the notes of my conversations with Fusi, I see Donald Makhura in places I had not seen him before. He is there, but he is not there. 'Donald Makhura also met with Van Rensburg,' I read. And a little later: 'Donald also spoke to Jacques Pauw.' His name is recorded but he is not a mover, not a cause of the story's course. He has not quite been erased. He has simply been rendered irrelevant.

I wonder why Fusi has done this. Is it simply that he needs to be the hero of his own story? That would be understandable, certainly, but it is still quite something to have forgotten the role played by the one who took your plight to the world.

Perhaps there is something deeper, something unspoken. On our very first evening together, as Fusi was driving me back into town and I felt his gentle presence beside me in the car, I had wondered out loud why he was not angrier. He had smiled to himself, smiled at my incomprehension, for the most shocking thing he had learnt in prison was that the power of his anger was killing him.

Perhaps Fusi has left Donald out of his story because he is angry. But for what reason I do not know.

Part III

Twenty-five

I am sitting at the desk I mistakenly remember occupying when I first read of Fusi Mofokeng. Across the road is the same brickwork. This time, I am reading the transcript of the 1992 trial that put Fusi and Tshokolo behind bars. It has been a long time coming; three years have passed since I met Fusi.

The audiotapes of the trial proceedings were lost when I began this project. All I had to work with was the newspaper coverage the trial had produced and the memories of those who were in the courtroom. This was not entirely surprising as the Free State High Court archives appeared not to be in good shape. But it was immensely frustrating. The prosecutor was dead. The judge was now in his late seventies and would not talk, for the story was abroad that he had convicted two innocent men and he regarded me as hostile.

I spoke instead to the two lawyers who had represented the defendants, Paul Heymanns and André Landman. Their memories were by now more than two decades old and the passage of time leaves the strangest marks on what people recall. Their respective rememberings were so very eccentric, so closely attuned to their own emotional lives.

Why the audiotapes suddenly resurface is something of a mystery. From out of the blue I receive an e-mail in March 2014 from a journalist at the Wits Justice Project, which is still working on Fusi and Tshokolo's case, saying that the tapes have been found. I begin that very day to raise money to have them transcribed. Six months later, a full transcript of the trial lands in my inbox in an attachment 2 117 pages long.

I sit down to read and within minutes I am wholly absorbed. A little more than twenty years have passed since these proceedings were recorded and yet they seem to have come from the furthest reaches of time. The pages are filled with the characters of another epoch: black servants whose apparent dedication to their white masters grows thicker as the pages turn; the presiding Judge, Koos Malherbe, who addresses black witnesses by their first names and calls the white men in their lives 'Baas Orsmond' and 'Baas Steyn' and who talks to white female witnesses as if they are the most delicate creatures, liable at any moment to crumble to dust.

As hard as one tries, it is impossible not to look upon these people knowingly – they are unaware that the words on their tongues and the thoughts in their heads are dying; within three or four years, nobody will behave like them in a courtroom ever again.

The transcript is as interesting for what is not reflected in its pages. Clement Ndabeni and Mandla Fokazi told the court that the only language they could follow was their native isiXhosa. And so testimony given in English and Afrikaans was translated into isiXhosa. And testimony offered in Sesotho was translated first into Afrikaans and then into isiXhosa. When Fusi, Tshokolo and Sikhalo addressed the court in their native Sesotho, they did so in brief bursts before waiting for their testimony to be rendered into two other languages. And the only part of the proceedings they heard in their native tongue was their own testimonies.

None of this is reflected in the pages I read; the transcript is in a seamless Afrikaans. Absent is the work of the court interpreters, the final arbiters on what it was that the accused meant to say.

I am not half an hour into reading when the story I have had in my head for the past three years about what happened on 2 April 1992 – a story I know is not entirely right, but which I have always assumed to be largely true, at least in its broadest outline – shatters.

Recall the essence of the tale Fusi told me when I met him, and the story his co-accused presented to the truth commission. Fusi was lying in bed on the morning of 2 April when his brother-in-law, Sikhalo Ncala, knocked on the door. Sikhalo and the men he brought with him were on their way to Inanda in Natal to assist their comrades in a battle against Inkatha. They stayed in Bethlehem for a few hours and drove on. On the outskirts of town, they were pulled over by police. Under standing orders to surrender neither themselves nor their weapons, they opened fire, killing Constable Oosthuizen and gravely injuring Constable Joubert. Then they scattered and fled.

That the shootout took place outside the residence of a wealthy white family by the name of Orsmond was sheer coincidence. The story the prosecution told in court – relying heavily on the testimony of young Thabo Mokoena – that the men had come to Bethlehem to rob the Orsmonds, that Fusi and Tshokolo had indeed explicitly *invited* the men to Bethlehem *in order* to rob the Orsmonds, was sheer fabrication.

But now, just pages into the transcript of the trial, to my mind it is clear, beyond any doubt, that the men who came to Bethlehem on the morning of 2 April did indeed intend to do ill on the Orsmond property; they failed only because they executed their task so poorly.

The first witness is a white woman, Mrs Mary Orsmond. But she is the first witness simply *because* she is a white woman: the prosecution, alive to the power of spectacle, and thus to the importance of how to begin, wants to show that this is an attack on the hearth of a decent white home.

The star witness, actually – the one whose testimony tears to pieces the story I have had in my head – is the second witness, a middle-aged black man named Simon Motaung.

On 2 April 1992, Motaung was working in the garden of Mr and Mrs Ret and Mary Orsmond in a neighbourhood of smallholdings on the outskirts of Bethlehem called Ballyduff. He had been in the Orsmonds' employ for eleven years, his wife, Martha, for thirteen. He tended the garden, Martha the house.

It was late morning, he believed, when his work in the Orsmonds' garden was disturbed by the sound of a vehicle. He looked up to find a bakkie, the cargo area concealed by a white canopy, making its way along the dirt road on the other side of the garden fence.

A little while later, Motaung heard what sounded like a person whistling. He lifted his eyes, thinking that Johnny, employed on the smallholding next door, was calling him. But nobody was there. And then all of a sudden two men were standing alongside him and greeting him, two black men; and when counsel enquired whether either of those men was in the court, Simon Motaung said yes, Accused Number Three was one of those two men. Accused Number Three was asked to stand and Sikhalo Ncala, Fusi Mofokeng's brother-in-law, rose from the dock.

Asked whether the man accompanying Accused Number Three was in the courtroom, Motaung says that he did not recall his face. He remembers only that the man wore a sleeveless jacket with a Mobil insignia on its breast and stood silently with his hands in his jacket pockets. Later in the trial, Clement Ndabeni will confirm that it was he who walked onto the Orsmond property with Sikhalo Ncala.

Accused Number Three, Motaung continues, said that he wanted to speak to Motaung's employer as he was looking for a job. There was only enough work on this smallholding for himself, Motaung replied, and suggested that the men go to his employer's place of business, Orsmond

Aviation, at the airfield nearby, for the business employed many people. The stranger then asked Motaung when his employer would return and Motaung replied that he had no idea, although he knew very well that Mr Orsmond would soon come home for lunch.

Motaung asked the men where they had come from and Sikhalo Ncala replied that they had walked from Ntshirela and would now continue to the airfield. At this, what remained of Motaung's credulity evaporated and he knew for certain that these men meant trouble; for Ntshirela referred to the mountains to the west of Bethlehem, quite some distance away; and besides, had they walked, he was certain he would have seen them coming. As he entertained these sceptical thoughts, he saw, over the shoulders of the two men, the bakkie with the white canopy emerge from a dip in the road.

A little later, Motaung took his lunch break with John Nkosi, who worked next door, the Johnny he had thought he heard whistling for him earlier. He told John Nkosi of the bakkie and of the men who had approached him and they discussed whether to tell Mr Orsmond, who had by now returned for lunch. They agreed that it was best not to alarm him, but Motaung resolved, and said out loud to John Nkosi, that if the bakkie were to return they should call the police. He also told his wife, Martha, what had happened and between them they agreed not to tell Mrs Orsmond for fear of scaring her.

Simon Motaung returned to his tasks in the garden, Ret Orsmond went back to the airfield and Mary Orsmond left on an errand with her seven-year-old daughter, Kate. The afternoon wore on and Motaung got lost in the rhythms of his work. Much later, the shadows of the trees stretching across the length of the Orsmonds' garden, he looked up to find that the bakkie had returned; it was now parked some distance up the dirt road, its bonnet open, its driver peering into the engine.

It occurred to Simon Motaung that this was precisely the situation in which he had envisaged calling the police. As he contemplated whether to see his resolve through, three men emerged on foot from the direction of the bakkie. One of them was Accused Number Three, Sikhalo Ncala. Motaung watched them make their way up the road separating the Orsmond property and the property next door, and then disappear right behind the Orsmonds' home.

Panicked, Motaung now ran to the house to phone for help. Just at this moment, Mary Orsmond returned home with her daughter Kate and Motaung told her that they were all in peril and that she must phone the police.

I believe that there is little question, then, that the men who came to Bethlehem on the morning of 2 April intended to do ill in the Orsmond home. They had driven Clement's bakkie all the way from Fusi's house to Ballyduff in the morning, had reconnoitred, had walked onto the property asking questions. And then they were back in the afternoon, three of them stealing around the back of the house, the rest of them in the bakkie around the front. They worked in so amateurish a manner that by the time they were ready to assail, the neighbourhood was in a state of high alarm.

As I read the transcript, another strand in the story Fusi told me, and the others told the truth commission, crumbles. They testified that the police pulled their bakkie over to the side of the road as they were leaving town. It was the most unfortunate coincidence, they suggested, running into a police van just when they did.

But it is clear from the trial record that running into the police was no coincidence at all. The men in the bakkie made such a spectacle of themselves during the course of the day that by the time they were ready to move onto the Orsmond property much of the neighbourhood was in a state of panic. Indeed, the police came *because they were called*.

Recall that Mary Orsmond left her home during the course of the afternoon with her daughter, Kate, to run errands in town. She returned at about 4:15 p.m. As she approached the bend in the dirt road outside her house, she passed a stationary bakkie, the bonnet raised, the driver peering into the engine.

'When I arrived home,' Orsmond tells the court, 'my garden boy and his wife, Simon and Martha, were waiting for me outside the back door. They were very agitated. Simon's first words to me [were]: "Please get hold of the police immediately."'

She called her husband at the airfield. He was harried; he was about to fly one of his company's planes to Johannesburg; he told her to shut the curtains and close the doors.

No sooner had she put down the phone than Simon rushed to her, shouting that the bakkie was now moving past the house. She went to the window and watched. The bakkie came to a halt some distance down the road, made a U-turn, came slowly back towards the house, and then stopped at the entrance to the Orsmond driveway, giving its occupants a clear view of her home.

And so three men had already stolen around the back of the house; and now the bakkie was blocking the front.

The driver got out and opened the bonnet once more. Then two more men emerged from the cargo area and stood looking at the house. Orsmond phoned her husband again and this time he agreed to postpone his flight to Johannesburg; he would call the police, he said, and then he would come home and ask the men in the bakkie what it was they wanted.

Mary Orsmond was about to phone the police herself when Martha came to say that a yellow police van had already arrived. It transpired that another black man employed by a white family on that road, Boorman

Nhlapo, had taken fright when the bakkie reappeared, and had advised his employer, Sue Robertson, to call the police.

Orsmond returned to the window and saw a police van parked nose to nose against the bakkie; and it strikes me as I imagine her looking at the scene at the end of her driveway that the men in the bakkie, their game now up, their armoury on the brink of discovery, understood themselves to be freeing their country from a white dictatorship. And yet at the faintest trace of their scent, the black servants of Ballyduff had smelled mortal danger and had screamed their alarm to their masters.

'I opened our front door,' Orsmond continued, 'and walked out onto the lawn to go and speak to the police. Then I noticed two police get out of the vehicle and I carried on, proceeding walking towards them. I noticed that at that stage all the black, all the gentlemen involved were all back in the bakkie when the policemen got out of their vehicle. Then the back section of the vehicle opened up. Then they just started shooting.'

Sue Robertson, the Orsmond's next-door neighbour, takes the stand. Her farmhand, she testifies, Boorman Nhlapo, had at about 4:15 p.m. reported a suspicious vehicle standing on the dirt road and advised her to call the police. She had done so at once, she said, and was told that a patrol vehicle was on the way.

From her window, she says, she watched a police van arrive and two police officers step out of their vehicle; and then, she says, she heard gunshots and saw balls of smoke in the air.

'*Die twee polisiemannetjies het omgespring*,' she said, '*en na ons kant toe gehardloop.*'

The word she chooses to describe the police officers, *mannetjies*, is literally translated as 'little men'. One might call a toddler a *mannetjie*, in jest, as he shoots his toy pistol, perhaps, or as he trips over his feet.

'The two little policemen turned around and ran towards our side. Constable Oosthuizen fell first and then Constable Joubert fell on our side of the road.'

The bakkie sped off, she continues, and *ek het gou die polisie geskakel en gesê hulle moet kom help want die kinders het geval.* 'I quickly phoned the police and told them to come and help because the children had fallen.'

She went out into the street to find that Constable Oosthuizen was dead. 'His back was covered in blood; his body lay crooked.'

As for Constable Joubert, standing over him it struck Sue Robertson that she knew him, vaguely, knew his parents, his family. He was bleeding fiercely from his left eye and from his stomach. He was conscious and trying to move, but one side of him seemed to be lame. She sat with him, she said, and spoke kindly to him, and waited for help to arrive.

The defence cross-examines Robertson and when they are done and she is about to leave the court, Judge Malherbe detains her a moment longer.

'On more than one occasion,' he remarks, 'you described the police officers as children.'

'That's right, Your Honour.'

'You knew one of them. Is that true?'

'That is correct.'

'Was he a child in your eyes because he was a young man?'

'That is correct, Your Honour.'

'Say again which one he was.'

'Constable Joubert.'

'How old was he?'

'About thirty.'

'Please tell the court how old you are.'

'I am fifty-five, Your Honour.'

And now Malherbe announces that it is posterity he is imagining; he wants the matriarchal scene he has witnessed recorded in words so that those who read the transcript will know.

'It's just that words alone don't convey what the court sees, ma'am. I see that you have grey hair and talk of the young men as children and that you shared with the court ...' and the rest of the sentence is inaudible to the stenographer.

'I just want to tell the court,' Robertson replies, 'that my son is twenty-seven. That is why I see them as children.'

'I am also nearly fifty-five,' Malherbe replies. 'Thank you, ma'am. You can go back now.'

I am in for another surprise.

When the police interrogated him in the early hours of 3 April 1992, Fusi had told me, they asked whom he had seen that day. He diligently recounted the names of the women who had come to the house; and he recalled that Thabo Motaung had come briefly in the morning and that Tshokolo Mokoena had stopped by in the afternoon. The police, he said, had latched on to Tshokolo's name, gone to his house and dragged him from his bed.

That is how Tshokolo got caught up in the whole business, Fusi told me.

But I now learn that there is a much closer and more suggestive connection between Tshokolo and the shooting incident outside the Orsmond home.

Early in Mary Orsmond's testimony, the prosecutor asks whether she knows any of the accused. She certainly does, she replies; she points to Tshokolo Mokoena and tells that court that he was employed at Orsmond Aviation, her husband's business.

'Now, at the time of this incident on April 2nd 1992, was he still in the employment of your husband?'

'No. No, he was not.'

'Did Accused Number One know where your home was?'

'He did.'

Later in the trial, when Tshokolo Mokoena is cross-examined, he confirms that he worked for Orsmond Aviation for ten months as a spray-painter. He left his employment at the aviation company at the end of February 1992, he says, just more than two months before 2 April. His last day at Orsmond Aviation was a Friday; by the Monday he had a new job at a small welding business in the centre of Bethlehem called Staal en Pyp.

Led by the prosecutor's questions, Tshokolo says that he parted ways with the Orsmonds on foul terms and was left with a bitter taste in his mouth.

'How much did Mr Orsmond pay you?' the prosecutor asked.

'R130 a week.'

'Why did you leave your employment with Mr Orsmond?'

'We did not agree on the wage he paid me,' Mokoena replied.

'What was wrong with the wage he paid you?'

'It was too little for the work that I did.'

'Were you unsatisfied about it?'

'I was unsatisfied about it.'

'And when you began working at Staal en Pyp, you earned R250 a week?'

'That is right.'

'It seems to me that you were also interested in buying an allotment and needed money for that.'

'That is right.'

And with that, the prosecutor ended his cross-examination.

I go back to the notes I took from my conversations with Tshokolo Mokoena. We spent two afternoons together, about a year before I read the transcript of the trial; I had asked him to tell me the story of his life in as much detail as he would care to give.

In the 1980s, he said, when he was a young man, he walked one day into the town centre of Odendaalsrus, the Free State hamlet in which he was born and raised, looking for work. On the premises of a business that made toys, he was asked what he could do.

'I can spray-paint,' he had said. He no longer recalled why this, of all possible vocations, came into his mind, but the following day he had a job painting toy fire engines and fighter jets.

The company was successful. It was expanding. It opened a factory in the town of Potchefstroom. Tshokolo went along when the new factory opened and worked there for four years, from 1986 to 1990, when it closed its doors, leaving him unemployed.

He went to live in Bethlehem in 1990, he said, because his grandmother lived there, and soon after settling found a job as a welder at an enterprise in the centre of town called Staal en Pyp. That is where he worked, he said, from early 1990 until 2 April 1992. He knocked off at 5:00 p.m. that evening, never to return.

He had edited out his time at Orsmond Aviation. It was no longer in the record of the life he told.

In the three years before I read the court transcript I spoke to all of the men who had been convicted for Constable Oosthuizen's murder. I spent many dozens of hours with Fusi and with various of his relatives and with men who knew him in prison. In none of their stories had Tshokolo ever worked at Orsmond Aviation. His employment there had no place in their pool of memory.

Twenty-six

R ecall that the witness who sank Fusi and Tshokolo was their friend Thabo Motaung. From out of the blue he appeared as a state witness testifying that he had been present when Fusi and Tshokolo hatched the plan to bring the men from Johannesburg to rob the Orsmonds.

Thabo Motaung's performance in the witness box makes for uncomfortable reading. It is clear that the prosecutor, Advocate Visser, has taken Motaung's measure as an awful witness, one who is unable to tell the story required. For it is the prosecutor who tells Motaung's tale as a series of questions to which Motaung simply replies 'yes', over and again.

From the prosecutor we hear that Thabo Motaung knew Fusi Mofokeng and Tshokolo Mokoena, that he was, indeed, Fusi's neighbour. And he was aware that Tshokolo worked at the airfield for Orsmond Aviation until early 1992.

At the end of 1991, the prosecutor says, and his witness affirms, Thabo met with Fusi and Tshokolo at Tshokolo's house in Bohlokong. There was talk about money; money was needed. Tshokolo remarked that at his employer's house there was a great deal of cash; Fusi said that he would call his brother-in-law in Johannesburg, Sikhalo Ncala.

After Christmas, the prosecutor continues, Fusi went to visit his brother-in-law in Johannesburg and was away for a month. The three met after Fusi returned. Fusi asked Tshokolo if he was sure there was money at the Orsmond house. Tshokolo was sure.

And now Judge Malherbe interrupts, for it appears that the interpreter is struggling to understand what Thabo Motaung is saying.

'You must please listen nicely and answer clearly,' he reprimands. 'Don't stand there and mumble so that the interpreter can't hear you.'

Now Fusi and Tshokolo's lawyer, André Landman, intervenes.

'This testimony consists of a string of leading questions,' he complains. 'I'm not sure if it is that the witness is unwilling, or whether he was warned about implicating himself as an accomplice, but I must object. The witness is being led from one place to another, all the way. Almost no evidence is coming from the witness's mouth.'

'I acknowledge that the questions are leading,' the prosecutor replies. 'But there is so much detail in this case. One wants to be sure that the backbone is there. If the court says I must ask less leading questions, I will accept.'

'I won't tell you how to ask questions,' Judge Malherbe says. 'But the more leading your questions are, the less credible the answers. You take that risk.'

The awkward duo continues. Thabo, his brother-in-law, Zulu, and Fusi met in the Bethlehem town centre on the morning of 2 April, Thabo says. Fusi informed them that the men from Johannesburg were here in town, that the plan was going ahead. Fusi, Thabo and Thabo's brother-in-law went to the bank. Then they visited Tshokolo at his place of work and informed him that the people from Johannesburg had arrived. Next, Thabo and his brother-in-law went home, dropping Fusi off at his place along the way.

Later, in the early evening, Thabo went to Fusi's house. While he was there, somebody Thabo did not recognise came to speak to Fusi. Fusi stepped outside to talk to the stranger and returned moments later and said: 'Come, we are going to meet my brother-in-law.'

Sikhalo Ncala was waiting at the end of the road. They met him and began walking towards a tavern and along the way they came across Tshokolo. Thabo decided that he did not want to drink and split off from the others and went home.

The following morning Thabo went to see Fusi to discover that he had been arrested.

Landman begins his cross-examination and within minutes Thabo Mokoena has rebelled against the whole business of being in the court-room. Although not reflected in the transcript, it appears that he has begun answering questions by simply repeating them.

'Why do you repeat the questions every so often?' Malherbe explodes. 'Is there something wrong with your hearing?'

'Just with one ear.'

'The one you're holding? The left ear?'

'Yes.'

'The right one is healthy?'

'Yes.'

'And the interpreter is sitting close enough to you?'

'Yes.'

'To your healthy ear?'

'Yes.'

'He speaks a language you understand?'

'Yes.'

'Not a strange language?'

'No.'

'So why do you waste time by repeating the questions every so often?'

To that Thabo Motaung does not reply.

Landman tries to continue his cross-examination.

'What standard at school have you reached?' he asked.

'Standard 3.'

But Malherbe is not quite done.

'What is wrong with your left ear?'

'Water went into it when I swam.'

Landman muscles his way back in.

'Can you remember anything that happened at the second meeting with Fusi Mofokeng and Tshokolo Mokoena, the one that took place after Mofokeng returned from Joburg?'

'I can't remember well any more. We were talking about so many things.'

'I just want to make sure you don't confuse yourself. The plans to rob the Osmonds were at the 1991 meeting?'

'No, this year.'

'You mean 1992?'

'Yes.'

'You spoke about it then?'

'We spoke about something, but I can't remember well.'

'You remember nothing?'

'I can't remember well any more.'

Landman wonders aloud why Thabo Motaung's brother-in-law, Zulu, has not been called by the state. After all, Thabo was with Zulu when he met with Fusi Mofokeng in the Bethlehem town centre on the morning of 2 April; Zulu would have heard that the men from Johannesburg had arrived; he had allegedly gone along with the others to Tshokolo's place of work to inform him that the men who were to rob the Orsmonds were here. Why was he not called? Was it because his story would not corroborate Thabo Motaung's? Nobody answers his question.

That Judge Malherbe accepted Thabo Motaung's testimony I find scan-
dalous. A small child can see that the evidence has been placed in his
mouth by the prosecution. He is incoherent. He contradicts himself at
every turn. And his moral anguish is palpable; he is desperate to be anywhere but in the courtroom.

His testimony is not the only scandal. Several of the accused complain that the police beat them viciously upon their arrest. And Tshokolo
Mokoena has the physical evidence to prove it; he was badly beaten all over
his head and has lost the vision in one of his eyes. Judge Malherbe appears
to be barely interested. At one point he asks Mokoena whether the police
beat him hard. His curiosity is idle. He seems merely to be passing the time.

And one of the accused, Donald Makhura, tells the court of being
tricked; the police at one point offered him a lighter sentence, at another,
a complete reprieve, if he provided them with information. He held his
side of the bargain and told them what they wanted to know. He was
given a document to sign so that the agreement was down on paper.
And then the document disappeared and the agreement vanished. Judge
Malherbe appeared to be not much interested in this story either.

This is no perfect trial by any measure. The evidence that Fusi and
Tshokolo conspired to bring the Johannesburg men to town to rob the
Orsmonds is suspect to say the least. But even imperfect trials offer incon-
testable truths. One is that the men from Johannesburg had ill intentions
upon the Orsmond property. Another is that Tshokolo Mokoena knew
the Orsmonds and their property and had reason to be furious with them.

All of this is new. It is not in the testimony that the men presented
to the truth commission. And it is not in the oral testimony I have been
gathering for three years. Indeed, it breaks the very backbone of the
story the men have for so long been telling: that they were just passing
through town, their business elsewhere; that they were unlucky enough
to be pulled over by the police just as they were leaving Bethlehem.

Twenty-seven

There is no image of Fusi Mofokeng in the witness box. A photograph was taken of him outside the Bethlehem Magistrate's Court when he was charged several months earlier, and another when he gave testimony at the amnesty hearing in Welkom in 1998. But what he looks like on the day he speaks in Judge Malherbe's court I can only guess. I imagine him with the long hair and the fresh face that attracted Isaac Ganda's attention. But that is improbable as he has been in jail many months and his head is surely shorn.

Early in the morning on 2 April, Fusi begins his testimony, the people from Johannesburg arrived. Sikhalo told Fusi that he was looking for Fusi's brother, Amos. On discovering that Amos was not home, Sikhalo said that he would leave at once for the petrol station where Amos worked. The others would remain in the house.

At about 9:00 a.m., before Sikhalo had left to find Amos, Thabo Motaung's brother-in-law, Zulu, came by, and asked Fusi to accompany him on a shopping expedition to Metro. Fusi agreed and said that he would meet Zulu and Thabo at Metro shortly. He told Sikhalo that there was a key to the house with the next-door neighbour and that he could come and go as he pleased.

Fusi walked to Metro where he found Zulu and Thabo Motaung. They shopped, they went back to Zulu's place in Zulu's car, they unpacked his groceries and then they watched videos together all afternoon. Fusi left at about 5:00 p.m.

When he got home, Fusi continues, the house was empty. He cleaned in the places where the visitors had left a mess. When Amos got home Fusi went out to buy bread; it was almost dark.

Nobody came or went, he said, until about 9:00 p.m., when Sikhalo arrived to say that he was in the deepest trouble.

The prosecutor's cross-examination of Fusi is long and meandering; it is often hard to discern the point of it. I am some fifteen pages in when he finally asks Fusi why he offered up Tshokolo Mokoena's name in the first hour or two after his arrest.

'Because Warrant Officer Steyn asked me who I drank with,' Fusi replies.

'Did you give the names of your other drinking companions?' Visser asks.

'No.'

'Why not?'

'Because I don't have any other drinking companions.'

I feel awfully hollow as I read these lines. Just a week earlier, Tshokolo had been in the witness stand; he was a teetotaller, he had testified, and had never set foot in a tavern. He knew Fusi, he said, because Fusi drank in a tavern across the street from his house and he would see Fusi when he looked through the window. But they had never spoken to one another.

I read the discrepancy between their respective testimonies and I wince. How hard could it have been for Fusi and Tshokolo to make sure to tell the same story? The trial began in late November 1992. It was not until February 1993 that Tshokolo took the stand. Tshokolo was livid that Fusi had led the police to him. But could they not have made peace and used those months to ensure that their tales aligned?

Fusi has told me that he was gutted before and during his trial. The news of Amos's death was still fresh; and he had been chronically ill and spent time in hospital. But his memories do not tell half of what was happening to him, I now see. To be so disarmed, so powerless, so confused; to be unable to collaborate with Tshokolo in the telling of a remotely consistent story. Fusi must have been terrifyingly alone.

The prosecutor does not have to break a sweat to show that Fusi and Tshokolo are lying. The fish is squirming in its narrow barrel; all Visser need do is shoot.

On reading further I see that Fusi must have been in even deeper trouble than his failure to sync his story with Tshokolo's suggests.

Recall that in the tale he tells of 2 April, he was at home when Sikhalo knocked on the door because he was ill and had taken off from work. Had Sikhalo come on another morning, a morning on which Fusi had been healthy, he would have been behind the cashier's till at Checkers, and Sikhalo would have found an empty house.

And the rest of Fusi's life would have turned out very differently.

But from his testimony in court another story emerges. His illness, it seems, was considerably more serious than a passing malady.

During the course of his cross-examination, Fusi tells Judge Malherbe that he was chronically ill at the time of his arrest.

'What sort of illness did you have?' Malherbe asks.

'I had headaches at certain times and also pain here in my side,' he replies.

And as Malherbe questions him further it emerges that he has left his job at Checkers because of his recurring illness; indeed, he went to Thokoza for the month of January not to spend time with Sikhalo Ncala, but to see a traditional doctor he hoped would cure him. And when he returned from his medical pilgrimage, his brother, Amos, supported him because Fusi worked at Checkers no more.

In the tale he recounted to me, the time before his arrest was the best of his life. He had a good job and he was flush. He had his brother, the beloved Amos, his cousin, Khulu, and his dear friend, Sengata. He adored these boys; each weekend the four went drinking and pursued girls, their pockets full of their wages.

It was not so. The Fusi on the witness stand is a young man who has been felled by pain in his head and in his side; it has robbed him of his job and sent him hunting for a cure. He is unemployed and penniless and reliant on his brother for food and shelter.

He is, it seems, a most unreliable guide, not just to what happened on 2 April 1992, but to the state he was in at that time.

Whether the roots of his illness lay in his emotional condition is impossible to say. But he had spent his teenage years with a violent father who had made him poor. He and Amos had had to stand on their own two feet and make their own home. I had been struck, when he first told me his story, by the contrast between the wretchedness of his condition and the sublimity of his memories. Now I have come to see that these memories are best treated with scepticism.

In retrospect, the most moving moment in the story Fusi first told me about 2 April was the beginning: the day had started with Fusi's father sending Thabo Motaung to see to his ailing son. He had fabricated an act of kindness, his father's kindness, and placed it at the start of the day.

Twenty-eight

When I phone Orsmond Aviation a woman answers.

'I am writing about a shooting incident that took place outside Ret Orsmond's home twenty-five years ago,' I explain. 'I want to ask him if he'll talk to me about what he remembers.'

'I remember it like it was yesterday,' the woman says. 'I am Ret's daughter, Kate. The shooting took place on 2 April 1992. I was seven years old. I was thinking about it just moments before you phoned. Actually, I think about it every day.'

Two pools of memory, entirely incompatible, have lain side by side, year in and year out, each quite oblivious of the other.

Tshokolo Mokoena and Fusi Mofokeng have most likely brushed shoulders with Kate Orsmond in Bethlehem's town centre, or with Ret or Mary Orsmond, or with their foreman or their workshop manager. There is little chance that they would recognise one another; Fusi and Tshokolo last clapped eyes on Mary and Ret in court a quarter of a century ago. Fusi and Tshokolo's lives have been shaped by their conviction for a murder of which they knew nothing. The Orsmonds' lives have been shaped by their memory of the day the family came within a hair's breadth of extinction because of what they believed to be the rage of a disgruntled employee.

The Orsmond pool of memory is not quite stable. Mary and Ret divorced several years after the shooting, which probably accounts for the discrepancies in what they recall; I guess that when people do not speak much, the stories they tell drift off in different directions.

The way Ret remembers it, the family almost died for the play-money in his children's board game. Somebody told him the story – whether his former wife Mary, who heard it in court, or the investigating officer, with whom they spoke again and again, he no longer recalls. Tshokolo caught wind from a fellow worker that piles of money lay around his employer's house. But there were never piles of money just lying about and so somebody had surmised – and, again, Ret cannot recall who worked it out – that one of the black workers had seen the kids' Monopoly money on the floor and mistaken it for the real thing.

The workers at the airfield often had reason to wander into the Orsmonds' home, for they were routinely called upon to help the family with domestic chores. There was a closed-circuit radio at the house in Ballyduff set to the same frequency as the radios the business used. If Kate needed a lift to dance class, or if her brothers were home from boarding school and were going to see friends, somebody would get on the radio and ask a worker to come and fetch them.

And so an employee – wide-eyed, unschooled and none too smart – had come to fetch Kate or one of her brothers, or to paint a door, or to install an appliance, and had seen money strewn all over the floor. The rumour did the rounds until it reached the ears of Tshokolo Mokoena, whose rage was growing, or so the tale goes.

Ret Orsmond is sitting in his office at the airfield when he tells me this tale. Oddly, he looks exactly as I imagined. The lenses of his aviator sunglasses are lost somewhere in the locks of his thick hair and he is still wearing his bomber jacket; just that morning, he flew his wife and his seventeen-year-old sons to Bethlehem from their holiday home in Plettenberg Bay; he used the twin-engine reserved for flying the family. He is a maverick entrepreneur who pursued his boyhood dream of flying in the face of furious paternal resistance. And he made a great success of it. He is courteous and warm and speaks as softly and unassumingly as Fusi does; and as he entertains the thought that his world might have died for the accoutrement of a board game, he blushes.

Mary Orsmond has no recollection of the Monopoly money. By her lights, the motive for the attack was not robbery, just revenge. The three men whom Simon Motaung spotted sneaking around the back of the house at 4:15 p.m. were hiding in a deep ditch behind the tennis court. Their task was to kill Mary and Kate and whoever else was in the house. The ones in the driveway were to kill Ret when he got home.

It was an unseasonably hot day, Mary remembers. Kate had spent much of the morning in the pool. Mother and daughter had taken a nap in the early afternoon. The whole house was open – the windows, the sliding doors.

Mary was a devout Roman Catholic back then. Now she has married a preacher and has come to believe that God is everywhere; one does not need to go to church to find Him. He was there in Ballyduff that afternoon, she says, for if He was not the men in the ditch would have figured out that the sliding doors were open and simply walked into the house.

Her sons might so easily have been at home. It happens that they were out with friends. What if they had been splashing around the swimming pool or playing tennis? Would their presence have alerted the men in the ditch to the fact that the house was all opened up and theirs for the taking?

It strikes me as I listen to Mary Orsmond that the image left most vividly in her mind, returning to her day after day, standing in for the whole grim affair, causing her and her children to die a thousand deaths, is an image nobody actually saw but was only ever surmised: Sikhalo Ncala, Donald Makhura and Mandla Fokazi waiting in the ditch behind the tennis court, until the sound of gunshots caused them to flee.

Nobody at Orsmond Aviation remembers Tshokolo Mokoena very well. Perhaps that should not be unexpected; he only worked there for ten months and it was a long time ago. But the extent to which he has faded surprises me, given the centrality of his place in the Orsmonds' collective memory.

When I ask Ret Orsmond what he remembers of Tshokolo Mokoena he pauses and thinks for a long time.

'Nothing,' he says. 'I don't remember him at all.'

'Do you remember the circumstances of his departure? It seems from the court transcript that it may have been ugly, that there was a scene.'

'We had a strike here once,' Ret replies. 'Maybe he was involved in that.'

He leaves the office to ask the woman at reception about the date of the strike; and it occurs to me while I wait that many of the people in this building have worked in this business for decades; it is an intimate organism that has grown from one man's love of guiding a machine through the air.

'The strike was in 2004,' he says when he returns: twelve years after Tshokolo left. And when I ask if there is anyone here who worked closely with Mokoena, he calls in a man called Tom Bezuidenhout, his workshop manager for the past forty years.

'I remember him well,' Tom says, but his body is as stiff as a corpse as he sits on Ret's couch, and his gaze is full of suspicion.

'He was militant. He and Daniel's brother stoked one another up. He was, how can I say, he was his own person, an intellectual. He did not just conform. For example, he wore his own cap, not the hard-topped cap we issue to the workers, but his own cap.'

'Who was Daniel's brother?' I ask.

'Another militant one. Very strong. Very independent. Very disgruntled.'

He pauses a long time and to fill the silence he continues.

'Ja, he was different, that one. It was in the way he dressed, and in this stoking up he did. I was not involved in the spray-painting. Something happened to make him leave, but I don't remember what.'

'Mike Williams was chief engineer,' Ret says. 'He would have worked with him. Mike did not take too much hassle. If somebody complained about wages, he would tell them where to get off. Maybe Mike fired him. I can't swear to it. But I think that's what I remember.'

Mike Williams, who is still in Bethlehem, working for another company, will not take my calls. Perhaps he does not want to talk about firing an employee who allegedly grew so bitter as to return with an army of men and automatic weapons. Perhaps there are wounds at which it is better not to pick, especially in the company of a curious stranger.

When I do eventually manage to track Mike Williams down, he is on a satellite phone in another country and the line is poor. He tells me he remembers nothing, nothing all, and as I push and prod he grows ever more insistent that he cannot recall a thing.

But later, when I talk to Kate Orsmond, she is more candid than these wary men. Throughout her childhood, she tells me, she understood that Mike Williams and Tshokolo had fought bitterly for some time, and that their feud ended when Tshokolo was fired.

I speak to a man named Petrus Motsoeneng. Ret hired him on the day Orsmond Aviation opened and for as long as anyone could remember he had been the company's foreman. He had been the immediate boss of every black employee Orsmond Aviation signed up in a period spanning more than forty years.

He is old now, and has retired, and we meet in his home in Bohlokong, just a stone's throw from Fusi's house, on a Sunday afternoon. Three generations of his family wander in and out of the living room, some to watch television, others to listen in on his tale and to offer their own comments.

At one point, I offer the story of the Monopoly money and ask how common it was for the workers to talk of what they saw in the Orsmond home.

Before Petrus Motsoeneng can reply, his daughter speaks in his stead.

'We all thought that white people's homes were strewn with cash,' she says. 'We compared their lives with our lives, their many things with our few things. This business of whether somebody saw the kids' play money is a red herring. We simply believed that there would be money all over the place. You did not have to see it with your own eyes.'

As for Petrus Motsoeneng, he nods when his daughter speaks, but he passes no comment.

And when he does begin to talk of that time, he holds forth with authority, does Petrus Motsoeneng, but he is an old man telling tales. Tshokolo Mokoena was not fired, he says; no, he wandered off a few days before the shooting at Ballyduff; he simply stopped reporting for work. And on the morning of 2 April, he continues, he himself, Petrus Motsoeneng, was in town, running an errand, and stopped to fill his car with petrol. Opposite him in the station forecourt was a bakkie with a white canopy, and as he passed the back of the vehicle he saw Tshokolo Mokoena in the cargo area, along with several other men. He greeted the errant Mokoena and Mokoena greeted him back; and he noted to himself that this AWOL employee must be up to a lot of nonsense.

It strikes me as I drive away, Motsoeneng and his daughter waving me goodbye, that if you begin with a single base assumption – that Tshokolo Mokoena brought the men in the bakkie to wreak revenge – any tale might grow, even in the heart of an honest-to-goodness man remembering the past as best as he is able.

Kate Orsmond was in her bedroom when the shooting began. Already, she was uneasy, if not downright afraid, for Simon and Martha had been in a state of near hysteria when she and her mother got home. Now, with the sound of automatic gunfire in the air, she ran and hid behind the curtains. And that is where Mary found her. She picked Kate up, carried her through the house, and literally threw her into Martha's arms.

'Go to the safe, fetch the gun, take the child and run!' Kate recalls Mary shouting.

Martha did not go to the safe; she simply took Kate by the hand and ran. Halfway across the garden, she stopped and turned, her hand still firmly gripping Kate's, and scuttled back into the house. She must have been so afraid, Kate surmises, that she lost all sense of what she was doing.

Kate never really recovered, she tells me. For years after, she would look behind the curtains whenever she came home. Still, now, all these years later, the sound of gunshots or crackers leaves her ill at ease. The incident has taken up a permanent abode inside her, sometimes in her conscious thoughts, sometimes less detectably, in the ways she apprehends the world. Her parents sent her to a child psychologist and that assisted her a little. But the greatest help, it seems, came from others, like Simon and Martha, who loved her like she was their own child.

And the Orsmonds must indeed have trusted Simon and Martha deeply. In the face of mortal danger, the safest image Mary Orsmond could conjure was of Martha running across her garden, a gun in one hand, her daughter's hand in the other.

Their lives went on, Kate tells me, and as the incident receded, democracy came. She was ten years old, she thinks, when her school began admitting black children for the first time. She promptly made friends with a black girl, Joyce Mokoena, and brought her home. She still talks to Joyce from time to time, she says. Joyce now works in police forensics. A few years ago, there was a break-in at Orsmond Aviation and, lo and behold, it was Joyce who came to sweep for fingerprints.

Back then, she says, when they were still children, she brought Joyce home one day after school. They were sitting side by side on the couch watching television, when Martha walked in.

As she took in the scene, Martha froze and stared. 'Your place is on the floor,' Kate remembers her saying sharply to Joyce. 'Not on the couch next to the white girl.'

I am wondering what to make of this scene. Did it speak to Martha's fierce devotion, not just to Kate, but to the system that made the Orsmonds high and the Motaungs low? Or was Martha afraid that if the white adults saw a black girl on their couch next to their daughter they would take offence? Martha is dead now, I am thinking to myself, and has taken the answers to such questions to the grave, when Kate begins telling me of another person who helped her in the wake of the shootings: Warrant Officer Steyn.

After the attack, the Orsmonds did not sleep under their own roof for another week. They spent the first night with Mary's parents and then left the next day for Mauritius on a family holiday they had long planned.

When they finally returned to their home, Warrant Officer Steyn was there waiting for them. He promised that he would place an all-night patrol at the bottom of the driveway, not just that night, but the next, and the night after that. Before going to sleep each evening, Kate would look through the curtains and see the blue lights; she drew a great deal of comfort from this, she says.

Warrant Officer Steyn kept visiting the house in Ballyduff, Kate recalls. He appeared to worry that the two men who escaped on 2 April were still out there and might come back. He would walk around the property, his eyes cast always on vulnerabilities: the locks, the windows, the ditch behind the tennis court.

He took a special interest in Kate, it seems. Whenever he visited he asked whether she was sleeping, whether she had nightmares, whether the sessions with the child psychologist were of help.

Two years after the incident, on 27 April 1994, South Africans of all races went to the polls to elect a democratic government. Ret and Mary left their home at about midday to vote. On TV that morning they had watched the queues at the polling stations grow forever longer and they warned that they may be gone a long while.

It was about lunchtime when Kate and her brother, George, who were swimming in the pool, heard their names being called. They swam to the side and looked out to find Warrant Officer Steyn standing in the garden.

'Take everyone inside and lock the doors,' he instructed George. 'This is not a good day to be outside.'

Of all the images Kate Orsmond has left me, this one remains among the most vivid in my mind.

In the dense forest through which Fusi Mofokeng has cut a path, so many other trails run. Those of the Orsmonds, Mary, Ret and Kate; those of Simon Motaung and his wife, Martha; that of Fusi's sister Victoria and of his brother-in-law, Sikhalo Ncala; of his mother, Maletsatsi Letia Mbele; of the charismatic Donald Makhura; of the parents of the late Constable Oosthuizen. Each of these trails might consume the length of a book.

Among them are the paths of Steyn and Robertshaw, two warriors who move back and forth each day across a frontier. On one side are the homes of black folk and the police stations of the eastern Free State; here they break down doors and lie and betray; they fasten young men in chains and loosen the faucets of a steady flow of pain.

On the other side are girls like Kate, so very exposed in their suburban homes, so urgently in need of protection.

How might it be to cross that frontier each day, to get home at night and shower, washing the violence and the love that is one's work off one's skin? How might a book about that sound and feel?

A quarter of a century after the events of 2 April, Fusi and Tshokolo walked onto the premises of the business in downtown Bethlehem run by Colin Anthony Packenham Robertshaw. They were accompanied by a journalist from the Wits Justice Project, Ruth Hopkins. Hopkins asked Robertshaw whether he remembered the two men and he looked at them blankly. She spoke their names. Once he understood what was going on he grew angry, and what came from his tongue, sharp and unadorned, was what I take to be the most vivid image in his mind associated with that day.

'You shot a policeman dead on the ground,' he said. 'We dug the bullets up; there was a trail of bullets in the ground where they stood over the policeman and shot him in his head.'

It is an execution he is describing. And as I listen to the recording of his voice Ruth Hopkins has given me, I recall something Paul Heymanns, one of the two lawyers who represented the accused, said to me when I interviewed him in his chambers in Bloemfontein.

'This was not an easy case for me personally,' Heymanns had said. 'This will not be reflected in the record, but outside the formal court proceedings, in the background, the police were saying that this was a setup, that these guys deliberately hung around looking suspicious to draw the police.

'So here I was representing these men in this very heightened emotional atmosphere; it was being whispered that these bastards were out to execute our young officers.'

All these years later, I think that this remains the understanding of the men who beat Tshokolo Mokoena, tormented Fusi Mofokeng, deceived Donald Makhura and forced a squirming Thabo Motaung into the witness box. No wonder Steyn kept coming back to see to Kate Orsmond; the men who descended on her house intended to take as many white lives as they could, he believed, and two of them were still out there.

Twenty-nine

What happened on 2 April 1992? Why did Sikhalo Ncala and his comrades come to Bethlehem?

When he testified in Malherbe's court, Sikhalo Ncala acknowledged that it was indeed he who had walked onto the Orsmond property that morning asking Simon Motaung to see his employer. And when Clement Ndabeni took the stand, he acknowledged that he had accompanied Sikhalo. But Sikhalo insisted that his intent had been benign; he was using his brief time in Bethlehem to look for work.

Sikhalo acknowledged, too, that he and his companions from Johannesburg were again outside the Orsmond residence in the afternoon, but he argued that this was sheer coincidence. It is a coincidence that strains credulity. The Orsmond residence is on an out-of-the-way dirt road beyond the edge of town. That Ncala and Ndabeni happened to wander onto the property in the morning while looking for work is difficult enough to swallow. That they ended up in the driveway of the very same property in the afternoon is too much.

As I read his testimony, it seems Sikhalo believed that the game was up. He did not even try to give his evidence an aura of credibility. For instance, in his cross-examination of Ncala, the prosecutor noted that, on arriving in Bethlehem on the morning of 2 April, Ncala had stopped first at the house of Amos and Fusi's father, David Mofokeng, for he thought that David's sons still lived with him. The door was answered by a man called Bernard Motwai. Motwai had testified earlier in the trial. When he opened the door to Sikhalo Ncala, he had told the court, Ncala had asked for Fusi Mofokeng.

'Why did you say you were looking for Fusi and not Amos?' Visser asked.

'There is no difference between Fusi and Amos,' Ncala replied, 'because they are brothers and they live together.'

And although not reflected in the record, it appears that Ncala chuckled at his own testimony.

'I see you're laughing again,' Visser observed. 'What's so funny?'

'I am not laughing,' Ncala replied. 'It is just my disposition.'

'This is a very serious matter,' Malherbe intervened. 'There is nothing to laugh about. Do you understand?'

'I do, but I wasn't laughing.'

'Bernard Motwai gave evidence that you asked for Fusi, not Amos,' Visser continued. 'Your advocate did not object. Now you say they're brothers and there's no difference between them. You must remember that the people listening to your evidence are not children.'

'I am aware of that, Your Honour.'

'I put it to you that you choose Amos now because you've heard in the interim that he died and is not here to give evidence.'

Ncala does not reply.

And what of the TRC? Having read the trial transcript, it is hard not to take a dim view of the Amnesty Committee hearing in Welkom in 1998. Judge Selwyn Miller, who chaired the hearing, kept asking whether the bonnet of the bakkie was open and whether the SDU men were travelling on a dirt road. One can surmise that he read a couple of pages of a summary of the judgment and took in only the matter of the bonnet and the dirt road; or that he speed-read the whole thing so carelessly that he forgot most of its content; or that he found much of the material in the summary of the judgment inconvenient and decided to ignore it.

These were SDU members on a mission, after all; that they were so had been confirmed by the ANC, which was paying for their lawyers. It was an uncontroversial case. The Amnesty Committee's workload was massive; there were so many cases to get through. To slow down and scrutinise a long judgment when the case appeared to be open and shut must have seemed an irrational use of time. The Amnesty Committee's business, it seems, was not to determine what had happened on 2 April, but to rubber-stamp decisions that had been made.

And so the story the applicants chose to tell the Amnesty Committee came to constitute the facts of the matter. The bits of the tale they sliced off simply vanished. Thus, Sikhalo Ncala was not seen on the Orsmond property hours before the shooting, asking when Ret Orsmond would be home. And Tshokolo Mokoena had never worked for Orsmond Aviation, let alone left acrimoniously two months earlier. And the bakkie had not parked at the end of the Orsmonds' drive, three of its occupants having walked around the back of the house, causing such alarm among the neighbourhood's employees that the police were called.

There was a hiccup, of course; if the story were true, two innocent men would be left in prison. They had more than a decade still to serve for a crime the Amnesty Committee deemed they had not committed. For if the others had indeed made full disclosures, and thus qualified for amnesty, Fusi Mofokeng and Tshokolo Mokoena had to be innocent. What to do? The amnesty machine seems not to have been designed to imbibe the unexpected. It was struggling enough just to process the routine. And so it simply ground on, leaving the two it deemed innocent to keep writing their ceaseless letters.

The Bethlehem men seemed terribly ill informed about the amnesty process. Did they know that, had they told the Committee that they had tried to rob the Orsmonds, they would still have received amnesty? All they had to say was that they were doing so under the instructions of their commander, their purpose to raise cash for their cause. And they could have testified that any one of them was their commander and had made the decision off his own bat. This would have been good enough for the Amnesty Committee.

Did they know that all the editing they did was not only unnecessary but would leave two of their number in jail?

One person in the community hall in Welkom that day did bring some of the missing facts to the commissioners' attention: the eloquent and unforgiving father of Constable Oosthuizen, one of three men shot to death on 2 April. Listening to a story that was part incomplete, part untrue, his anger rose. By the time he took the stand he was positively furious. The Amnesty Committee had by now long since learnt how to interpret such fury. It belonged to those who, understandably, but disappointingly, could not forgive.

What of Fusi and Tshokolo's connection to the events of 2 April? Did they have anything to do with the fact that the men from Johannesburg spent the day scouting the Orsmond property?

Thabo Motaung testified that he was present when Fusi and Tshokolo conspired to bring the Johannesburg men to Bethlehem to rob the Orsmonds. But his testimony reeks. That it was coerced from him is written all over it. Indeed, it was the prosecutor who told Motaung's story, Motaung's tortured reluctance to play along quite obvious. His evidence should surely be discounted.

But that is not the end of the matter. If the Johannesburg men did indeed arrive at the Orsmond property with ill intent – and it is certain that they did – how did they come to target the Orsmonds?

The police took Fusi from his home late on the evening of 2 April. By 3:00 the following morning he was in a police vehicle pointing the way to Tshokolo's house. The police dragged Tshokolo from his bed, shackled him to a chair and beat him. Why did Fusi lead them immediately to Tshokolo? At the trial, he said they asked him with whom he drank. Why pick out Tshokolo when he drank with so many others? And why did the police go after Tshokolo with such urgency?

By the time I met him, Fusi's account of 2 April contained a slightly more credible story. The police wanted to know who had visited the house that day, he said. Two women had come, but they did not interest the police. It was the men who had captured their attention. Thabo Motaung had come in the morning, Tshokolo Mokoena in the late afternoon; and so the interest of the police had alighted immediately upon them.

The question remains why the police pounced so quickly on Tshokolo in particular. What about Amos? They were happy to release him first thing in the morning of 3 April and had no business with him again. Fusi says this is because Amos had an alibi; he was at work all day on 2 April. But what sort of alibi is that? The conspiracy of which Fusi and Tshokolo stood accused took place before 2 April. Where the conspirators were when the shooting outside the Orsmonds took place is not at the heart of the matter.

And so the question remains: Why did Fusi lead the police so quickly to Tshokolo, and not to anybody else? And why, when they arrested Tshokolo, were they so certain that he was involved?

Thirty

It is a Saturday evening in early September 2014. I am heading south on the highway along the border between the Free State and Lesotho. It is a magnificent road in the daylight hours. Behind vast, flat fields of green lucerne, Lesotho's mountains rise to the sky. They are purple and blue and in the shadows almost black and they climb the horizon with thundering majesty. You are on the very cusp of the plateau and the escarpment, and you feel you are nudging a membrane between two planets; at any moment you will break through to find yourself in another world.

But it is pitch-dark now, and all I see is the tunnel my headlights carve.

Six weeks have passed since the transcript of the trial arrived in my inbox. I have spent the days in between at my desk, half a world from here, reading page upon page.

At first, I sent Fusi the transcript and requested that he read it. But within days he wrote to say that he had stopped; he was struggling with the Afrikaans, he explained, which puzzled me a little, as he has been around Afrikaans all his life.

A couple of weeks later I phoned to let him know when I would be coming to South Africa. My reading of the transcript had led to so many questions, I said; I had lost count of how many I had to ask and some of them were so troubling that I lay awake at night.

He offered immediately to take two days off work to give us all the time we needed.

I'm sure that won't be necessary, I said. Let's meet at the end of the working day and take it from there.

Now, I am here. I arrived in South Africa just this morning. But he has told me on the phone that he is not in Bethlehem; he is in Maseru, the capital of Lesotho, with his wife-to-be, Teboho, and her ten-year-old daughter, Lebo. He is so very excited. It is his first time outside of South Africa. He is in another country. The people are different, he says. The very air feels different when he breathes it into his lungs. Will I join him? He is with family of Teboho's. He would love for me to meet them.

I am staying in a village not far from Bethlehem. It is in fact just a stone's throw from Fusi's beloved Oorsprong. I would settle in and wait for him, I said, and suggested that he and his family stop at my place for Sunday lunch on their way home from their travels.

He thanked me and said that he would very much like to come for lunch, but would I please join him now, tonight, in Maseru. It was so special here, he said, and his voice was animated in a way I had not heard before. This quiet and cautious and so very deliberate man was acting on a whim, fuelled, it seemed, by joy.

Infected by his enthusiasm, I agreed.

Dusk had already fallen and Maseru was two hours away at least.

'Just get in your car and go,' he told me. 'Go now. Phone me when you are thirty kilometres away; I will meet you on the Lesotho side of the border post.'

I drive south into the darkness with Lesotho out of sight on my left and the Free State on my right; thirty kilometres from the border crossing, I phone Fusi on his mobile to find it goes to voicemail. I phone again when I am fifteen kilometres away and once more as I wait on the South African side of the border post. And then I am through and on the other side and the evening is entirely deserted, just the road from the border, empty, without pedestrians, Maseru itself obscured by the hill ahead.

I park on the shoulder, put on my hazard lights and wait for Fusi to call. The world around me seems awfully lonely and all of a sudden I feel spooked and turn the key in the ignition and drive back into South Africa.

Heading north, the farmland and the mountains invisible, the oddest feeling falls upon me. I felt so estranged from Fusi as the pages of the trial transcript turned. The more I read, the less I could guess what was in his heart.

Was he innocent, as he had spent the last twenty-two years explaining? Or had he forgotten the fact of his involvement in what had happened on 2 April? It is certainly not inconceivable. His outrage at being swept one night from his house and convicted of murder might well have transmogrified, over time, into a false belief that he had had nothing to do with the crime. I simply do not know. The trial transcript had informed me of so much. But it had not revealed whether Fusi had been implicated and it certainly did not tell me what was happening inside him.

Has my reading of the transcript caused him to fear me? What does he think I have found? He was so insistent that I drive through the night to Maseru only to vanish without a word.

I stop in Ficksburg and find a steakhouse in which to eat dinner. As I wait for my meal a feeling of foolishness comes over me. Fusi's unexpected disappearance, for which there are a thousand possible reasons, almost all of them innocuous, has caused such trouble. I understand, if only in flashes, that the hostility I feel may well be my own. I have spent the last six weeks unpicking a man's story, and although it has been a silent and solitary endeavour, it has about it a whiff of violence.

I am paying the bill when my phone rings.

'I was having my hair cut,' Fusi says, his voice anxious and concerned. 'I did not realise that there was no phone reception where I was. I walked out of the barber and there were six missed calls from you.'

I should turn around and come back, he tells me; he would like very much for me still to come.

But I am far from the border crossing now, and it is late, and I tell I will see him for lunch tomorrow.

He says okay, but I can tell from his voice that he is disappointed and upset, the simplest arrangement having gone so awry on this light and joyful evening.

At lunch the next day he is as merry as I have ever seen him. He arrives in his red Toyota, Teboho in the passenger seat, Lebo in the back, a trailer for their luggage tagging behind. He hired the trailer from a rental agency, he tells me. There were so many things to take to Lesotho, and so many things to take home. Leaving without the trailer would have been unthinkable: where would the human beings have gone?

The rental company wanted to charge him R600 to attach the trailer to the car. But he had looked at it closely and then at the back of his Toyota, and he had found a way to do it himself: he removed the car's bumper, stored it safely in the boot, and harnessed the trailer to the car's naked frame.

I have for a while now admired his absorption in mechanical matters. During the untold hours we have spent alone on the road, he has explained to me, with the lucidity of one who is thinking always of these matters as his mind ticks over, why our car moves forward when I press down on the accelerator, what happens to the engine when I change gears, why the brakes stop the car, what causes the electronic tag on the windscreen to beep when we pass through a toll gate, the mechanism that connects the reverse gear to the white lights on the car's tail, what the 'cell' is in a cellular network and why my phone will never receive a signal sent directly from the transmission tower of a rival company.

I have told him that I did not think much about these matters and knew next to nothing of the machines I used every day.

He flashed me a look, a moment of unguarded astonishment, and showed me what he was thinking: that in the body alongside him was a soul not just different from his own, but profoundly strange.

And I glimpsed, very dimly, something of what had happened inside him since his release from prison. He had been away for so long; now, he had walked into a world whose machines had changed and each offered itself to him anew for understanding.

I bring chairs out onto the porch and the family settles itself in the sun while we wait for lunch to finish cooking. I am sitting among them, but it feels as if I have drifted up and am watching them from the line of the tin roof. I am marvelling at what Fusi has done since his release. The feeling of alienation that descended upon him in his first days of freedom – his lying awake at night listening to the noises of a world that was foreign; his daytime excursions through a town that was both his home town and a place grown strange – has long receded. Indeed, he has calibrated himself to the world, and the people around him, far better than most of those who have spent their adult lives free. It has been just three years and in this short time he has conjured from nothing what I see before me: a paterfamilias, benign and happy, his loved ones about him, a successful family excursion in tow.

When he and Tshokolo were released from prison, each was given a lowly job in the Bethlehem municipality, an apology, after a fashion, offered by members of the Free State's political elite, for their heedless suffering. Tshokolo was employed as a welder at a municipal workshop, Fusi as an assistant mechanic.

Among the villages whose road graders and transport vehicles Fusi was assigned to service was Rosendal, the hamlet in which we now sit, waiting to eat lunch. It is a long journey from Bethlehem, well over half an hour, the roads poor, the driving slow. En route, he would pass within spitting distance of Oorsprong.

As the wide blond world opened up and the mountains of his childhood came into view, the feelings that seized him were so commanding that he would stop his car and walk into the veld. In the shade of a tree he would sit and close his eyes and listen to the silence and open them again to see the land he had walked as a boy.

He made a habit of doing this, each time he was called to Rosendal: stopping the car when he came near to Oorsprong, going to sit in the veld. He is not sure he knows what he was thinking when he sat there; indeed, what came over him perhaps arrived in a medium that bore little resemblance to words. In part, he thinks, he was making up for the time in prison, where there was no silence, not even in the depth of the night.

He knew that those hours of solitude, so urgent and so necessary that he was driven to seek them, were integral to his healing. Although the healing must surely have begun much earlier, when Thabang Mokotedi believed that he was innocent, and when Gerrit Steyn taught him that to fight with the past would kill him.

And yet it would be a mistake to say that he became Zen-like or otherworldly, for in this state of healing he grew ever so pragmatic, perhaps even a little cynical. He joined the ANC, whose indifference to his plight had been nothing less than contemptuous, for he lived in a town whose public service was dominated by the ruling party, and he knew that if he wanted to advance he must get to know the right people.

And so in the months preceding elections he would come home from work, change clothes and go out into the streets to canvass for a party about which he must surely have felt ambivalent. And on Sundays he accompanied Teboho to church, despite the ebbing of his religious feeling, for it had been decided that the ANC's campaigners must be visible in places of worship.

In these extramural activities there was not just pragmatism but the highest degree of discipline. So many hours of his days were spent paving, with a meticulousness that did not falter, the road to his advance.

And advanced he has. Within a year of leaving prison, he was promoted from his lowly job, and six months later he was promoted again. On the day we meet for lunch he has his eye on a managerial position in the municipality's logistics department and he is certain that if he plays his cards right he will get it. Having emerged from prison in a state of poverty he is making his steady way into his country's middle class.

I wonder whence his competence comes. He walked into freedom aged forty-four, his last stint of gainful employment two decades in the past. Around him, much of the world was jobless, grown men lining his street throughout the daylight hours. And yet he worked as if he had been working all his life, his technical and political smarts as sharp as the crack of a whip.

Lunch is ready and I serve. There is steak and sweet potato and a salad. I give Teboho her plate and sit down next to her. She is plump and middle-aged and very quiet, much quieter than I would like. For the longest time now, my presence has made her uneasy. She looks at me curiously but is not sure what to say. I have not been any more competent. I have asked her about her work – for a pitiful wage, she manages a crèche a few blocks from the home she and Fusi share – and about her ambitions to start her own business, a hairdresser's salon. Neither conversation has gone very far.

But now, in the wake of their successful excursion, she is positively loquacious. She tells me that half her family is from Lesotho, half from South Africa, and she relates something of the history that caused them to end up on opposite sides of the border. Fusi has no relatives in Lesotho and the international dimensions of Teboho's family network fill him with excitement.

Some eighteen months back, before he and Teboho met, we were on the road, where we were going I no longer recall, when he began talking, out of the blue, of the need to pace himself.

During his first months of freedom, he said, he was kept awake at night by the thought that he had no wife, no home of his own, no children. The idea that he might grow old without a family filled him with dread.

What do I do, he thought to himself: find a woman much younger than I am, a woman of childbearing age? Do I begin siring a family at the age of forty-five or forty-six?

I do not yet have a job that will permit me to feed and clothe them and educate them, he thought. I need to accept my situation. I need to under-stand that I have been in prison and missed out on having children. It is illogical to try and take everything that was denied me. I will simply trip over my feet and fall down.

He told me all of this in so uncharacteristic a manner, re-enacting the dialogue that had bounced night after night against the walls of his head.

And then, on my next visit, there was Teboho and her daughter Lebo, and her nineteen-year-old son, Thabo, and they and Fusi were all living together in the very modest home Teboho rented in Bohlokong. He was absorbed in the business of supporting them and this required managing levels of debt that appeared to be driving him crazy.

He had bought Teboho a Samsung smartphone and Thabo a Blackberry, both on credit, the terms nothing less than extortionary. As we drove each day across the Free State, visiting one-time prison inmates from Fusi's past, and the court in Bloemfontein where he had been tried, and the hall in Welkom that had hosted his TRC hearing, and elderly warders in their retirement homes, he pulled at the skin on his fingers and stared constantly at a point on the horizon, his face the very picture of worry.

It was on the tip of my tongue to ask why he was doing this to himself. These fancy phones were luxuries, surely: could Thabo not wait for his while the debt on Teboho's was being paid down?

Before the words were out of my mouth, I was struck by my own obtuseness and held my tongue. He was going through this pain to show them that he was for keeps. It was so plain once I saw it. He could not have children of his own, but if the down payment was sufficiently hefty, the risk sharp enough to put sweat on his brow, the children could become his, truly, his love for them as deep as if they were his own.

On the afternoon the family joins me for lunch Thabo is away. He has just found work hundreds of kilometres from here as an unskilled labourer on a construction site. Fusi worries about the distance and about the work. Thabo is a small boy: he stands no more than five foot six, his frame narrow and thin. Will the work entail heavy lifting, Fusi wonders. He knows from his own experience that pushing a wheelbarrow packed with slabs of concrete or piled with bricks is work for a man with broad shoulders and a strong back. He has told Thabo that if he is not coping he must get in a taxi and come home. There is no shame in refusing work that will hurt you, he has counselled; it may take time, but we will find something more in line with your strengths and your skills.

It is not easy, though. Thabo has had diabetes since his early teenage years. It went undiagnosed for far too long, and, when it was diagnosed, it was not treated with competence. A sickly teenager, he fell so far behind at school that he threw in the towel and dropped out.

Thabo is a challenge, Fusi has told me. To find a vocation for a frail and poorly educated boy is hard. If anybody knows anything about South Africa it is that the country cannot provide nearly enough work. He thinks that Thabo may have a future as a truck driver. There is plenty of work and it is not badly paid. He bought Thabo the books from which to study for his licence and in the evenings they went through them together line by line. But when the day of the test came, Thabo discovered to his horror that it was in English, not Sesotho, and that he was sure to fail.

It is just a small setback, Fusi has said. Out in Steynsrus the test is conducted in Sesotho. If the construction job doesn't work out and Thabo returns home, we will make a truck driver of him yet.

This business of steering a child into adulthood is not easy, and who knows whether he will succeed, but Fusi takes to it like an old hand. During those years behind bars – when he himself was made to be a child, unable to decide when to turn out the lights, when to eat in the morning, when to exercise and when to rest – a father matured in his mental life, an imaginary Fusi rehearsed and rehearsed, waiting for a place in the world.

I have been in his presence when he has taken to admiring the life he has made. There is no arrogance in this, I don't think, and certainly no complacency; but there is wonder.

A quarter of a century ago there was Fusi and Amos, Khulu and Sengata. Amos and Khulu are dead, one because he drove drunk of an evening from Phuthaditjhaba, the other of Aids. As for Sengata, his life is something of a mess. He has children from three women and his attempts to support them perennially bankrupt him. And when he is flush he gambles away what he has. His body has become middle-aged, but his soul, it seems, has remained in the boy who stole his grandmother's car one Friday evening and drove through the night to a girl far away.

Many years ago, there were these four boys. From out of the blue a tragedy befell one of them; he was taken away and did not return for a very long time. Now, these decades later, he is the only one among them to partake with heart and soul in the regeneration of life, the ones he is shepherding borrowed from the seed of other men.

The family has eaten and left. Tomorrow is Monday; Lebo must go to school, Fusi and Teboho to work.

I wash the dishes, leave the house and walk to the village restaurant and bar. There is football on TV and an assortment of men has gathered. I order a drink and stare out of the window as the world darkens and the sun goes down.

Thirty-one

Fusi's place of work is on the edge of Bethlehem's town centre, just where the shops and the warehouses give way to suburban homes. At 4:30 p.m. sharp he emerges from the building and settles in the passenger seat of my car.

I have been rehearsing this conversation for more than a month. Now that I am finally here I am not sure how to begin and I end up choosing the most pragmatic of matters. His lawyers are preparing a case to have his criminal record expunged; if and when they succeed he wants to sue the state for wrongful conviction.

This course of action was lodged in his mind many years ago, long before he was released from prison. It was a running joke between Fusi and Thabang Mokotedi. 'You are suffering now,' Mokotedi would tell him over and again. 'But the whole business will end with a pot of gold. How many days have you been behind bars? It is coming up to five thousand. What is one day's suffering worth? R5 000 at least. I hope you will remember to spread the love.'

Now, I tell him that I do not want to do anything to damage his case. I am not even sure I want to continue writing the book at all, I say, until I have a better sense of what happened on 2 April.

He sits impassively, saying nothing, his body quite still.

I tell him I want to go through the version of events as he first recounted them to me.

The eight men leave Bethlehem in their bakkie in the late afternoon. They are just out of town, on the highway to Natal, when they see a police roadblock ahead of them. They turn left onto a dirt road. An unmarked car is following them and they grow increasingly nervous. And then all of a sudden a yellow police van is heading towards them. Clement stops the car, lifts the bonnet and peers under it. The police van stops, two cops get out, and Joe gives the order to shoot.

I tell him of what I have read in the transcript. It is barely plausible that the shooting took place outside the Orsmonds by coincidence, I say, because Sikhalo Ncala and Clement Ndabeni walked onto the Orsmond property in the morning asking if there was work.

'It was their strategy to agree to that,' Fusi says.

'But why?'

'Because Ncala wanted to distract attention from the others.'

'But this put much more attention on all of them. To say that Ncala and Ndabeni were there in morning is to say they were targeting that place.'

'I think maybe they blundered.'

I am not sure what to say next. Fusi's co-workers are now streaming out of the building and onto the street. Some head off in the direction of Bohlokong, ambling, at leisure, in no hurry to get home. Others wait in groups of two or three. Through the closed window come the sounds of muffled chatter.

I go on doggedly.

'There is something I don't understand,' I say. 'The bakkie was parked on the road outside the house a long time. All the black employees on that road were in a state of alarm. Sikhalo, Donald and Mandla then slipped around the back of the house. Then the bakkie moved into the Orsmond's front driveway. The police did not happen to be going by; they were

called because the neighbourhood was in a state of panic.'

'I think I vaguely remember the Ormond neighbour giving this evi-dence,' Fusi says. 'I have forgotten her name.'

'Sue Robertson,' I say.

He nods and then repeats her name, as if trying out the sound of it.

'It was not just Sue Robertson,' I continue. 'Three others gave similar testimony.'

'But I remember very clearly,' he replies. 'I remember Clement giving his testimony in court. He said they were driving on the Ballyduff road and when he saw a yellow police van coming he stopped the car and opened the bonnet.'

'That is in fact what he said at the TRC,' I say, 'when there were no eye-witnesses to disagree with him and whatever he said became the truth.'

Fusi stares ahead of him and sighs.

'We were all telling so many stories at the time of the trial,' he says. 'Some we were telling to each other in the cells, some we were telling the court. It is hard to keep track.'

'Another thing,' I continue. 'I did not know until I read the transcript that Tshokolo worked at Ormond Aviation for ten months, that he left just two months earlier because of a dispute over wages.'

He raises his eyebrows in surprise. 'No, he must have worked there much longer ago than that. Since we met the previous year, when he was gambling on horses, he worked in town and lived in Bohlokong.'

'He agreed on the witness stand that he left Ormond Aviation at the end of January 1992.'

'Tshokolo said many things on the witness stand that were not true,' he replies. 'I don't know why he said that.'

'But why would he have told a lie that made matters much worse for him?' I asked. 'If it were not true that he had worked for the Ormonds until two months before the shooting, he or his lawyer would have said

so. If it were not true that he parted with Ormond Aviation on very bad terms, he would have said so in court.'

From the beginning, Fusi has been impassive, inscrutable, his voice as soft and as even as ever. But now he turns his head and looks at me the face on and in his voice there is a new intensity.

'I wish Thabo were still alive,' he says. 'I wish I knew what happened between Thabo and the police. Did they threaten him? Did they pay him? They tried the same with me. They wanted me to go with them to the scene of the crime.'

'Thabo's evidence is terrible,' I say. 'He was clearly dragged kicking and screaming onto the witness stand. He was unable to tell a coherent story. And right there on the stand, he rebelled. He simply stopped cooperating with the prosecutor.

'But even if we forget Thabo's testimony, if we look only at what was accepted by all the parties in the courtroom about what happened in the morning and in the afternoon ...'

'It all comes down to Thabo,' he interrupts. 'Thabo is dead. I wish he could speak from the grave ...'

'It seems clear that the intention of the men from Phola Park was to rob the Ormonds,' I say. 'Many SDU members were using their weapons to commit robbery. It was not at all uncommon.'

'I know,' he replies. 'Even at the TRC it was said that many SDU members were using their weapons for that purpose. But not in this case. How would they know of the Ormond property? I had never heard of it. Thabo had never heard of it. They themselves had never heard of it.'

'I do not know any more what happened that day,' I say. 'But I know that the story you initially told me, when we first met, is not right.'

'I understand,' he says quietly. 'I think you must talk again to Ncala and Fokazi. You must ask them these questions.'

He looks me square in the face again, the intensity so unusual for him,

and I am astonished when I discover that he has changed the subject.

'I was told that there was a story in yesterday's *Sunday Times* about Tshokolo and me,' he says. 'I am very anxious to find a copy. It is already late Monday afternoon, maybe it is too late, but if we go to the corner shops now, quickly, maybe they have not yet thrown their extra copies away.'

And so we drive off, leaving Fusi's co-workers waiting for their taxis, and head into the late-afternoon traffic of downtown Bethlehem; we rake the corner shops on the main streets, one after the other, Fusi rushing in while I remain in the idling car. But none still has a copy of the *Sunday Times*.

And now Fusi insists that we drive to the mayor's house in the suburbs, for if anyone keeps the newspaper, surely it is the mayor of Bethlehem. He is anxious, he says, because if the story says anything negative about the Justice department, or about the government in general, maybe his case to be pardoned will not go well. There was a time, a year or so ago, when somebody from the Wits Justice Project wrote an angry article about Fusi and Tshokolo's case and Fusi's lawyers were up in arms because they said maybe the article would antagonise the Justice department.

We arrive at the mayor's place, a large ranch-style home in the suburbs, and although the mayor is not home his security detail is alarmed by a strange car appearing in the drive and we are met by a flurry of men in suits. Fusi gets out of the car and explains his predicament and they all shrug their shoulders, at ease now that it is just a supplicant from the township. They read *City Press* on the weekend, they tell him, not the *Sunday Times*.

And as we drive off, mission unaccomplished, towards Fusi's house, where Teboho and Lebo will be waiting, it strikes me that throughout our conversation about the transcript, a conversation I have for some time now been dreading, he was politely waiting for me to finish my business so that he could get on with his.

ONE DAY IN BETHLEHEM

I do not believe that he knows any more what took place on 2 April 1992. The story the men told to the truth commission in 1998 has become the truth. He has pasted it over the real events of that day. And so when I tell him that Ncala and Ndabeni spent the morning casing out the Ormond property and that the men from Phola Park descended upon the property in the afternoon, I am telling him a tale he simply does not recognise. And when I say that his friend, Tshokolo, worked for the Ormonds and left in anger, I am telling him something he has long since erased, for at the truth commission hearing there was no mention of Tshokolo's dispute with the Ormonds.

Thirty-two

Two months pass before I see Fusi again. Embarrassingly, I lose my way to Teboho's house, despite having visited many times before; I retreat to a petrol station at the edge of Bohlokong and call him.

Ten minutes later, a motorbike pulls up alongside me and the driver gives a tentative wave. His face is obscured by a crash helmet, his torso sheathed in a black leather jacket. I have only ever seen Fusi in stolid, middle-aged attire – his golf shirts, his windbreakers and his polyester slacks, his head forever shaved clean. I am caught by the fancy that an altered Fusi will emerge from behind this garb, brusque and more bluntly masculine than the man I have come to know.

His legs still straddling the bike, he lifts his visor and smiles. In an instant his disguise vanishes. The rest of his face covered, he is distilled to his essence, for it is with his eyes that he smiles. They are brown and liquid and very kind and they speak heavily of caution; I imagine him ten minutes earlier, sitting in an armchair in his living room, frowning at his phone, wondering why I am calling him instead of knocking on the door, as arranged.

I follow him through the township. It is 28 December today, the midst of the Christmas season; nobody is at work during this time and the

whole of Bohlokong appears to have come outside. People have taken over the streets, some of them in parties of a dozen or more; they stand in the middle of the main thoroughfares chatting away as if they are in their own backyards. There is scarcely space for vehicles and the back of Fusi's helmet keeps vanishing in the crowd.

At his home I discover the rest of the family is out visiting and that we are alone. Usually, the television is blaring, the kids staring at it as if in wonder; in the quiet his living room suddenly seems unfamiliar, as if I have just walked into a stranger's house.

He tells me that he is on call. The moment a public vehicle breaks down anywhere across the municipality he will have to go out and fix it. It could happen now, it could happen at 10:00 this evening. For all he knows, he will spend the night under an asphalt presser in some village at the end of a dirt road.

This is his third Christmas in a row on duty, he tells me. He is the only one who can be relied on during the holiday season; the rest are too drunk to pick up their phones.

Not for the first time I watch him marvel at his steadiness in the midst of disorder, his powers of concentration among those who drift and stray. He tells me that the motorbike on which he came to fetch me is borrowed; his own bike is broken and his car, too, is idle, for the brake pads are worn. He has spent much of the Christmas period disassembling the engines of both vehicles and scouring municipal workshops for spares. He has found a pair of brake pads, he says, and they are almost new. And since he will perform the labour himself, the whole business will not cost a cent.

And now he is talking of a trip the entire family will take to Johannes-burg. Thabo has come into money, he explains; an uncle died and has left him a small inheritance. But there is a woman in Johannesburg making trouble; she has hired a lawyer and is claiming that the money ought to

be hers. Thabo is too young and inexperienced to deal with the matter on his own and so Fusi is to accompany him when he visits the Master of the High Court. And besides, he says, it is not unknown for people to assassinate the beneficiaries of relatives' estates; Thabo should not be walking around Johannesburg alone while the matter remains unsettled; Fusi should be at his side.

He is wrapped up in his affairs – his vehicles, the interests of his foster children, his progress up the municipality's hierarchy – and to the extent that I can glimpse inside his head it is working incessantly on practical matters, always, each waking moment. That is what he is now in his life outside of prison, a head crammed with problems to be solved and calculations to be made.

I wait for a lull in the conversation. I have talked again to Sikhalo Ncala and I have matters to discuss and news to bear.

The Bethlehem men are dispersed across the country and every round of interviews takes time. I have taken to meeting each of them in a customary place. Clement Ndabeni I buy lunch at a restaurant called Steve's Grill in his hometown of Port St Johns. Mandla Fokazi I visit at his house in a Transkei village and Donald Makhura, of course, I meet in prison. As for Sikhalo Ncala, our encounters take place in the Wimpy in the sprawling Alberton Mall, a short journey from Phola Park. We met just four days earlier, on Christmas Eve, the mall around us heaving with thousands upon thousands of people.

'I asked Sikhalo whether he walked into the Ormonds' garden, along with Clement Ndabeni, on the morning of 2 April,' I begin.

Fusi is sitting on the couch opposite me, his hands resting on his thighs. He is still as he listens.

'Sikhalo said that it was him on the property,' I say, 'and that the one accompanying him was Clement. He said that he never intended to go with the others to Natal; he was always going only as far as Bethlehem

to borrow money from Amos to pay his debt to Sebenzile. But nor was he intending to return to Phola Park. Before they even embarked on the journey he decided that he would stay in Bethlehem and look for work. He was desperate, he said; the fighting in Phola Park was too hard.

'That morning, he said, he walked onto many properties to look for work. It was only much later, in court, when the Ormonds' employee, Simon Motaung, took the stand, that he understood that the property outside which the shootout happened was one of the places at which he had enquired earlier in the day. He must have visited twenty places that morning, he said, so many that he could not tell one from the other.

'I do not believe him,' I say, 'It would be the craziest coincidence …'

'I do not understand that,' Fusi interrupts, 'Sikhalo and Clement could not have gone out together in the morning. At no stage did Sikhalo leave me alone with the others in the house. Nozulu was behaving so strangely towards me and there was a bulge on his hip, clearly a gun. I was afraid of him. And when they went out to get breakfast, it was all of them who left. I even remember saying, ''If that man goes out he will be arrested because there is a bulge on his hip.'' They ignored my advice and laughed.'

I am silent. I do not point out what he had said in Malherbe's court: that he himself left home at 9:00 a.m., little more than an hour after the men from Phola Park had arrived. He met Thabo Mokoena and Thabo's cousin, Zulu, in town. And when he returned to Bohlokong it was not to his home but to Zulu's place. He idled there for hours, watching videos, and only got home after 5:00 p.m.

When were his memories of 2 April lost? When did he no longer know that he left home at 9:00 a.m. that day? And when did he forget that Sikh-alo and Clement walked onto the Ormonds' property during the course of the morning? When did he no longer know that Tshokolo worked for the Ormonds and that the men who came from Johannesburg tried to rob the Ormonds in the afternoon? Are these memories merely hidden in the

shadows cast by subsequent stories? Is it simply a question of letting the sun shine on them once more?

'I asked Sikhalo what happened in the afternoon,' I continue. 'He said Sebenzile was getting angrier and angrier with him and that he needed to get out of the car to save himself. By that stage, Donald and Fokazi were so troubled by Sebenzile's behaviour that they decided to abandon the mission to Natal. So they got out of the bakkie and walked away with Sikhalo. He claims that they just happened to walk past the Orsmond house on their shortcut to Bohlokong. And when Clement went into Ballyduff to find them, it was outside the Ormond house that he happened to stop. But really, Fusi, that is a ridiculous story; I don't know how he expected anyone to believe it.'

He is listening intently now.

'What bothers me most about the story,' he says, 'is why did they stop in Bethlehem? This business with Ncala paying the debt and then going back to Phola Park bothers me. It is not right. April the second was a Thursday. When Ncala arrived, he told me he would see me again on the Sunday night when the men were coming back from Inanda. He was planning to go with the others to Natal, I am certain of that.'

He is leaning forward now, his elbows on his thighs, his fingers locked together in front of him. This talking without hands, without gestures, lends his words gravity, as if each sentence, each phrase comes from the most careful deliberation.

'I have my own idea about why they stopped in Bethlehem. It comes from things that Donald Makhura told me later.

'When those SDU people travelled armed they only travelled at night. That was their strict rule, only at night. If they had left Phola Park earlier, at 10:00 p.m., say, they could have driven to Inanda through the night. But they would not leave without *ntelezi* to protect them. And the *nyanga* kept them waiting. He was busy dosing other people. They only got to

leave in the early hours of the morning. The plan was to stop in Bethlehem at sunrise because Sikhalo knew it. They would take cover there
during the day and leave again at sunset.

'After they arrived at my place, they decided that they were hungry,
so they would go to town to buy boerewors. That is when I pointed to
Nozulu and said: '"That one must not go to town; you will be arrested."
But they all went. And afterwards some of them were saying that they
got caught because there was pork in the boerewors. That is the rule with
ntelezi: once the *nyanga* has put it on you, you cannot have sex or carry
silver coins in your pocket or eat pork. If you do, it will not work: the
bullets will hit you.

'So, in my mind, that is why they stopped in Bethlehem. This connection between Tshokolo and the men from Phola Park: it did not exist.
There was nobody who could have told them about the Ormonds.'

'By they *were* targeting the Ormonds, Fusi,' I say. 'There is no doubt.
It is so clear in the court record. And there is a reason why, even now,
they will not admit it. Whenever I see Sikhalo and Mandla and Clement, each of them describes himself to me as a military veteran. They all
want the benefits that come with that: a free house, a military pension.
All these years later, there is bickering among the people who fought in
the early 1990s about who is a true veteran and who is not. And so if the
story is abroad that they were in Bethlehem to rob somebody maybe their
case will weaken. They are waiting, year after year after year, to be com-
pensated for what they did. And so their story is still alive; they believe
that it has consequences; they need to protect their legacy as soldiers.'

'What you say is true,' he replies. 'But the point remains: who would
have told them about the Ormonds?'

There is a long silence.

'I would like to ask you,' I say, 'whether I can continue writing the
story. When I first read the transcript, I thought it would be better if

I just stopped. But I think I would like to go on. Only with your permission, though. If you say no, I will simply stop, no more discussion. Because I am not writing the story we both thought I would when you agreed to this. Now I am writing a book that says that I do not know what happened on 2 April. That is not what you bargained for.'

His reply astonishes me. It comes out pat, rehearsed, as if he had already said it earlier to the empty room.

'I do not know a lot about books. But from what I have read, sometimes you meet a person and you think you know who they are, but it becomes more complicated. You say you will write that you no longer know what happened. As long as that is what you do it is fine. You present the many versions, and the reader decides what happened.'

His answer is too generous, too capacious, too fair by half. I am tempted to advise him to think again. But I am too grateful to do that, and too lucky.

It is late afternoon when the family returns. Teboho greets me tentatively, as always, and retreats to the kitchen to prepare dinner. Lebo disappears to the room at the back. As for Thabo, he stands in the middle of the living room staring at the TV, wondering why on earth it is blank. He finds the remote control, turns it on and sits down on the couch.

There is a Samuel L. Jackson thriller playing and the scene on which we stumble is raunchy; Jackson's torso is naked, a gold chain on his bare chest, his tongue in a woman's mouth. As the camera draws back he cups her buttock in a big hand.

The scene ill fits this very proper, Christmas-time house, and I expect Fusi to frown or change the channel. But he sits back in his chair and beams benignly, as if to say: what is on the screen is on the screen and what is in my home is in my home.

Thabo is staring unblinkingly at the screen. There is a large faux diamond in his left ear and the tongues of his trainers stand up against the bottom of his shins, stiffened by brilliant white starch.

The construction job upcountry did not work out and Thabo has found work at the local taxi rank. Fusi is displeased. The taxi business is for older men, he says; he does not like the sorts of youths who spend their time around the rank. He must find Thabo something more suitable.

I watch them, the gentle patriarch and the boy who has become his son, each staring without expression at the television set that dominates the room. We are in the same space in which Fusi and I discussed the past not an hour ago. The presence of the young one has chased that conversation away; it seems to have taken place elsewhere, in a tunnel or a hollow where the ground underfoot is muddy and unstable, the air damp, the light too dim. The task of steering children into adulthood requires fresh air and light.

Thirty-three

S ometime after Fusi agreed to work with me, he mentioned that he had kept all the letters he received when he was in prison. I asked whether I could see them.

They were with a man in Johannesburg who, oddly enough, was preparing to write a book about Fusi. I contacted him, went to his office to collect Fusi's letters, photocopied them, and returned them the following day.

There were more than four hundred in all. The vast majority were written in Sesotho. Just seventeen, all of them penned by Donald Makhura, were in English.

I put Donald's letters aside and concentrated on the rest. I do not read Sesotho and wanted to find just the right person to help me understand them. I went searching for somebody with whom I could sit down and discuss the meaning of the most important ones line by line.

What with all the attention the Sesotho letters consumed, I simply forgot about the ones Donald had written. I cannot explain it. I was travelling the four corners of South Africa to find anybody and everybody who had once known Fusi. All the while, a contemporaneous correspondence from his co-defendant was lying in a file three paces from the chair in which I wrote this book. I don't remember now what caused me to leap from my chair and retrieve those letters.

263

Donald's correspondence with Fusi begins in mid-1995, shortly after the two found themselves for the first time in separate prisons. It ends just after the men appeared before the Amnesty Committee of the truth commission.

The letters are surprising in so many ways that I am not sure where to begin. Perhaps with the fact that Donald took it on himself to orchestrate the testimony that the entire group would give to the truth commission. He was the most educated among them, he reminded Fusi several times; he was the intellectual; without his intelligence and his learning they were doomed.

And yet as smart as Donald was – and I am soon to learn that he is a formidably intelligent man – he did not understand the law. He believed, adamantly – for the strangest and most cockeyed reasons, reasons only a layperson confronted with the abstruseness of the law might conjure – that if the men admitted to the truth commission that they intended to rob the Ormonds their case was sunk.

'Fusi,' Donald wrote in a letter dated 23 November 1995, 'I want to tell you something from my heart. The possibility of this Truth Commission helping us is 10 % ... Fusi this commission want nothing else, but the truth. If there is no truth from our side we must forget about it (commission) ... Now, what does the Commission understand by the Truth? [T]his commission will be having all the files or records of our case ... Fusi, thorough investigations about this case are still going to be made by the commission. I know how it is going to work. The state is going to argue that this is not political ... Fusi I am clever. I can see what is going to happen. The big question is at T/Commission: Why do we say this case is politically? ... Fusi let's be careful of taking chances. The law is very tough this time.'

Donald, working without expert advice, had made three assumptions about the work of the TRC's Amnesty Committee. He was wrong on all three counts.

His first assumption was that the TRC's investigators would scour the court record with a fine-tooth comb. From other letters, it is apparent that he thought that they'd do much more: teams of investigators would descend on Bethlehem to interview scores of people. His estimate of the TRC's bureaucratic capabilities was vastly overblown. He had no clue that the body's workload was many times larger than its capacity.

His second mistake lay in his interpretation of what the TRC meant by 'politically motivated'. The Amnesty Committee would grant amnesty to those who met two conditions. First, the Committee would have to be satisfied that the amnesty applicant had made a full disclosure about the crime he or she had committed. Second, the crime had to have been committed to further the aims of a political organisation.

Donald appeared to think that conspiring to rob the Ormonds did not count as political. He was wrong. Were he to have testified that the commander of the group had ordered his men to commit robbery to acquire resources for the mission to Natal, this would have been enough for the Amnesty Committee.

There is a sense in which Donald erred because he knew too much. He understood better than most that, circa April 1992, self-defence units were more an expression of the anarchy descending on parts of the country than the disciplined organs of political movements. He himself had crossed into South Africa, heavily armed, off his own bat, without instruction from his MK commanders. He was himself an embodiment of the anarchy of the times. He did not appreciate that the TRC understood this; its interpretation of 'furthering the aims of a political organisation' was flexible enough to accommodate the wildness of that era.

Donald's third mistake lay in his understanding of what the Amnesty Committee meant by 'truth'. He appeared to believe that what he and his co-accused had testified at their trial was sacrosanct; they would have to stick to their original story when they appeared before the TRC.

He seemed not to understand that he could simply tell the Amnesty Committee that they had all lied to Judge Koos Malherbe. He thought that only an appeal court could wipe clean the slate that had been writ-ten at the trial.

This is the oddest of Donald's three assumptions. The first two are entirely understandable. The third seems to derive from an understand-ing of court evidence as a kind of religious doctrine. As if what was said in a courtroom had the status of papal infallibility until a subse-quent pope said otherwise. And, besides, the men *were* going to tell the Amnesty Committee that they had been dishonest in Malherbe's court; for they had concealed that they were SDU members en route to fight, and had lied about the purpose of their journey. And so, in addi-tion to being extremely eccentric, Donald's reasoning was riddled with contradictions.

It is possible that Donald was well aware of the inconsistencies in his reasoning and that his real intention was to bamboozle Fusi. For here is the second surprising fact Donald's letters reveal: He was out to screw Fusi and Tshokolo; his letters to Fusi were a macabre serenade, an attempt to convince a man to condemn himself.

Donald is acutely aware that he is advising Fusi to sink himself. It is such horrible advice that he cannot give it directly. Members of the ANC's legal department have come to see him, he writes, and he is in the process of 'filling in forms'. He is, in other words, applying for amnesty.

'Mind you,' he hastens to continue, 'Tshokolo, Morena [Sikhalo] and you must never fill in forms.'

It is just a brief line, but its import is enormous. Tshokolo, Sikhalo and Fusi must under no circumstances apply for amnesty, Donald is saying. Why not? Because they must stick to the story they told in Malherbe's court, otherwise they will not be telling the Truth. And in the trial court, Fusi and Tshokolo had said that they had no business with the men who

arrived from Phola Park; Sikhalo had said he had come only to settle a debt and to look for work. They should thus not apply for amnesty because they had committed no crime. Were they to confess to a crime the TRC would deny everyone amnesty.

In a later letter to Fusi, Donald spells this out more clearly.

'I hereby want to make the following points straight with you,' he writes. 'I am referring to the issue of Morena [Sikhalo] not applying for amnesty. Look at the following points: We wanted our statements to be the same with the statements from the court. You will recall that Morena said in the court that he was going to give Sebenzile his money at Bohlokong. Secondly, in Bohlokong he went out to look for work at Ballyduff. He also said he did not know we were carrying arms. Fusi I coached Morena in Virginia in the cell. I did not want him to be judged a liar by the committee.'

In the year leading up to the hearing, Donald, who by now understood that Fusi *would* appear at the hearing, whether or not he applied for amnesty, positively begged Fusi to tell the Amnesty Committee only what he had told Malherbe's court.

'Fusi, please stick to the original version when we go to the committee. Don't ever implicate yourself,' he wrote on 13 July 1998, four months before the Amnesty hearing.

Which leads to the final revelation contained in Donald's letters. Fusi had told me that, on the morning he went to the Amnesty Committee to testify, he believed that it would free him. When they told him he had come to plead his case in the wrong forum and that they could not help him, he was shocked to the core. But Donald had told Fusi that he could not possibly get amnesty if he admitted to no crime.

In October, the month before the hearing, Donald spelled everything out.

'You must know that we are all going to be at the hearing even if you

did not apply for amnesty,' he wrote. 'You are my co-accused and therefore you will also be there … Fusi you are not automatically going to be
freed in case I am freed. Be clear on this. The Amnesty Committee has no
powers to release a person who does not seek amnesty. You are innocent
in this case. There is nothing you are going to tell the committee. Only
those who confess and want amnesty will be considered by the committee. Your issue together with Ncala and Tshokolo will definitely be
referred to the court which will have no option but to release you, or to
give you bail.'

I am not sure whether Donald knew that Fusi and Tshokolo's appeal
had already failed. I can thus only guess whether he was hoodwinking
them when he said that they must entrust their fate to the courts.

Fusi must have defied Donald because he did in the end apply for
amnesty. He must have understood that Donald was looking after his own
interests and was throwing Fusi to the lions. But he seems not to have
absorbed the one vital truth Donald's admonitions contained: that if Fusi
went to the TRC to proclaim his innocence he would remain in jail.

It is no wonder that on his release Donald moved heaven and earth to
get Fusi and Tshokolo out of prison; he felt responsible for their continued incarceration.

And it is also no wonder that Fusi has erased the role Donald played
in bringing his case to the attention of the world, for beneath his placid
exterior he must have been furious.

When I next see Fusi I tell him what I have read in Donald's letters.

'The way you remember it,' I say, 'you arrived at the amnesty hearing
certain that the TRC would free you. When it did not, you were devas-
tated. But Donald had already told you that the TRC could do nothing for
a person who professed his innocence.'

'Now that you say it,' he replies, 'I remember Donald writing that. I did not believe him. I did not trust his advice. I must have just put what he had written out of my mind.'

In the end, Donald had his way. Clement and Mandla testified precisely as Donald wanted them to: they were en route to Inanda in Natal on a military mission; their stop in Bethlehem was incidental; they were unlucky enough to have been approached by police officers on their way out of town.

Donald believed that the men had 'a 10% chance' of getting amnesty because he doubted that the Committee would buy this story; after all, a simple reading of the transcript of the 1992 trial would give up its lies. In his letters Donald worried a great deal about what the late Constable Oosthuizen's father would say in his testimony. How relieved he must have been when the commissioners did not ask Oosthuizen a single question. And how astonished he must have been to discover that the chair of the Amnesty Committee had not even read a transcript of the trial.

In the wake of the hearing, before the Amnesty Committee had announced its verdict, Donald could not quite believe that they'd got away with it.

'Yes, it is surprising how few questions the commissioners asked,' he writes. 'But we should not get our hopes up. Maybe their investigations are ongoing.'

Only on the day he finally walked out of prison, his story still uncontested, did he truly understand that there was never going to be an investigation, that what he had said at the hearing was the final word.

The testimonies of the Bethlehem men were guided by the thinking of a layperson with heavily vested interests, limited access to information

and little knowledge of the law. There is some irony in this. The TRC was meant to be as accessible as possible to ordinary people caught up in South Africa's violence, whether as perpetrators or as victims. What would the men have testified had they spent just an hour with a well-informed lawyer? What would have transpired had Booker Mohlaba had the time to meet them a month before their hearing, instead of an hour?

Thirty-four

The visiting room at the maximum-security prison at Baviaanspoort, the facility that houses Donald Makhura, is a long,
wide rectangle like the classrooms of my childhood. In the far
corner there is a makeshift tuckshop – a table displaying neat rows of
chips and cold drinks, tobacco pouches and matches; it is staffed by a
prisoner in his orange overalls and a warder in his browns. Scattered
across the rest of the room are pairs of plastic chairs, one for the inmate,
the other for his visitor; and it strikes me as I take in the scene that almost
every man here is with his lover, knees pressed against knees, hands
holding hands, each couple a replica of the next.

Donald Makhura sits alone, his arms folded tightly across his chest, the
chair opposite him empty. His paunch shows through his prison shirt,
his thin, shapeless thighs through his prison trousers; in his ageing body
he cuts a vulnerable figure. He is in profile and I cannot properly see
his face, but his arms wrap his torso as if in a straitjacket and I wonder
whether he expects a visitor bearing bad news.

He looks up and when he finds my face his disappointment is palpable.

'I was expecting somebody else,' he says. 'A man called Mr Bruwer.'

'I brought these papers in case it was Bruwer. Let me give them to the
warder for safekeeping.'

He picks a bulging plastic bag up off the floor and holds it up.

He gets up, clutching his bag of papers, and makes his way to the warder at the door. Their exchange is brief and friendly. The warder takes the prisoner's bag and puts it carefully under his desk.

Mr Bruwer is the lawyer who represented Donald Makhura at the trial in which he was convicted of murdering his daughter and her boyfriend. When I spoke to Bruwer on the phone he told me that he had stopped practising law nearly two years earlier.

This is an unfortunate start, I think. I breeze in, a stranger, with news that is not so good, news that exudes my power as a man who is free, his impotence as a man who is not.

I tell him I bring greetings from Fusi, from Clement, from Sikhalo, from Tshokolo, from Mandla Fokazi. I tell him of the book I am writing about Fusi. And to get it out of the way, I tell him that I have spoken to Bruwer who informed me that he no longer practises law.

Donald cocks his head to the side and scratches his chin. Then he looks at me and starts to say something, but thinks better of it.

I am racking my brain for how to find him a new lawyer, and a decent one at that. I have come here to take, and I do not want to leave without giving something in return.

'What have you brought for me?' he asks, as if reading my mind. 'Did Fusi tell you that I have asked for a pair of shoes?'

His voice is resonant and strong; and as he speaks, his chest puffs out and his chin rises, as if he is strutting while sitting down. The trans-formation is something to behold. Even in these two brief questions he betrays that his place is on a stage.

He stares at me gravely, waiting for a response. His eyes are set wide apart atop high cheekbones, the breadth of the ensemble exuding a cer-tain power.

'He did not,' I say. 'But he told me how you use tobacco to trade in prison. Can I buy you some?'

'Yes, you can,' he says quietly, 'I would be very grateful for that.'

'Okay. Let's talk and ...'

'No, now,' he says. 'Get the tobacco now and then we will see about your business.'

So I queue at the tuckshop and return with four pouches of tobacco. He holds out both hands to take them and rests them on his lap. But he does not like this arrangement, it seems, for now he gets up again and makes his way back to the warder at the front of the room and gives him the tobacco for safekeeping.

When he returns he has his bag of papers with him again.

'I want to show you something,' he says as he sits down.

He places the bag carefully on his lap, its open top facing him. With his right hand he pulls out a thick sheaf of typed pages and holds them up in the air.

'This is the transcript of my trial.'

With his left he takes out three exercise books and hands them to me. They are identical, each foolscap and blue, each wrapped in a protective covering of transparent adhesive plastic. The covering has been applied with great care, the corners tight and precisely square.

'Open them,' he says. 'Look.'

He leans back in his chair, leaving behind him the stench of his breath. He does not trade much in the tobacco I have bought him, it seems; he smokes it. The odour is stale and pungent, as if it has been percolating in his mouth for years.

I open one of the notebooks. It is filled with dense handwritten script, the writing big like a child's and as perfect as a monk's.

'I have copied out the transcript,' he says. 'Not the whole thing. Just the relevant parts, the parts I need to work with. The typed transcript I must keep clean. This one,' he says, jabbing a finger at the open page on my lap, 'is so that I can take notes.'

And, indeed, much of the text is highlighted in an assortment of colours – red, blue, green, yellow, purple, pink – and in the margins, in the tiniest script, are the notes he has taken.

I turn the pages and each is the same, right to the end of the last exercise book: the big text of transcribed trial proceedings, the tiny script of his notes and the many colours of his highlighters. All in all, he has filled more than a hundred and fifty pages. They are a work of art, I think to myself; there is no less intensity here, no less obsession, than in a finely observed landscape. An image forms in my mind of Donald Makhura in a darkened cell, just a reading light shining; he is hunched over a narrow desk, hour upon hour upon hour.

As I turn the pages he tells me he is interested primarily in one person's testimony, the expert witness employed by MTN, the phone company. On the night of 4 November 2009, she testified, between 10:00 p.m. and 11:30 p.m., shortly after Donald's daughter and her boyfriend were shot to death in their car, the phone in Donald's possession was picking up a signal from a mast in Mamelodi township called Mamelodi Three.

Now he takes from his bag another document, this one a large folded sheet of paper. It is of a much better quality than the pages in his exercise book: thick and creamy and without lines. He opens it up carefully and spreads it across his lap.

It is a crayon-drawn map, the sort one might find in a board game. The only objects represented on it are five cell phone masts, each enormously large, reaching up like a skyscraper, each meticulously drawn in green, red, orange and brown. In bold black letters, so uniform that they appear to have been made with a stencil, are the names of each mast.

He points to the one called 'Mamelodi Three'.

'See,' he says, 'this mast is at the far northern end of Mamelodi. The murder took place in the south of the township. If my phone had been at the scene of the murder, it would have picked up a signal not from that

one.' He points a finger at Mamelodi Three. 'Not even this one.' He taps the next mast. 'Not even *this* one,' he waves an accusing finger at the next crayon drawing. 'The one closest to the scene of the murder was *five masts away. I was nowhere near the murder.'*

'Why did nobody point this out in court?' I ask.

It is as if my question has released a spring from under him. He grows higher in his chair, his arms spread in wonder, his eyebrows rise.

'The judge, Judge Ismael, he does not know the geography of Mamelodi. The prosecutor, Mrs Cronje, she does not know the geography of Mamelodi. The expert witness from MTN, she doesn't know the geography of Mamelodi. As for Mr Bruwer, he is supposed to be representing *me, my* interests – he does not bother to ask where in Mamelodi is this mast. All of them, they make the same mistake. The mast is in Mamelodi; the murder scene is in Mamelodi; therefore Donald Makhura was at the scene.'

He pauses, his face frozen, his eyes staring at me fiercely.

'Do you know what a scandal this is going to cause? I, Donald Makhura, representing myself, as a layperson, I am going to *humiliate* the National Prosecuting Authority. They are going to have to sell their teacups to find the money they will owe me. I will clean them out. They will have no money to pay their salaries.'

'Why didn't you say something to Bruwer in court?' I ask. 'Did you not know that the mast was in the wrong place?'

'I didn't know!' he shouts. 'My fate was being determined in front of me and I did not know!'

Months ago, he tells me, he requested the police docket and, once it arrived, he studied it through the night. He scrutinised every line on every page, he says. Examining the cell phone transmission record he found, to his astonishment, that there was not just one cell phone mast in Mamelodi: there were five.

The following week, he feigned a terrific toothache and requested an

urgent appointment with a dentist. Baviaanspoort Prison lies directly to the south of Mamelodi. The surgery of the dentist contracted to treat the prison's inmates lies on Mamelodi's northern border. The journey from the prison to the surgery runs across the length of the township.

'I had a lovely view through the window in the side of the van,' Donald says. 'As we are driving, I count the cell phone masts — one, two, three, four, five. I get back from the dentist, I draw this beautiful map, while it is all fresh in my mind.'

There were two eyewitnesses to the murder. Donald Makhura's ex-wife, Miriam, was at her next-door neighbour's house when she heard gun-shots in the street. She and her neighbour opened the front door to see a man they both identified as Makhura walking away from his daughter's car. Miriam knew it was her husband, even before she saw him, she said, for he had threatened to kill her and her daughter again and again. But see him she did: having lived with him for years, she testified, she knew how he moved when he was angry; he betrayed his identity as he walked away.

If the eyewitness testimony seems shaky, Miriam's account of her ex-husband's violence must have made it seem firmer. A few months earlier, she had acquired a protection order forbidding him from coming to the house for she said that he had beaten and sexually assaulted both mother and daughter.

'He told me that even if I run away, South Africa is a small place and he will hunt me down and kill me,' she told the court.

'He said I will cut your veins and you will bleed to death. I will cut your eyeballs with a razor blade. I will kill your child because you rely on this child.'

Makhura's own evidence did not help. He had left Mamelodi earlier in

the evening, he testified, and was on the road to Limpopo when the shots were fired. The MTN expert's evidence, which placed him in Mamelodi a full hour after his daughter was shot, put paid to his alibi.

I am not sure why Donald believes that his new evidence about the cell phone mast will help him. It would have taken him five or ten minutes to drive from the murder scene to the part of the township within range of Mamelodi Three. His evidence seems not to give him an alibi at all.

I close his exercise books carefully and hand them back to him.

'I know that you are thinking of your case,' I say. 'And maybe it is hard to get your mind to jump out of it, but I would like to talk about the past.'

'The past?' He frowns, a flash of unmasked confusion crossing his features. 'I don't have room to think of the past.' He taps his finger against his transcript and his exercise books, which are now piled on his lap. 'My mind is so much in these. Every waking hour. Even when I am sleeping.'

He puts the documents carefully back in their bag and gets up yet again to give it to the warder for safekeeping. I am wondering what he thinks may happen were he to leave the bag here at his side. I want to ask him, but fear that the question is too nosy.

'What do you want to know about the past?' he asks when he returns. 'You want to know about Fusi? Fusi is a priest. In Grootvlei, at the beginning of our sentence, all he did was meditate on things and study. He could concentrate for hours.'

'And you?'

'Me? I was wild. I tried to organise a rebellion.'

'Why did you work so hard to get him and Tshokolo out of prison?' I ask.

'Because I felt bad for them. They were not even trained to handle weapons. We parked outside their house in a car full of AK-47s and we

did not even tell them about these weapons. I hardly noticed Fusi. I felt nothing for him. I didn't even know him. Ncala knew him. He had some business in Bethlehem; I did not care what.

'Afterwards, I felt responsible for Fusi. The TRC: he did not understand that the process was not for him. He was not an educated man. He didn't comprehend the legal context.'

He is, uncharacteristically, silent for a long moment.

'I left no stone unturned,' he says finally. 'I knocked on the doors of some influential people. Jacques Pauw was the only one who was interested.'

I tell him I want to go back to 1992. What did he think of having to stop in Bethlehem for some inconsequential piece of business? Their vehicle was full of weapons, their mission was dangerous. Was he not annoyed?

'I did not care. Back then I was what they say in Afrikaans is a *wilde-kop*. I wanted action. I did not care if we stopped along the way.'

A moment ago he was beseeching me not to ask him to think of the past. Now he has crossed a threshold and he is in it. He is staring intently at his hands, which he holds out in front of him like a man in prayer.

'I was not the driver. I knew nothing about the trip. I did not care. I was wild then. I had been back from exile only two months. I had done wild things in Phola Park. I had killed people. I was full of *ntelezi*. You know *ntelezi*? We just drove from Thokoza to Bethlehem. It is a long way. There could be lots of roadblocks. We did not care. We were under orders not to surrender if we went into a roadblock; we were under orders to use our weapons. You know *ntelezi*? We were not allowed to wear watches or to carry silver coins.'

'Is that why you were caught that day in Bethlehem?' I ask. 'Because one of you was wearing a watch?'

'I don't remember. It was a long time ago.'

'Fusi says you told him many years ago that it was because there had

'Those guys had *ntelezi* inside them. They were wild. They did not later murdered.

The men on strike had all been dosed with *ntelezi* by a *nyanga* who was He is referring to a massacre of striking mineworkers by police in 2012.

you about the *nyanga*. You know about the *nyanga* at Marikana?'

thing goes way up, people who are very influential today, I will not talk to happened the night before. I am not going to tell you about them. This 'The *nyanga* did not keep us waiting the night before. Many things

whatever was occupying his Saturday morning before I arrived.

situation; he will storm off, retrieve his bag from the warder, and return to back curves. His body is primed, I fear, to eject itself from this unwelcome His foot taps the floor while I am speaking. His shoulders hunch and his

medicine.'

because you had to wait half the night for the *nyanga* to administer the has told me that you and your comrades only stopped in Bethlehem at all 'My business is to understand what happened on 2 April,' I say. 'Fusi

bad can come of you. That is how we were raised.'

about somebody, say, about the *nyanga* who did the *ntelezi*, something cannot talk to you about that. There are consequences. If you talk badly 'You want to know about the *nyanga* who administered the *ntelezi*: I

you can just write about it. For me as a black person, it is not light.

divulge certain things. This business of *ntelezi*: for you as a white person, 'I will never tell you the full story. Never. I have undertaken not to

'I want to know all I can about what happened that day,' I reply.

'What is it you want to know about those times?'

furrows cut across his forehead.

previous night, but I have barely begun when his face darkens and deep I begin to ask him about the *nyanga* who administered the *ntelezi* the

'It could have been that I was eating pork at the time.'

been pork in the sausages you ate that morning.'

think that anything could touch them. And that *nyanga* was assassinated afterwards. These things are very sensitive; I am not going to talk to you about *ntelezi*. You should not have brought it up.'

'You brought it up,' I say with a grin.

'No, you did,' he shoots back.

The warder at the door has looked at his watch and is making his way towards us. It is a good time for my visit to end.

'I do not want our conversation to make you uncomfortable,' I say. 'But I do want to talk more.'

It is a Saturday morning. Tomorrow, Sunday, is another visiting day. I ask if I can come back.

'You can,' he says quietly. The grooves in his forehead are gone and his body has uncoiled. His hands are in his pockets, the very picture of a man who has recovered his ease.

He thanks me for the tobacco, very graciously, and tells me how important it is to him. It is the most valuable currency in this prison, he says. With it, there is no end to what he can buy.

I stand up to leave and am halfway across the room when he calls me back. He is still sitting in his chair, as I left him.

'Sit,' he says. 'There is something I forgot to tell you.'

I sit. He is staring at me, his face full of concentration.

He reaches for my right arm and gently twists it so that its pale underside faces the ceiling.

'We take *ntelezi* at certain times, to fight, and it sits in us and nobody takes it out.'

With his index finger, he traces a line down a vein in my forearm as if making an incision.

'There is a term for this in English,' he says. 'Post-traumatic stress disorder.'

He lets go of my arm.

I nod and tell him I understand; I have heard what he has said.

I get up and leave. In the doorway, I turn and glance at him. He is still in his chair, leaning back, his hands in his pockets. He is staring ahead of him, looking satisfied.

When I return the following morning Donald wants to talk about Bruwer. When did I speak to him? How do I know that he is no longer practising law?' He wonders aloud whether Bruwer's abandonment of his profession has something do with his case.

'You must watch me,' he says. 'I am going to make history. I am a lay-person and I am going to overturn a High Court decision. It has never happened before. I have already made history by getting the judges to agree that there are grounds for appeal. Just Donald Makhura, no legal representative, standing before a full bench of the High Court.

'The judge was Bertelsman. He said: "Mr Makhura, you have raised the possibility that the court has made a mistake. But I cannot proceed on the basis of your hand-drawn map. We must have a proper map commissioned. Then we can proceed."

'There will be consequences for Mrs Cronjé and maybe for Bruwer, too. When I have won this appeal, I will make sure that the Judicial Services Commission investigates the matter. And perhaps the Law Society too.'

I am wondering how I am going to turn the conversation to the past. He is consumed. The violence he did to himself yesterday when he wrenched his mind from his case has issued a warning. I fear that his tolerance for the things I wish to discuss might snap at any time.

'I spoke to Fusi last night on the phone,' I say. 'He sends his greetings.'

He stares at me impassively.

'Did you notice that I did not ask after Fusi? Not yesterday. Not today. You tell me you have come from Fusi and I do not say what I should be

normal in such a situation: "How is Fusi?"'

'I noticed,' I say.

I notice, too, that he speaks only with his mouth, the rest of his face as still as a stone. He is a model of severity.

'Do you know why?'

'No, I don't.'

'Because I am angry with Fusi. He has not acknowledged that I got him out of prison. I went on a single-minded campaign. I went to see Tsotsi, one of the three judges who presided over the Amnesty Committee hearing. I went to see Charles Ngakula, a Cabinet minister. I was a colonel in the Air Force at that time. Each of these meetings I attended in my Air Force uniform. I went to see Bishop Tutu. I went to see the man who is currently the ambassador to Mozambique. The only person who picked it up and ran with it was Jacques Pauw.

'If you look at the lengths I went to for Fusi it is not so clear that when Donald Makhura dies he will not go to heaven.'

I study his face for irony – the hint of a smile, perhaps, or some mirth in his eyes. He is deadpan.

'Why did you try so hard?' I asked.

'Because I am the one who took responsibility. I stood up at the TRC and said that what happened that day was Donald's work.'

He looks at me gravely. There is disappointment in his eyes. He fears that I have not understood.

'Look at Fusi. He is a priest. He cannot handle a gun. He is not a soldier. I am a soldier. I am a killing machine. What happened in 1992 was Donald. Donald is the soldier. Donald is the killing machine, one of the most dangerous people in this country.'

He stares at me once more, as if to see whether I have absorbed what he is saying.

'Fusi and Tshokolo were not administered with *ntelezi*. Only we were.

Do you understand? They were not wild. They did not have this business in their blood.

'You asked yesterday about the night before. Yes, we were administered *ntelezi* the night before. Do you realise how dangerous the thing is?

'The previous *nyanga* who used to doctor us was killed scaling the wall of the hostel. We were attacking the hostel, we were found out, he was shot off the wall. A new *nyanga* came from the Eastern Cape.

'That was a rule, the *nyanga* must come from the Eastern Cape. When you are fighting with the Xhosas you must do *ntelezi* as they do. Otherwise they will not fight with you. I am Pedi, we have our own power, it is not like theirs. But when with them you must do as they do.'

He leans into me, coming close, and lowers his voice.

'It is heavy stuff. They instruct to fetch from the hostels one of those Zulu men with the heavy, flapping ears. They need his genitals for the *ntelezi*. It is necessary that they cut out his genitals with a blunt knife. The more painful it is, the more the *ntelezi* will work.

'You are listening to this and you are thinking that this is something barbaric, something primitive from previous times. I cannot tell you more about the *nyanga*. It is dangerous. It implicates people in high places. I have a brother living in Thokoza. I am imprisoned. I cannot protect him. You know that this is a violent country. You drive out of this prison, you know that you could get carjacked at the first traffic light.'

I say nothing. We sit in silence for a while.

'We were not meant to travel during the day,' he continues. 'Fusi is right about that. And Fusi is right that the *nyanga* treated us late that night. He also treated our weapons. Why? Because they were not weapons for our personal use. They were war weapons. We were delivering them. Others were going to use them to fight. This is my way of saying that we could not use the weapons to commit a crime in Bethlehem because they were not ours. Besides, how much money could that man have had on his farm?

How many banks did we pass on the way to Bethlehem?'

'There was no ill-discipline?' I ask. 'No SDU member ever used his automatic weapon to commit a crime?'

'There was plenty of ill-discipline. Let me tell you a story. A white man was gunned down for his car. The lady in the passenger seat ran away. There were people from the Bethlehem group there, people you have interviewed: I will not tell you who. We went searching for the lady. I stood on her. She was hiding in the grass, curled up in the position of a foetus with her hands over her head. I was carrying an AK-47. I could have shot her. She looked at me with her blue eyes. She had blonde hair. She was beautiful. I put my finger to my lips. She nodded. That is why I say to you that when I die it is not impossible that I will go to heaven.'

He has said this last sentence like a priest delivering a sermon, his index finger raised instructively.

'So, yes, people broke discipline. The Xhosas in Phola Park were divided into Pondos and Xhosas. It is like the Catholics versus the Protestants in Northern Ireland. It is complicated. They kill each other. At that time, two-thirds of adult men in Phola Park were armed with an AK-47. There can be big trouble. It was a very dangerous place. Go today to Khumalo Street and look at the memorial for the dead. Thousands were killed.

'It was the same on the other side, in the hostels. At that time, you would see a Zulu woman walking in front of the marchers from the hostel. She wore no shirt, her breasts were swinging to and fro. She had a broom and was sweeping the street in front of her. It was their *ntelezi*. Behind her were men with AK-47s. It was a very dangerous time.'

I have by now been swept up into his tale. It has not taken long. He is a gifted storyteller, his voice honed to transmit much more than words.

The other surviving men who drove to Bethlehem that morning I have interviewed many times. It is only Donald Makhura who still inhabits the truth of that day. By truth I do not mean facts — he seems to me a compulsive fabricator of tales. I mean a truth harder to grasp than facts, a truth that struggles to find expression in language at all; I am talking of the spirit propelling that journey.

The others have moved on. They are at peace, no longer reliable witnesses to the feelings of that time. Between who they are now and who they were then lies a membrane. Why labour to break that membrane? It can only lead to trouble.

Donald aside, the only other surviving witness to this spirit is Fusi, oddly enough. When the men piled into his small home, he felt their menace at once. The one called Nozulu, especially: he seemed crazed and ready to kill. Fusi did not want to be left in the house with that man. Nor did he think it safe for that man to go to town. His very being was shouting murder, it seemed.

Donald is watching me in my reverie. He knows that he has me locked in.

'You want to know what it was like to be in that SDU,' he says. 'It is difficult, but I will try to tell you.

'I was in exile. In February 1992, I returned to Thokoza with other guys from MK. One of them was called Frelimo. Lots of youngsters in MK who had grown up on the East Rand or in Natal started coming in from exile to fight. There was civil war in our homes and communities. We wanted to defend them. We did not ask our commanders. We just came.

'Frelimo and I came to Thokoza with automatic weapons. I knew the place very well. I had spent part of my childhood there. We approached the Phola Park SDU. They wanted me to do some terrible things before they would accept me.'

He looks hard at me and sighs.

'It is very, very complex. It will take a long time for you to get a commanding knowledge of the situation. You must talk to a lot of people, including to Inkatha people and hear about their experience of the SDUs.'

He puts on his gravest mask, the one that is still like granite, only his mouth moving as he speaks.

'There are lots of things Fokazi and the others will not talk about because it involves the orphans they have left. The SDUs were not always disciplined, not always under control. You give people AK-47s, they are now empowered, they go and use them to rob. Did we use our weapons against other SDU people? Yes we did. It was a wild time, a time in which you either kill or be killed.

'And there were many mistakes made. Things Fokazi will not tell you. Like when some members of the Zion Christian Church were crossing the graveyard at the edge of Thokoza. One of the silver stars they wear on their chests flashed in the evening light and somebody thought that they were police. They were killed, all of them. Go and look at that wall of remembrance in Phola Park; there are a lot of names there.'

'Tell me what happened on 2 April,' I say.

'I will tell. I have been resisting telling you. But I will.

'Our SDU was in demand; when there was killing to do, we were called, Shell House called us. That mission we were sent on on 2 April, look who was in that mission: Nozulu, the most dangerous killer; Sebenzile, an expert sniper. Why was such a high-skilled team being assembled? Think about it. What was our mission? What were we sent to do? Without naming names, a high-profile member of a political party was going to be killed, triggering a civil war. With all those people in the car, we absolutely knew that we would be stopped in a roadblock. We did not care.'

He is telling me that the High Command of Umkhonto we Sizwe had sent them on a mission to assassinate Inkatha's leader, Mangosuthu Buthelezi. I am weighing up whether to offer that this cannot be true.

Why Donald and his comrades set out for Inanda with a car full of weapons on 2 April I do not know. Communication between ANC-aligned defence units was growing at the time and it is quite possible that, through personal connections, comrades in Inanda had asked them to assist. But by April 1992, the High Command of Umkhonto we Sizwe had not made contact with the Phola Park SDU; it was a black box, quite unknowable, until September of that year, when the High Command sent Robert McBride to make contact. And what he found was sheer anarchy, the sort that Donald so vividly describes.

'What happened in Bethlehem?' I ask. 'Why did you never get to Inanda?'

He rubs his hands together and then rests them on his knees.

'I was in the back of the bakkie,' he says. 'Clement, Nozulu, Sebenzile and Sikhalo were in the cabin. When you are in the back, you cannot hear so good what is happening at the front. But there was a fight happening and Nozulu is crazy, gun happy, dangerous. They say that I am dangerous, but Nozulu was very dangerous. I knew that if we go further we will have a dead body.

'So I bail out – I say, "Gentlemen, in my view the mission cannot go on; the bad blood is imperilling this mission to an extent that it must be abandoned" – and Ncala and Fokazi come with me. Ncala is from the area. He knows a shortcut. So we walk into Ballyduff.

'As to what happened in the bakkie, I was not there any more. But I was told afterwards, in prison. They are now three men down. They cannot continue with the mission short of numbers. So they decide to abandon it. They turn around to follow us back into the township.'

'There are so many coincidences,' I say. 'Sikhalo and Clement were on that very same property hours earlier, looking for work. And as for the bakkie making its way back to the township: that seems improbable. It was in the street outside the Orsmond property for more than half an hour. But the time the police were called, every black worker employed on that road was scared out of his wits. Then there is also the coincidence of Tshokolo: he worked for the man who owned that property and was fired earlier that year.'

'Circumstantial!' he snaps. 'That is all circumstantial!'

'Circumstances can be compelling,' I say. 'Sometimes the circumstances add up and add up until they point in just one direction.'

'Precisely!' he says. 'You have hit the nail on the head! Given the times, Judge Malherbe made the right call. If I had been in his shoes, I would have arrived at the same verdict. There was all that circumstantial evidence. And on top of that, there was the testimony of the young boy Thabo Motaung.

'You need to look at the times. The courtroom was full. Everyone with a skin like mine' – he brushes his forearm with his fingers – 'wants us to walk. Everyone with a skin like yours' – he reaches across and squeezes my bicep – 'wants us to go down. You cannot look at the matter from after 1994. You need to see it in its own time. If Judge Malherbe was here, sitting where you are now, would I be angry with him? No. I would say: "My Lord, you did well; you came to the only conclusion you could."'

He leans back in his chair and smiles. For the first time, he seems truly, deeply satisfied with his performance.

There is a warder lingering and he tells us that our time is up. Donald rises briskly, shakes my hand, wishes me well and strides out of the room, his gait full of purpose.

Why does he hold on to this barely believable story now, all these years later? The first time I interviewed Mandla Fokazi, he told me that the ANC had treated him and his comrades unfairly. They had fought for freedom, he said, and they had sacrificed a great deal. The very least they should get in return was a military pension.

The first time I met with Clement Ndabeni, he said the same. He had been jailed as a young man, he said. His wife left him when he was behind bars. His life had been broken and could never be put back together again. He had been a soldier and should receive a free house at the very least.

Sikhalo Ncala had said the same. When he returned from prison, he said, his career as a construction contractor was ruined. He spent the first year after his release unemployed. Why had the ANC not helped them? He had sacrificed his career for the struggle, after all. And still, now, these many years later, he was awaiting compensation.

And so, perhaps, in telling me the story he did, Donald is sticking up for them all. They were ordinary men in the early 1990s. In the encroaching chaos they took it upon themselves to become soldiers. They were swept into a life way beyond the realm of ordinary human experience. They saw death from close quarters, again and again. And it ended only when they were caught and tortured and they lost their best years to prison.

And so it is vitally important that 2 April 1992, the day that ended their military careers, be remembered as a day of soldiering, pure and simple, a day that leaves them noble and worthy of a soldier's pension.

Thirty-five

It was the winter of 2011, about two months after Fusi's release from prison. The world was still new and very hard. Matters that everyone else took for granted – finding one's way home in the evenings without getting lost, for instance – remained a daily toil.

On one of these difficult, distracted days, an odd text message appeared on his cell phone's screen.

'This is Nnyalleng. I want to talk to you.'

His cousin's daughter was called Nnyalleng and he assumed that the message was from her. It was an odd message for her to send. Although they were family, she and Fusi had met only a couple of times; he could not imagine what she wanted. He would be seeing her soon, at a family gathering, and he saw no reason to respond.

A week later, as he was washing his red Toyota at a car wash in town, a man he vaguely knew came to him with a message. 'There is a girl who works at the casino,' he said. 'Her name is Nnyalleng. She says she is desperate to talk to you.'

Fusi thanked the man for the message and went about his business. Again he assumed that this Nnyalleng was his cousin's niece. She can wait, he thought to himself; nothing could be so urgent that he must put down what he is doing and come.

But when he saw Nnyalleng a few weeks later and asked why it was so urgent that they should talk, she stared at him in bemusement. She did not work at the casino, she said, and the number from which the message was sent was not hers.

He was puzzled, to be sure, and for a few days the faceless Nnyalleng lingered until she quietly fell out of his mind. He was concentrating so very hard on just getting by. He had neither the time nor the confidence to go wandering into the unknown.

A long time passed. More than four years. The text message and the car wash emissary had long disappeared from his thoughts.

And then from out of the blue, in November 2015, she wrote to him once more. Her message was much clearer this time.

'This is Nnyalleng. I am your daughter.'

He texted her back and asked her where she was. She was at an address in Bohlokong, a fifteen-minute drive from work. It was a little after noon; his lunch hour was at 1:00 p.m.; he put down his tools, got on his motorbike and rode.

It always seems so mysterious in retrospect – how a piece of information, and not just any information, but the knowledge that one is a father, can lie there for years in the vast filing system of one's mind. It is neither remembered nor forgotten: it occupies a nameless room in between.

On the journey from work to Bohlokong he pieced it all together; by the time he turned into Nnyalleng's road he knew exactly who she was.

In 1986, Fusi met a girl called Tabita. They slept together, on and off, before finally breaking up for good in 1989. When he went to prison three years later she wrote to him to say that she had given birth to a daughter in the months after they parted. She had a new boyfriend by then, and for the sake of their relationship she told him that he was the father. But the girl was Fusi's, she said in her letter, and when the little one was old enough she should know the true story of her paternity.

Tabita died in 1999, still a young woman, barely thirty, and after she was buried, her younger sister took up her pen. She wrote to Fusi three, perhaps four times to tell him that Nnyalleng was growing, that she was nearly in her teens now, that his daughter was about and in the world.

He had taken in the news like a stone in his porridge; he had removed it from his mouth and put it carefully to the side. What could he do with the knowledge that he was a father? He had no roof under which he might house her, no money, no means to care for a child. He was fighting for his freedom and it consumed every piece of him. Of the people outside, there was his mother and Victoria; he had no space for others; they were surplus to requirements.

Nnyalleng was waiting outside her house. She was not expecting him to arrive on a motorbike and she barely turned her head when he approached. His crash helmet concealing his face, he stopped close to her, a mere fifty paces or so away; he could watch her unnoticed for as long as he liked.

She turned from him, and as she showed him her profile, he gasped. He could almost say that he was looking at his mother. Not the sickly woman who had come to visit him in Kroonstad, nor the wan corpse he had seen lying in the morgue. It was the woman who had appeared at Easter on Oorsprong, still young, still unfamiliar and a little strange, a gift from the city in her hands.

He took off his helmet and walked towards her. The moment she saw him he stopped in his tracks. She came to him briskly and without inhibition wrapped him in an embrace and squeezed him, her head buried in his chest.

He is not a demonstrative man, his intimacies cautious and hard-won. As he held her he felt acutely the oddness of this moment for the girl in his arms was a stranger. But as their embrace lingered, another feeling took root, deeper than familiarity, too mysterious easily to name. It was a longing, a pining, a reaching for something unnamed. And he understood that it had always been inside him although he was meeting it, now, for the first time.

It is a Saturday morning in the winter of 2017. Fusi and I are to go to Oorsprong today. It is something we have been planning for a while.

Winter is a good time for this expedition, I am thinking, for the mountains will be stark, the grass yellow, the sky large and clear and pale blue.

We stop first at the barber at the end of Fusi's street. His head has not been shaved for more than a week, he says; it is itchy and distracting and there will not be an opportunity for a haircut again this weekend.

The salon consists of just one small room and it is filled with men waiting for their heads to be shorn. We find a space to sit. Fusi is soon absorbed with something on his cell phone while I watch the barber work.

He is young, thirty at most, I think. He wears blue-and-white Converse All Stars and a tight-fitting polo-neck sweater that shows his back and his shoulders to be strong. He works fast, each man in the barber's chair no more than six or seven minutes, I guess, before making way for the next in the line.

With both of his hands he massages into the head before him a thick, creamy lather, like a man pasting over a globe of the world. Then he takes from its packet a new razor and shaves with his left hand. His right he uses as a cup into which he scoops a growing stew of black hair and beige cream. The cream gathers, the hand fills; the moment it begins to overflow, he deposits its contents with one deft flick onto a part of the head that has already been shaved. There it stands, a lopsided, creamy crown, its owner looking momentarily ridiculous, until the barber sweeps it away in a fell swoop and throws it in the dustbin at his side.

Fusi hands me his cell phone; on the screen there is a photograph of father and daughter, Fusi and Nnyalleng. Her eyes are closed in embarrassment, it seems, on her face a broad self-conscious smile. Her left hand rests on Fusi's thigh, her right on her swollen belly. She is seven months pregnant when the picture is taken, the little one inside her a boy.

As for Fusi, his eyes are downcast, his face expressionless, as if cameras are best avoided. Had I never met the man in the photograph, I would have guessed him to be shy, perhaps a little sullen and ever so reserved.

They decided at the beginning to take it slowly; Nnyalleng went to see him each day in the early evening and texted him each night before going to sleep. As for Fusi, he paid a formal visit to her family and sat with them in his quiet way.

But matters soon progressed for there was much fathering to be done. When they met, Nnyalleng was unemployed and living with a man Fusi did not like at all. He clearly made his living outside the law and he often missed paying his monthly rent. After work each day, Fusi would make quiet enquiries about his past and it turned out that he had a bad way with women.

Fusi not confront Nnyalleng. He schemed and hatched plans and was about to act when she left this man of her own accord. One thing followed another, and soon she was living with Victoria, in the house the government had given Maletsatsi Mbele, and Fusi was paying her way.

Then she met another man, this one decent, from a good family, holding down an honest, humble job. And then she was pregnant and Fusi was negotiating bridewealth with the family, his thoughts attuned to the extraordinary fact that he would be a grandfather soon.

It is his turn in the barber's chair now, and I find that I have been anticipating this moment. For there is a brief episode at the end of each haircut, a flash performance so startling that it has astonished me every time.

When the shaving is done and the razor thrown away, a lacquer is sprayed over the bald head and cheeks and then the cheeks are rubbed with a towel. It is a moment of exquisite vulnerability: the eyes closed, the brow creased, the face is robbed of the persona it presents to the world. It is steeled against invasion and that is all. When it is over and the eyes dare to open, the look they offer the mirror is momentarily confused, as if they are seeing the face that appears there for the first time.

The lacquer is sprayed on Fusi's head and cheeks and the towel comes down on his eyes. His reserve vanishes, his face creases and frowns; he resembles a newborn straight from the womb, the months of reverie so violently ended, in front of him a world he must stumble through blind.

It is the briefest parenthesis: it lasts no more than a second or two. And then he is Fusi again, a grandfather-to-be, at the beginning of a journey to Oorsprong. He has not passed through its front gates since he was a young man.

In the car I tell him a story.

Something extraordinary happened the other day, I say, and it came from out of the blue.

I was working in my office in Johannesburg when there was a knock on my door. It was a colleague, and beside her stood a middle-aged man.

'This is Mr TN,' she said – for in telling this story I ought not to use his name – 'he came in to ask to be put on our mailing list. We got chatting and it turns out that he grew up in the eastern Free State. I thought that the two of you should meet.'

With that, she turned around and disappeared, leaving Mr TN and me to talk.

He was in his mid-fifties, I think, grey, lined and handsome. He wore the signature clothes of an academic at work: chinos, a collared shirt, a casual jacket, a rucksack slung over his shoulder.

We began talking and when I asked whether he had spent any time in Bohlokong his ears pricked up.

'So you know the eastern Free State pretty well.'

Sitting alone in my office, hour upon hour, day upon day, Fusi's world had been filling my head; now, with Mr TN for an unexpected audience, tales came from my mouth in a spasm of telling.

I recounted the evening in 1964 when Jan Mbele fell into a hole; the family's eviction from Lucia and the journey through the snow; the young men like Sikhalo who fled the farms to find themselves in the midst of an urban war; women like Maletsatsi and Victoria and the scars they bore for marrying dysfunctional men; the aging Rose and Nono Mbele, whose declining capacity to offer Madipela their labour prolonged the family's slipping hold on Oorsprong.

I told him of how Fusi was shipped from home to home, first that of an aunt, then Oorsprong, then his uncle Jack's house on the East Rand. I told of his teenage decision to defy his family and live with his shamed and drunken father. And then I told of his arrest and his incarceration. These were just ordinary lives, I said, but they were filled with hardship and at times even with a horror that can only be described as extraordinary.

Mr TN, who has insisted by now that I call him T, has suddenly grown emotional. His bottom lip is quivering and he is stumbling with his words.

'I have put my childhood away,' he says uncertainly. 'I know the things you are speaking of.'

He is battling to speak. He is heaving the words out one by one as if each is a heavy boulder.

'The childhood is there. There are memories. But it is as if they are someone else's. I have stored them far, far away.'

'Do you have children?' I ask.

He does. They are busy, successful professionals.

'Do you ever take them to where you grew up?'

'Never. Never, ever. I shield them. I do not want them to know.'

He begins to weep, and he is clearly as startled as I am. He is a grown man, after all, distinguished and certain; the mien that accompanied him into the room was so comfortably self-possessed. He has walked into a stranger's office and within minutes he has fallen apart.

'I am so sorry,' he says. 'I can't believe that this is happening.'

'It's really fine,' I say. 'Really, it is.'

I fish in my bag for a packet of tissues and hand it to him.

'Do you mind if I stay until I recompose myself? I do not want to wander out there like this.'

'Of course.'

He blows his nose loudly and sits down. Then he stands again. He clears his throat and begins speaking about his father.

'He lived at a place called X.'

'I know it,' I say. 'I went there with Fusi just the other day.'

He stares at me. On his face there is no less than an accusation.

'Why did you come here this afternoon?' he asks. 'What is it that brought you here?'

And now he is weeping again and I turn my back and look out of the window.

'I did very well in school,' he says, 'so well that I received a bursary to study at university. These were the days when they were not certain that blacks could think abstractly. It was difficult being black and at a liberal university in the thick of apartheid. There were hard decisions to be made.'

The talking had begun to unburden him. He was now sitting comfortably in his chair. He began speaking of his father.

He was a preacher, T said. On a Sunday he would ride his bicycle to four, five congregations to preach. His congregants were farm workers. He knew them. Knew their lives, their problems.

T didn't get to see his father much. He was registered as living out on the farms and was therefore not allowed to enter the town where T lived without official permission. He would have to go to the municipal office to apply to see his children; he would be granted a permit good for forty-eight hours.

At the end of his father's weekend visits, T would see him off to the station. Each time he would ask his father when he would return. He would never say.

'I took this as abandonment,' T said sadly. 'He was clearly unable to explain the real reason. Perhaps it was just too mortifying.

'Once,' T continued, 'I walked into the municipal office with him. A young Afrikaans man was on duty. What happened next I simply did not understand. My father began mumbling, grovelling. He was such a neat, polished, respectable man, always wearing polished shoes, a collared shirt, a jacket. I did not understand what was happening. Afterwards, as we walked out, I tried to catch his eye. He would not look at me. He would not look me in the eye.'

He had a mind to weep again, but checked himself and turned his thoughts elsewhere.

'This remains a difficult country for black people,' he said. 'I know too many black graduates without jobs. I am a successful professional but I want to give up my profession to devote myself full-time to helping.

We sat in silence for a while.

'It is good that you are writing these stories,' he said finally. 'The suffering you are writing about is not acknowledged. But tell me, how do you feel as a white South African recording such stories? Do you feel guilt?'

This turning of the lens was uncomfortable. I am not sure that I am a faithful recorder of how I replied. I think I said that it was hard to absorb such suffering, that I was humbled by its presence, but that writing was itself a means of acquiring distance from it.

He noted this, silently.

He desired to be in touch with Fusi, he said. They should talk on the phone. And perhaps, then, T might pay a rare visit to Bethlehem and the two could meet in person.

I would be seeing Fusi the following week, I said. I would tell him all about T, and then, if Fusi permitted, I would give T his contact details.

We exchanged numbers and e-mail addresses. We shook hands. And then he was gone.

I wandered into the corridor and walked the distance to the office of the colleague who had brought T to me. I was in something of a daze. She was at her desk, hard at work, quite oblivious to what she had made.

'Thank you,' I said.

Now, in the car, en route to Oorsprong, I tell Fusi of my encounter with TN. I try to forget nothing; I want to include every detail.

When I am done, he says nothing. But from the mood enveloping the car it is apparent that he is puzzled.

'I do not know of TN,' he says finally. 'But you are welcome to give him my number. It would be a pleasure to meet him.'

'What do you think of his story?'

He shrugs. Then he stifles a nervous laugh.

'I am sorry that his memories are so painful,' he says carefully. And then he is silent once more.

There is, on reflection, little in TN's story that Fusi shares. That one might flee the eastern Free State, that one might go so far as to conceal the place from one's children – this came from a foreign place.

When Fusi was released, an opportunity arose to apply for a post at the Wits Justice Project. He thought about it a long time before declining to apply. In part, he did not want to turn his fate as an innocent man into a profession. He was free now, and he felt the urge to start anew.

More profoundly, though, he did not want to leave Bethlehem for it was deep in his bones. Those trips to Rosendal in the months after his release, when on drawing near to Oorsprong he would leave his car and sit in silence, are a part of him now. The landscape on which he gazed was as much in his soul and as it was outside. To exile himself from it makes little sense.

In the stillness of the mountains and in the wideness of the veld he found his deepest sense of his childhood. And his memories are uniformly wonderful. I have never seen him more at peace than when remembering Oorsprong, never more excited than when recounting his weekends with Amos, Sengata and Khulu. He is taken to falling into the soft embrace of those times.

I do not trust these memories. He is, I think, the poorest witness to his past. For all the hours that we have spoken, for all the people I have met who knew him when he was young, it is, perversely, in his testimony to Judge Malherbe that I see the flash of a wincing truth.

He was ill; he had been so for months. And he did not know what was wrong. He was travelling far from home in search of a cure.

His illness had robbed him of his job; he was unemployed. Occasionally, when his health permitted, he laboured in the garden of Thabo Motaung's uncle. It was lowly work, and barely paid, I'm sure.

There are no reliable witnesses to what was ailing him. But perhaps his own reconstruction of the past provides the faintest clue. In his recollections, 2 April begins with the kindness of his father; in the fiction he has created, his father's first thought as he wakes is that his son is ill and needs breakfast; and so he instructs Thabo Motaung to go and cook for Fusi. And so in his imagination he has made the father he craves, just as he has scattered magic across the whole breadth of his past.

I share TN's story with Fusi because it seems to me to contain the very memories of childhood Fusi has suppressed. In offering TN's memories, slowly, with care, with intimacy, might they provoke from Fusi a response? They have provoked nothing at all; he simply does not recognise them; between the past he knows and the past TN remembers there is little in common.

Who would Fusi have become had Sikhalo not knocked on his door? Would he have shared the same soul as the man sitting next to me now? Or would his past come to him as TN's does, his feelings tortured and sad?

There is no knowing. Of the three men with whom he shared his youth, two are dead, the other lost. It is the one whom a tragedy befell who has turned out well. But those three boys are not proxies for Fusi, are they? They are themselves.

Who knows? Perhaps I am entirely wrong. But I think that becoming an innocent man healed him.

Whether he was innocent on 2 April I do not know. But in its wake he knew himself to be unjustly imprisoned. And in his quest for justice he became all he is now – a person whose past has been washed in pastels: the past of a decent man whose happiness is growing.

And whether he was innocent in fact, there is little doubt that he was existentially innocent. For he was the son of labour tenants, the most downtrodden people in the entire land, and a civil war was raging and lives were being turned upside down, ordinary people turned into killers, gentle people ground into dust; and nothing in his history gave him the wherewithal to navigate this world. That, above all, is why he was thrown in jail in the early hours of 3 April 1992, and why he did not see the outside world for another nineteen years.

We are driving through the valley where Oorsprong lies. On our left is a grand, sprawling hill and he is pointing to a stretch of veld at its base.

'There were people living there,' he says. 'Before I went to prison, that area was full of houses. Maybe twelve of them. We knew every family. Now it is as if nobody was ever there. It is just veld.

'This whole valley, in fact: it is astonishing to think that it is empty now when hundreds of black people lived here.'

He is clearly deeply moved. And he is unusually loquacious.

'When democracy came,' he continues, 'the government passed a law giving the tenants on white farmers' land security of tenure. The farmers responded to the new law by chasing people away. The government had given people rights, but it did not remember to tell them.

'It was quite a shock when I came out of prison. The township was so much fuller than before. The new people were the ones who had been chased off the farms. Many of them were hungry. Many of them, you could see from the look in their eyes that they were suffering deep inside. People did not have that look before I went to prison. It is something new.'

I am astonished. He has never spoken to me like this before. His fortunes are so closely tied to the favour of powerful people; when he looks about him, it has always seemed to me, he keeps one eye on the side on which his bread is buttered. To offer so biting a critique of the world over which the ANC presides is out of character.

Perhaps the proximity to Oorsprong has brought forth a subterranean conversation. Perhaps, below the surface of his steady pragmatism, he speaks this way to himself all the time.

'While you were being forgotten inside prison,' I say, 'your family was being forgotten out here on the farms.'

'That is true,' he says. 'We are ordinary people. We tend to be forgotten.'

We are approaching Oorsprong now, and his memories are growing more particular.

'Little Dirkie and I swam together in that pool,' he says with pleasure. 'He came to Oorsprong during the school holidays to stay with his grandmother, Madipela. He spoke no Sesotho. I spoke no Afrikaans. We communicated with our faces, with the way we looked at one another. He was a funny boy, a kind boy, I can say.'

Now we are at the gates of the farmhouse and an elderly white man has come out to see who is visiting. Three Giant Schnauzers are dancing around him. Three more dart through the hedges and across the lawn. They are young, all of them, and light on their paws, our visit cause for delight and celebration.

Their owner does not seem as pleased. His face, grooved with lines so deep they seem to cut inside him, shows nothing at all. He simply stares at us without expression. I feel Fusi tensing; he is not sure what to expect.

We get out of the car and walk to the fence.

'Can I help, gentlemen?' the old man asks crisply.

Fusi stops a short distance away, his head bowed.

'My name is Fusi Mofokeng,' he begins diffidently. 'I knew this farm as a child. My grandparents moved here in 1964. They were here the rest of their lives. Their name was Mbele. They were on my mother's side. They both died on this farm, in fact. They are actually buried here.'

He points to the hill on his right.

'I would like to ask your permission to visit the place where we lived.'

'Of course,' the old man says at once. 'I myself am only a tenant here. But first you must come inside and drink coffee and eat the cake my wife has baked.'

His face is still utterly impassive as if made of the roughest stone. And his voice is blunt and flat, like he is giving us directions instead of inviting us into his home. But what he has said is so unexpectedly warm and so gracious that we are happy to comply.

'Will your dogs not bite?' Fusi asks.

Now, for the first time, he smiles in amusement.

'They are friendly creatures,' he says. 'They have never bitten a soul.'

We walk through the garden and the dogs provide a riotous retinue;

they trace jagged circles around us and then dart in to sniff our heels. The braver ones jump on our chests and our backs; they are enormous and on their hind legs they meet us eye to eye.

Fusi is petrified but he dutifully soldiers on. He has resigned himself to being bitten, it seems; he is just waiting for it to be over and done with.

The house before us is quite beautiful. It is a Free State sandstone, wide and square and unadorned. Under its green tin roof runs a fringe of intricate ironwork. It is well preserved, its terracotta veranda freshly painted and smelling of polish. It must have been standing here for at least a hundred years.

The old man leads us through a darkened lounge, the curtains drawn. He settles us in the kitchen, puts on the kettle and begins preparing the coffee. We sit on high stools around a kitchen island; it is a small space and Fusi and I sit shoulder to shoulder.

He pays no rent, the old man tells us as he busies himself. He sounds a little astonished as he says this, as if he is discovering it for the first time. The place belongs to relatives, a big farming family that has bought up many farms over the years. Usually they flatten the farmhouse on the land they buy. But this one – it is just too beautiful to tear down. And so they kept it standing and invited the old man and his wife, who are just distant relatives, to move in.

The walls of the kitchen are thick with photographs. They all show the old man when he was young. In each he is wearing a running vest and holding a trophy, sometimes on his own, sometimes in a group of other young men. I look him over and marvel at how his body has aged. It is thin and bent and seems as brittle as a stick. In the photographs he is a model of athletic beauty, his shoulders thick and strong.

He was a policeman most of his life, he explains, at the physical train-ing college in Pretoria. He was a high jumper, and, at the risk of sounding boastful, he says, a very good one.

304

He points to a photograph. He is wearing his vest and a pair of shorts, his hands on his hips. He smiles straight at the camera, his face posed and pleased.

'This was taken in the United Kingdom in 1967,' he says. 'There was a very big athletics meeting. It was the height of apartheid. It was only in the UK that South Africans could go to compete. All of the best South African track and field athletes were there. If South Africa had been allowed to compete in the Olympics, this is the team that would have gone. Aside from myself, only one other policeman made it into that tour. He did the hundred metres.

'Mind you,' he says, addressing Fusi, 'there was a black athlete among the South Africans. His name was Sydney Maree.'

I am racking my brain, making sure that I have not made a mistake. I am fairly certain that Sydney Maree became famous more than a decade after the old man's visit to the UK. In the late 1960s Maree was still a schoolboy, in the small town of Cullinan, just a stone's throw from Baviaanspoort Prison, where Donald Makhura is being held. I am wondering what compelled the old man to place him in the story.

'I know of Sydney Maree,' Fusi beams. 'I saw that he is living in South Africa again after many years abroad.'

The old man is such a chatterbox that I have paid no attention to Fusi. Now I see that he is looking around the house in wonder.

'I have been in this room before,' he says. 'My mother worked here. She prepared breakfast right where you are standing for the woman who owned the farm. But time has moved on. This kitchen has been renovated. This big island was not here before. And some of the walls have been knocked down.'

'That's right,' the old man says. 'In all of these old houses, the kitchen was walled off. The food was served into the dining room through a hole in the wall.'

It comes from out of the blue, apropos of nothing at all.

'You know,' the old man says, now facing Fusi square-on, 'even though I worked for the police, I knew nothing about Eugene de Kock.'

De Kock was the police officer who ran the assassination squad exposed in the early 1990s by Jacques Pauw. He subsequently became a figure of infamy, a byword for state-sanctioned murder.

'Those were very dark days,' he continues. 'It does not leave one feeling proud, even if one did not know personally what was going on.'

I look around. I take in the renovated house, the photographs of the old man when he was young, the view of the yellow hill outside. I freeze the moment in my mind's eye.

The old man has told Fusi that he feels crap about the past. On behalf of himself, on behalf of Eugene de Kock and me and all white people, he has said that he does not feel good.

When our coffee cups are empty, he says, and the cake is gone from our plates, we must wander the farm. We should feel free to go wherever we want and to stay for as long as we like.

Fusi nods and says thank you. And when the old man escorts us to the gate he is still chattering on. He and his wife used to sell bottled water, he tells us. They would start with ordinary municipal water, treat it nine times and then inject it with oxygen. It was a good business, he says, but being a travelling salesman when you have passed the age of seventy is no life. Now they breed Giant Schnauzers. The female they imported from California, the male from Poland. She has had four healthy litters and each pup sells for R6 000.

'So many dogs,' Fusi says neutrally.

The old man offers first Fusi and then me his hand.

'Good luck,' he says, and he waits at the gate until we are driving off and then shuffles back to the house.

We drive up the hill on a rutted farm road until we come to a closed gate.

'My uncle made this gate,' Fusi says softly. 'Jack's brother.' And we park the car and walk through the gate Fusi's uncle made and we are on wide, open veld.

We walk eastwards along the contour of the hill. The house from which we have come lies out of sight in the valley below. The breeze is stiff, the world around us very quiet.

'It is here,' Fusi says. 'I am fairly certain it is here. On this spot was my grandparents' house. I can tell because the view of the valley is exactly the same. I know that view so well. And on that spot there was the Ncalas' house and over there was a very big house; the man who owned it kept cattle on farms all over the district.'

There isn't a trace of any of these houses. It is just us and the yellow grass on the hillside and the wind.

'My grandfather, Nono, built the house,' Fusi says, 'out of mud from the river. The material for the entire home was carried by one man in one wheelbarrow, over and over again, over and over again.'

We wander on until we reach the place Fusi insists must have been the tenants' graveyard. We search through the grass and find nothing; Fusi is beginning to doubt his memory when he stumbles over a protrusion in the grass. We get on our hands and knees and tear the grass away to discover the remnants of a cross. Faded, but still clearly visible is the name 'Ncala' and a date, '1987'.

'It is Sikhalo's father,' Fusi says quietly.

We take pictures from various angles. And now we are back on our hands and knees for this is the only way we will find his grandparents' graves.

Duly, we come across the stump of a tombstone, then another, then a third and a fourth. Two of them must belong to Nono and Rose, Fusi thinks, but his memory is failing him; their funerals were decades ago, in another life, and he cannot possibly recall where he stood when they were buried.

The uncertainty seems to frustrate him, for now he wants to see the dam. We abandon the graveyard and walk sideways down the hill's steepest slope.

We round a corner and there it is, standing modestly some distance below us. It is a simple farm dam, its surface dark and rippled by the wind, its shore lined with blue gums.

'Look at the trees,' he says in astonishment. 'Look at how old they are.'

'You remember them being smaller?' I ask.

He examines me warily as if what I have said is nothing less than daft.

'I was here on the day they were planted. I was on holiday from Thokoza. I helped with the planting.'

He is staring at them in wonder.

I leave him to his reverie and descend the hill. At the bottom I potter around and throw stones at the surface of the dam. Then I climb the hill to join him again.

He is just as I left him, staring down below.

'I still can't get over those trees,' he says.

He gives me a frustrated look. If he had a thousand years, he seems to be saying, he would not find the words to tell me what he is feeling, or he would find them at last but I'd fail to understand.

Perhaps he is startled because the trees have measured his age. Or because of their sheer indifference to him. He planted them, after all, with the help of the ones buried further up the hill. One day he too will be gone and the trees will still be growing.

Epilogue

In South African law, if a person has been convicted of a crime, and if their appeal against their conviction has been lost in the appeal courts, they have reached the end of the road. There is no legal apparatus that might permit a court to reopen the case. This is an egregious omission in the country's statutory law. What if compelling new evidence arises? There is no judicial forum in which an unjust decision can be reversed.

Instead, there exists a strange piece of legislation, Section 327 of the Criminal Procedure Act, which envisages an awkward and unsatisfactory fusion of judicial and executive action. A convicted person petitions the Minister of Justice, making a case that evidence has arisen to question the original verdict of the court. If the minister finds the new evidence compelling, he or she refers the matter to the court in which the conviction occurred – in Fusi and Tshokolo's case, the Free State High Court in Bloemfontein. The court, in turn, evaluates the evidence. But it does not make its evaluation public. Instead, it advises the President of the Republic of South Africa whether the new evidence is strong enough to overturn the original conviction. The President has the power, at his or her discretion, to expunge the conviction from all official records.

It is a deeply inadequate piece of legislation. The Minister of Justice is not compelled to provide reasons for referring, or deciding not to refer, the matter to a judge. And the judge is in fact legally compelled *not* to make his evaluation public. Nor is the President obliged to provide reasons either for expunging, or deciding not to expunge, the criminal record. It is hard to imagine that the procedures envisaged here satisfy the right to access to justice.

When Fusi and Tshokolo were released on parole, they urgently wanted to submit a Section 327 petition to have their criminal records expunged. Among other motivations, they wished to sue the South African state for the suffering they had incurred over the previous nineteen years. They lodged a petition in August 2017. At the time of writing, in April 2019, twenty months later, the Minister of Justice has given no indication whether he will refer the matter to a judge. If precedent is anything to go by, he never will; as far as I have been able to tell, no Minister of Justice *has ever* referred a Section 327 application to a court.

Sometime in 2013, Ruth Hopkins, formerly of the Wits Justice Project, asked a senior Department of Justice official why Section 327 petitions never make it to court. His standard response to such petitions, he told her – off the record, of course – was to stuff them in a drawer, unread.

Acknowledgements

My primary debt, as anyone who has read these pages can see, is to Fusi Mofokeng. If I have done anything right in this book, it is, I hope, to have captured something of his spirit.

I would like to express my heartfelt thanks to Jeremy Gordin. In his former role as director of the Wits Justice Project, Jeremy threw himself heart and soul into Fusi and Tshokolo's case. He also brokered my relationship with Fusi at the beginning, making this book possible. I am enormously grateful, too, to Ruth Hopkins, also formerly of the Wits Justice Project, who worked tirelessly, year after year, on Fusi and Tshokolo's quest to expunge their criminal records. Ruth was unfailingly generous in sharing documents, information and her perspective on the case.

I am grateful to the Millennium Trust, which provided the funds for transcribing the audio recording of the original 1992 trial. The cost was well beyond my means and the work was vital to this enterprise.

I wrote the final chapters of this book during a fellowship at the Stellenbosch Institute for Advanced Study (STIAS), as salubrious a place for productive work as one could imagine. Many thanks.

In Johannesburg I was accommodated with generosity and grace by the Wits Institute for Social and Economic Research (WiSER).

Sebabatso Manoeli translated several dozen of the letters Fusi received during his incarceration from Sesotho to English. She did so with her customary rigour and insight, and her eye for detail. Thank you, Sabi.

Many thanks to Jeremy Boraine and everyone else at Jonathan Ball Publishers, which has been publishing my books for seventeen years now, and to Angela Voges, whose copy-editing is superb.

Several people read drafts of the manuscript. Mark Gevisser is a reader of unrivalled talent, and Carol Steinberg and Jocelyn Alexander both possess a wisdom every writer should be so lucky to borrow. Commissioned by the publisher, Sisonke Msimang and Angela Voges provided enormously valuable reader's reports. Thank you to you all.